THE *Seinfeld* SCRIPTS

THE FIRST AND SECOND SEASONS

HarperPerennial

A Division of HarperCollinsPublishers

HarperCollins books may be purchased for educational, business, or sales promotional use. For information please write: Special Markets Department, HarperCollins Publishers, Inc., 10 East 53rd Street, New York, NY 10022.

FIRST EDITION

Designed by Elliott Beard

ISBN 0-06-095303-9

98 99 00 01 02 ❖ /RRD 10 9 8 7 6 5 4 3 2 1

Contents

Cast List VII

SEASON ONE

The Seinfeld Chronicles 3

The Stake Out 29

The Robbery 65

Male Unbonding 95

The Stock Tip 125

SEASON TWO

The Ex-Girlfriend 155

The Pony Remark 185

The Jacket 215

THE PHONE MESSAGE 247

THE APARTMENT 279

THE STATUE 311

THE REVENGE 347

THE HEART ATTACK 379

THE DEAL 409

THE BABY SHOWER 441

THE CHINESE RESTAURANT 471

THE BUSBOY 499

CONTENTS

Cast List

JERRY SEINFELD...........................JERRY SEINFELD

GEORGE COSTANZA................. JASON ALEXANDER

ELAINE BENES ....JULIA LOUIS-DREYFUS

COSMO KRAMER .... MICHAEL RICHARDS

SEASON ONE

THE Seinfeld SCRIPTS

THE
SEINFELD
CHRONICLES

WRITTEN BY

LARRY DAVID & JERRY SEINFELD

DIRECTED BY

ART WOLFF

AS BROADCAST JULY 5, 1989

TEASER

INT. NIGHTCLUB—NIGHT A

Opening credits over the following:

JERRY

Do you know what this is all about? Do you know why
we're here? To be out. This is out. Out is one of the
single most enjoyable experiences of life. People—you
know how many people come home at night—"We
should go out?" This is what they're talking about. This
whole thing—we're all out, no one is home.
Not one person here is home. We're all out. There are
people trying to find us. They don't know where we
are. "Did you—I can't find them, where did he go? I
don't know. He didn't tell me where he was going. He
must have gone out." You want to go out. You get
ready, you pick out the clothes, right? You take the
shower, get all ready. Get the cash, get your friends, the
car, the spot, the reservations, when you stand around,
what do you do? You go, "We gotta be getting back."
Once you're out, you want to get back. You want to go
to sleep, you want to get up, you want to go out again
tomorrow, right? Wherever you are in life, it's my
feeling, you've gotta go.

End opening credits.

ACT I

SCENE A

FADE IN:

EXT. COFFEE SHOP—ESTABLISHING SHOT—DAY (STOCK)

INT. COFFEE SHOP—LATE AFTERNOON (DAY 1)

A typical New York City coffee shop. It's not rush hour, but there's activity and we hear that unmistakable din. Jerry and a longtime friend, George, are sitting at a table. George, slightly insecure, has an opinion on everything. He lives life at a higher intensity level than Jerry.

JERRY
See, now to me, that button is in the worst possible spot. The second button literally makes or breaks the shirt. Look at it, it's too high, it's in no-man's-land. You look like you live with your mother.

GEORGE
Are you through?

JERRY
You do, of course, try on when you buy.

GEORGE
Yes, it was purple, I liked it. I don't recall considering the button.

JERRY
Oh, you don't recall.

GEORGE

(USING PEN LIKE A MICROPHONE) No, not at this time.

JERRY

Well, Senator, I'd like to know what you knew and when you knew it.

A waitress, Claire, *approaches* the table. *Obviously overqualified, she always gets the joke. She pours coffee from two pots of coffee.*

CLAIRE

Mr. Seinfeld . . . Mr. Costanza.

GEORGE

Are you sure that one's decaf? Where's the orange indicator?

CLAIRE

It's missing. I have to do it in my head. "Decaf left, regular right . . . Decaf left, regular right." It's very challenging work.

JERRY

Can you relax? It's a cup of coffee. Claire's a professional waitress.

CLAIRE

Trust me, George. No one has any interest in seeing you on caffeine.

Claire exits.

GEORGE

How come you're not doing the second show tomorrow?

JERRY

Well, there's this woman might be coming in.

GEORGE

(TAKEN ABACK) Wait a second, wait a second, what coming in? What woman is coming in?

JERRY

I told you about Laura. The girl I met in Michigan.

GEORGE

No, you didn't.

JERRY

I thought I told you about her. Yeah, she teaches political science. I met her the night I did that show in Lansing. (TRIES TO POUR MILK) There's no milk in here, what is the story, what—

GEORGE

Wait, wait, what, what is she like?

JERRY

Oh, she's really great. She's got like a real warmth about her, and she's really bright, and really pretty, and uh, and the conversation though, I mean, it was—talking with her is like talking to you but, you know, obviously, much better.

GEORGE

So what happened?

JERRY

Oh, uh, nothing happened, you know. But it was great.

GEORGE

Oh, nothing happened, but it was—Well, this is great. So, you know, she called and she said she wanted to go out with you tomorrow night? God bless. Devil, you.

JERRY

Yeah, well, not exactly. I mean she said—you know, she called this morning and said she had to come in for a seminar and maybe we'd get together. So—

GEORGE

(WHISTLES FOR JERRY TO STOP) Yo, whoa, whoa, whoa—"had to"? "Had to come in"?

JERRY

Yeah . . .

GEORGE

"Had to come in"?

JERRY

Yeah, but . . .

GEORGE

"And maybe we'll get together"? "Had to" and "maybe"?

JERRY

Yeah.

GEORGE

No. No. No. I hate to tell you this. You're not going to see this woman.

JERRY

What? Are you serious? (NOT CONVINCED) Why, why did she call?

GEORGE

What do I know? Maybe, you know, maybe she wanted to be polite.

JERRY

"To be polite." You are insane.

GEORGE

Alright, alright, I didn't want to tell you this, you want to know why she called? You're a back-up. You're a second line, a just-in-case, a "B" plan, a contingency . . .

JERRY

Oh, I get it. This is about the button.

GEORGE

Claire, Claire, you're a woman, right?

CLAIRE

What gave it away, George?

GEORGE

I'd like to ask you, ask you to analyze a hypothetical phone call you know, from a female point of view.

JERRY

Oh, come on now, what are you asking her—now what is she going to know?

GEORGE

A woman calls me and says she has to come to New
York on business . . .

JERRY

Oh, you are beautiful.

GEORGE

. . . and maybe she'll see me when she gets here. Does
this woman intend to spend time with me?

CLAIRE

I would have to say . . . uh . . . no.

George holds up pad that says "no."

GEORGE

So why did she call?

CLAIRE

To be polite.

GEORGE

(TO JERRY) "To be polite." I rest my case.

JERRY

Good, good. Did you have fun? You have no idea what
you're talking about. Now come on, come with me, I
gotta go get my clothes out of the dryer anyway.

GEORGE

I am not going to watch you do laundry.

JERRY

Come on. Be a "come with" guy.

GEORGE

Come on, I'm tired.

George and Jerry get up.

CLAIRE

Don't worry. I gave him a little caffeine. He'll perk up.

GEORGE

I knew I felt something. I did.

Claire *laughs and* exits.

CUT TO:

SEASON ONE

ACT ONE
SCENE B

INT. LAUNDROMAT—LATER

George is staring at the window of a churning clothes dryer.

GEORGE (V.O.)
This is the dullest moment I have ever experienced.

A man next to Jerry and George is utilizing all manner of laundry products with great facility.

JERRY
Oh, look at this guy. Lookit, he's got everything, he's got detergents, sprays, fabric softener. This is not his first load.

GEORGE
I need a break, Jerry. You know, I gotta get out of the city, I feel so cramped . . .

JERRY
(INTERRUPTING) And you didn't even hear how she sounded.

GEORGE
What?

JERRY
Laura.

GEORGE
I can't believe—We already discussed this.

JERRY
Yeah, but how can you be so sure?

GEORGE
'Cause it's signals. (SNAPS FINGERS) Jerry, it's signals. Don't you—Alright, did she even ask you what you were doing tomorrow night? If you're busy?

JERRY
No.

GEORGE

She calls you today, she doesn't make a plan for tomorrow? It's Saturday night.

JERRY

Yeah.

GEORGE

What is that? It's ridiculous. You don't even know what hotel she's staying at. You can't call her. That's a signal, Jerry. *That's* a signal. (SNAPS FINGERS)

JERRY

Maybe you're right.

GEORGE

Maybe I'm right. Of course I'm right.

JERRY

This is insane. You know, I don't even know where she's staying . . . She's not going to call me. It's unbelievable.

George shrugs sympathetically.

GEORGE

I know, I know. (ABOUT THE CLOTHES) Listen, your stuff has to be done by now. Why don't you just see if it's dry?

JERRY

No, no, no. Don't interrupt the cycle. The machine is working. It knows what it's doing. Let it finish.

GEORGE

You're going to overdry it.

JERRY

You can't overdry.

GEORGE

Why not?

JERRY

For the same reason you can't overwet. Once something is wet, it's wet. Same thing with death.

Like once you die, you're dead, right? Let's say you drop dead and I shoot you. You're not going to die again, you're already dead. You can't overdie, you can't overdry.

A crowd has formed.

GEORGE

Any questions?

JERRY

How could she not tell me where she was staying?

George helps the dryer stop. The cycle comes to an end.

GEORGE

Look at that, they're done. They're done.

DISSOLVE TO:

ACT ONE
SCENE C

INT. NIGHTCLUB—NIGHT A

Jerry's on stage.

JERRY

Laundry day is the only exciting day in the life of clothes. It is. No, think about it. The washing machine is the nightclub of clothes. You know, it's dark. There's bubbles happening. They're all kind of dancing around in there. The shirt grabs the underwear, "Come on, babe, let's go." You come by, you open up the lid and they all—(MIMES FREEZE) Socks are the most amazing article of clothing. They hate their lives. They're in the shoes with stinky feet. The boring drawers. The dryer is their only chance to escape and they all know it. They do escape from the dryer. They plan it, in the hamper, the night before. "Tomorrow, the dryer. I'm going. You

wait here." The dryer door swings open. The sock is waiting up against the side wall. He hopes you don't see him. Then he goes down the road. They get buttons sewn on their face, join a puppet show. So they're showing me, on television, the detergents getting out bloodstains. Is this a violent image to anybody? Bloodstains? I mean, come on, you got a T-shirt with bloodstains all over it, maybe laundry isn't your biggest problem right now. Maybe you oughta' get the harpoon out of your chest first.

CUT TO:

ACT ONE
SCENE D

Ext. Jerry's apartment building—establishing shot—night (stock)

Int. Jerry's apartment—night (night 1)

A small walk-up studio with a kitchenette on Manhattan's West Side where house plants wage a daily struggle for survival. Jerry gets milk from the fridge and carries a bowl of cold cereal over to his convertible sofa. There is a baseball game on TV. He sits.

sfx: phone rings

JERRY
(INTO PHONE) If you know what happened in the Met game, don't say anything. I taped it. Hello. No, I'm sorry, you have the wrong number . . . yeah, no—

sfx: knock at door

JERRY (CONT'D)
Yeah?

KESSLER (O.S.)
You up?

Kessler enters.

JERRY

(TO KESSLER) Yeah. (INTO PHONE) People do move. Have you ever seen the big trucks out on the street? Yeah . . . No problem. (HANGS UP)

KESSLER

Boy, the Mets blew it tonight, huh?

JERRY

(BESIDE HIMSELF) Ahhh! What are you doing? Kessler, it's a tape. I taped the game. It's one o'clock in the morning. I avoided human contact all night to watch this . . .

KESSLER

Hey, I'm sorry. I—you know, I thought you knew about it. (HOLDING UP TWO SLICES OF BREAD) You got any meat?

JERRY

Meat? I don't know. Go. Hunt. (AS KESSLER CROSSES) What happened in the game, anyway?

KESSLER

(HEAD IN FRIDGE) What happened? Well, they stunk! That's what happened. (HEAD OUT OF FRIDGE) You know, I almost wound up going to that game.

JERRY

Yeah, you almost went to the game. You haven't been out of the building in ten years.

KESSLER

Yeah.

Kessler returns, meat on sandwich, which he eats throughout scene, chewing. He looks at Jerry. Jerry looks at Kessler. After a quick evaluation, Jerry reluctantly picks up the papers from the couch. Kessler has permission to stay. He sits.

KESSLER

(LEAFING THROUGH MAGAZINE AND TEARING A PAGE) You done with this?

JERRY

No.

Kessler tries to put the page back.

KESSLER

When you're done, let me know.

JERRY

Yeah, yeah. You can have it tomorrow.

KESSLER

I thought I wasn't allowed to be in here this weekend.

JERRY

No, it's okay now. That girl's not coming. I misread the whole thing.

KESSLER

You want me to talk to her?

JERRY

I don't think so.

KESSLER

I can be very persuasive. You know that I was almost a lawyer.

He makes a "missed by inches" gesture with thumb and index finger.

JERRY

That close, huh?

KESSLER

You better believe it.

SFX: phone rings

JERRY

(INTO PHONE) Hello? . . . (VOICE GOING UP AN OCTAVE) Oh, hi, Laura . . .

KESSLER

Oh, give me it, let me talk to her. Let me talk to her.

JERRY

(INTO PHONE) No, believe me, I'm always up at this

time. How are you? . . . Great. Sure . . . What time does the plane get in? . . . I'll get my friend George to take me.

KESSLER

(ENGROSSED IN THE GAME) Slide! Oh!

JERRY

It's my neighbor. Yeah, I got it, ten-fifteen. No, don't be silly. Go ahead and ask . . . (SURPRISED) Yeah, sure. Okay. Great. No, no, it's no trouble at all. I'll see you tomorrow. Great. Bye. (HANGS UP, CONFUSED) I don't believe it. That was her. She wants to stay here.

FADE OUT:

END OF ACT ONE

ACT TWO

SCENE E

FADE IN:

EXT. JERRY'S APARTMENT BUILDING—ESTABLISHING SHOT—NIGHT (STOCK)

INT. JERRY'S APARTMENT—NIGHT (NIGHT 2)

George and Jerry have deposited a queen-size futon into the living room.

GEORGE

You know, I can't believe you're bringing in an extra bed for a woman that wants to sleep with you. Why don't you bring in an extra guy, too?

JERRY

Look, it's a very awkward situation. I don't want to be presumptuous.

GEORGE

Alright, alright, one more time. One more time. What was the exact phrasing of the request?

JERRY

Alright, she said she couldn't find a decent hotel room . . .

GEORGE

A *decent* hotel room . . .

JERRY

Yeah, a decent hotel room, would it be terribly inconvenient if she stayed at my place.

GEORGE

You can't be serious. This is New York City. There must be eleven million decent hotel rooms. What do you need, a flag? (WAVES HANKY) This is the signal, Jerry, this is the signal.

JERRY

This is the signal. Thank you, Mr. Signal. Where were you yesterday?

GEORGE

I think I was affected by the caffeine.

The door opens and Ralph, a somewhat hyper Labrador, bounds in, followed by Kessler. Ralph jumps on George.

GEORGE

Whoa, whoa, whoa, good dog, good dog, alright! Good dog.

KESSLER

He really likes you, George.

GEORGE

Well, that's flattering.

Ralph runs into the bathroom.

KESSLER

Ah, he's getting a drink of water.

Kessler sees the futon.

KESSLER

Is this for that girl?

JERRY

Yeah.

KESSLER

Why even give her an option?

JERRY

This is a person I like. It's not "how to score on spring break."

GEORGE

Can we go? I'm double-parked. I'm going to get a ticket.

JERRY

Yeah. Okay. Oh, wait a second, I forgot to clean the bathroom.

GEORGE

So what? That's good.

JERRY

Now how could that be good?

GEORGE

Because filth is good. What do you think, rock stars have sponges and ammonia lying around the bathroom? You think they have women coming over, they gotta tidy up? In these matters, never do what your instincts tell you. Always, always do the opposite.

JERRY

This is how you operate?

GEORGE

Yeah, I wish.

JERRY

Let me just wipe the sink.

KESSLER

Why even give her an option for?

Jerry exits, *leaving George alone with Kessler.*

KESSLER (CONT'D)

Unbelievable. (BEAT) How's the real estate business?

GEORGE

It's not bad. It's coming along. Why? Did you need something?

KESSLER

You handle any of that commercial real estate?

GEORGE

Well, I might be getting into that.

KESSLER

You keep me posted.

GEORGE

I'm aware of you. (LOSING PATIENCE) Alright, let's go.

Jerry returns.

GEORGE (CONT'D)

Let's go. You're on stage in twenty-five minutes.

DISSOLVE TO:

ACT TWO
SCENE H

INT. NIGHTCLUB—NIGHT B

Jerry's on stage.

JERRY

The dating world is not a fun world. It's a pressure world, it's a world of tension, it's a world of pain. And you know, if a woman comes over to my house, I gotta get that bathroom ready, 'cause she needs things. Women need equipment. I don't know what they need. I know I don't have it—I know that. You know what they need? Women seem to need a lot of cotton balls. I don't have cotton balls. I've never had a cotton ball. I've never bought a cotton ball. Women need cotton balls. I've never been in a situation where I thought to myself, I could use a cotton ball right now. The only time I ever see them is in the bottom of your little wastebasket. There's two or three that look like they've

THE SEINFELD CHRONICLES

been through some horrible experience. Tortured, interrogated—I don't know what happened to them. I once went out with a woman. She left a little Ziploc baggie of cotton balls over at my house. I didn't know what to do. I took them out, I put them on the kitchen floor like little tumbleweeds. I thought maybe the cockroaches would see it, figure, "This is a dead town, let's move on." The dating world is a world of pressure. Let's face it, a date is a job interview that lasts all night. The only difference between a date and a job interview is not at many job interviews is there a chance you'll end up naked at the end of it. You know, "Well, Bill, the boss thinks you're the man for the position, why don't you strip down and meet some of the people you'll be working with?"

CUT TO:

ACT TWO
SCENE J

EXT. AIRPORT TERMINAL—NIGHT—(STOCK)

INT. AIRPORT—GATE FORTY-THREE—NIGHT (NIGHT 2)

Jerry and George are sitting on a bench, watching people go by.

JERRY
Wouldn't it be great if you could ask a woman what she's thinking?

GEORGE
What a world that would be. If you could ask a woman what she's thinking.

JERRY
You know, instead, I'm like a detective, I've got to pick up clues, the whole thing is like a murder investigation.

GEORGE

Don't get worked up. Because you're going to know the whole story the minute she steps off the plane.

JERRY

Really, how?

GEORGE

It's all in the greeting.

JERRY

Uh-huh.

GEORGE

Alright. If she puts her bags down before she greets you. That's a good sign.

JERRY

Right.

GEORGE

You know anything in the lip area is good.

JERRY

Lip area.

GEORGE

A hug is definitely good.

JERRY

A hug is definitely good.

GEORGE

Sure.

JERRY

Although what if it's one of those numbers where the shoulders are touching, but the hips are eight feet apart?

GEORGE

Brutal.

JERRY

You know how they do that?

GEORGE

A shake is bad.

JERRY

A shake is bad. But what if it's the two-hander? The hand on the bottom, the hand on the top, the warm look in the eyes. Hand sandwich.

GEORGE

Right. Well, that's open to interpretation because so much depends on the layering, the quality of the wetness in the eyes—

Passengers start filing out. *After a few moments, Laura sneaks up behind Jerry and covers his eyes with her hands.*

LAURA

Guess who?

JERRY

Hey, hey—

JERRY/LAURA

(HOLDING HANDS) Heeeey. Heeeey. Heeeey.

JERRY

Good to see you. This is my friend George.

LAURA

Oh, hi. Hi, nice to meet you.

GEORGE

Hi. How are you? Good. Laura. Sure.

JERRY

I can't believe you're here. Wow.

A beat. Laura motions to her bags. Jerry and George rush over and pick them up.

JERRY

The bags. The bags. Oh, I'm sorry.

LAURA

Well, thank you.

They start to walk off.

JERRY

Well, that was an interesting greeting, did you notice
that, George?

GEORGE

(STUMPED) Yes, the surprise blindfold greeting . . . That
wasn't in the manual.

CUT TO:

ACT TWO
SCENE K

INT. JERRY'S APARTMENT—LATER

Jerry and Laura enter. *He* turns on *the* lamp.

JERRY

So, uh, what do you think?

LAURA

Oh. This place isn't so bad.

JERRY

It kinda motivates me to work on the road. So, make
yourself at home.

She sits on the couch and takes off her shoes.

JERRY (CONT'D)

So, can I get you anything? Bread? Water? Salad
dressing?

LAURA

Actually . . . do you have any wine?

JERRY

Yeah, I think I do.

LAURA

(ABOUT LAMP) Oh, do you mind if I turn this down?

JERRY

No—yeah, go right ahead.

Jerry moves toward kitchen area.

LAURA

Jerry, I was wondering . . . would it be possible, and if it's not, fine, for me to stay here tomorrow night, too?

JERRY

Yeah, yeah, sure, yeah, why don't you stay? What is your—what is your schedule for tomorrow? Are you doing anything?

LAURA

No, I'd love to do something. I have my seminar in the morning, but after that I'm wide open.

JERRY

Really? What would you like to do?

LAURA

Well, I know this sounds touristy, but I'd just love to go on one of those five-hour boat rides around Manhattan.

JERRY

Yeah, we could do that . . . why not? Why not?

Jerry sits on the couch.

JERRY

I'm just—I'm really glad you're here.

SFX: phone rings

JERRY (CONT'D)

(INTO PHONE) Hello . . . yeah . . . yes, she is. Hold on. It's for you.

LAURA

(INTO PHONE) Hello? Hi . . . No, no, it was great. Right on time. No, I'm gonna stay here tomorrow. Yes, yes, it's fine. No, we're going on a boat ride. Don't be silly . . . I'm not gonna have this conversation. Look, I'll call you tomorrow. Okay. Bye.

Laura hangs up.

LAURA (CONT'D)

Never get engaged.

JERRY

You're engaged?

LAURA

You know, you really have no idea what it's like until you actually do it. You know, I'm on this emotional rollercoaster.

JERRY

You're engaged?

LAURA

I can't believe it myself sometimes. You have to start thinking in terms of we. It's a very stressful situation.

JERRY

You're engaged.

LAURA

Yeah, he's a great guy. You'd really like him . . . (BEAT) I can't wait to get on that boat.

JERRY

Me, too.

On Jerry's look we:

CUT TO:

**ACT TWO
SCENE P**

INT. NIGHTCLUB—NIGHT C

Jerry's on stage.

JERRY

I swear I have absolutely no idea what women are

thinking. I don't get it, okay? I admit, I'm not getting
the signals. I am not getting it. Women, they're so
subtle. They're little—everything they do is subtle. Men
are not subtle. We are obvious. Women know what
men want, men know what men want. What do we
want? We want women. That's it. It's the only thing we
know for sure. It really is. We want women. How do
we get them? Oh, we don't know about that, we don't
know. The next step after that we have no idea. This is
why you see men honking car horns, yelling from
construction sites, these are the best ideas we've had so
far. The car horn honk. Is that the beauty? Have you
seen men doing this? What is—the man is in the car.
The woman walks by the front of the car. He
honks—(MAKES SOUND) Beep, beep, beeeep, beeeep.
This man is out of ideas. The amazing thing is that we
still get women, don't we? Men—I mean, men are with
women. You see men with women. How are men
getting women, many people wonder? Let me tell you
a little bit about our organization. Wherever women
are, we have a man working on the situation right now.
Now, he may not be our best man, okay, we have a lot
of areas to cover—but someone from our staff is on the
scene. That's why I think men get frustrated when we
see women reading articles like, "Where to Meet Men."
We're here, we're everywhere, we're honking our horns
to serve you better.

FADE OUT:

END OF SHOW

THE Seinfeld SCRIPTS

THE
STAKE
OUT

WRITTEN BY
LARRY DAVID & JERRY SEINFELD

DIRECTED BY
TOM CHERONES

AS BROADCAST MAY 31, 1990

ELAINE

Oh, Jerry . . .

JERRY (V.O.)

Oh no, not now.

Jerry turns to Elaine.

ELAINE

I had this dream last night, and you were in it.

JERRY

Really?

ELAINE

Yeah.

JERRY (V.O.)

Oh, God. I gotta get out of this.

ELAINE

You were you, but you weren't you.

JERRY

No kidding?

JERRY (V.O.)

Why is this happening? Please, make her stop.

ELAINE

I think . . . I think we were in my house where I grew up and you were standing there, you were looking out the window.

JERRY (V.O.)

This is brutal.

ELAINE

And you turned around and you had these wooden teeth.

JERRY

How do you like that?

JERRY (V.O.)

Can I turn now? Is this over? No, I can't. I can't. I'm stuck.

ELAINE

Jerry, are you listening to me?

JERRY

Yes, I heard you.

PAMELA

Elaine, what's the name of that jewelry store you took me to that time?

JERRY (V.O.)

Thank you, Pamela.

Jerry exits his conversation and turns back towards Vanessa.

JERRY

So, you're a lawyer.

VANESSA

Sagman, Bennett, Robbins, Oppenheim and Taff.

JERRY (V.O.)

(QUICKLY MEMORIZING) Sagman, Bennett, Robbins, Oppenheim and Taff. Sagman, Bennett, Robbins, Oppenheim and Taff.

JERRY

Of course. They handled my tattoo removal lawsuit.

VANESSA

Oh, that was you?

JERRY

Imagine? Spelling "mom" with two "o's"?

VANESSA

Very funny. What do you do?

JERRY

Comedian.

VANESSA

Really? That explains it.

JERRY (V.O.)

(STILL MEMORIZING) Sagman, Bennett, Robbins,

Oppenheim and Taff. Sagman, Bennett, Robbins, Oppenheim and Taff.

ROGER

Are you ready?

Vanessa gets up. Jerry's stunned.

VANESSA

We gotta run. Happy birthday. Bye everyone.

Everyone ad-libs goodbyes.

PAMELA

Thanks for coming.

VANESSA

(TO JERRY) Bye.

JERRY (V.O.)

I can't believe it. I've got nothing. I don't even know her name . . . Sagman, Bennett, Robbins, Oppenheim and Taff. Sagman, Bennett, Robbins, Oppenheim and Taff . . .

Jerry turns to Elaine, who gives him a look.

CUT TO:

ACT ONE
SCENE D

EXT. TAXI—NIGHT

INT. TAXICAB—NIGHT—A FEW MINUTES LATER (2)

Jerry and Elaine are riding along in silence for a few moments.

JERRY

. . . that wasn't so bad really.

Elaine doesn't respond, then:

ELAINE

You know, uh, you could use a little work on your manners.

JERRY

Why? What did I do?

ELAINE

Well . . . well I just don't appreciate these little courtesy responses, like I'm selling you aluminum siding.

JERRY

I was listening.

ELAINE

No. You couldn't wait to get back to your little conversation.

JERRY

No, you . . . you were talking about the, uh, the dream, you had—where you were, uh, you had wooden teeth . . .

ELAINE

No! No! You had wooden teeth. You had wooden teeth. I didn't have wooden teeth. *You* did.

JERRY

Alright. So *I* had wooden teeth. So what?

ELAINE

So . . . so nothing. Nothing!

As Elaine stares out the window:

CUT TO:

ACT ONE
SCENE DD

INT. NIGHTCLUB—NIGHT
(*Jerry, Extras*)

JERRY

Apparently, Plato, who came up with the concept of the platonic relationship, was pretty excited about it. He named it after himself. He said, "Yeah, I got this new thing, 'platonic.' My idea, my name, called it after myself. What I do is, I go out with the girls, I talk with them, don't do anything and go right home. What do you think? I think it's going to be big." I bet you, there were other guys in history that tried to get relationships named after them—but it didn't work. You know, I bet you, there were guys who tried to do it—just went, uh, "Hi, uh, name's Rico, would you like to go to bed immediately?" Hey, it's a Riconic relationship.

CUT TO:

ACT ONE
SCENE E

INT. JERRY'S APARTMENT—LATER THAT NIGHT (2)

Jerry enters. *His parents are under the covers in Jerry's folded-out sofa bed, reading and watching TV.*

JERRY

Hey . . .

FATHER

. . . There he is.

JERRY

This is what I like. See? You come home, your parents are in your bed.

MOTHER

You know, Jerry, we don't have to do this.

JERRY

What are you talking about? It's fine. I love having you here.

MOTHER

Tomorrow we'll go to a hotel.

JERRY

Ma, will you stop?

MOTHER

No, why should we take over your apartment?

JERRY

I don't care, I'm sleeping next door.

MOTHER

Your friend Kramer doesn't mind?

JERRY

No, he's making a bouillabase . . . So, Dad, let me ask you a question. How many people work at these big law offices?

FATHER

Depends on the firm.

JERRY

Yeah, but if you called up and described someone, do you think they would know who it was?

FATHER

What's the matter? You need a lawyer?

JERRY

No. I met someone at this party and I know where she works but I don't know her name.

MOTHER

So, why don't you ask someone who was at the party?

JERRY

No, the only one I could ask is Elaine and I can't ask her.

THE STAKE OUT

FATHER

Why not?

JERRY

Because it's complicated. There's some tension there.

MOTHER

He used to go with her.

FATHER

Which one is she?

MOTHER

From Maryland. The one that brought the chocolate covered cherries you didn't like.

FATHER

Oh, yeah, very alert . . . warm person.

JERRY

Oh, yeah, she's great.

MOTHER

So how come nothing materialized there?

JERRY

Well, it's a tough thing to talk about, uh, I don't know.

MOTHER

I know what it was.

JERRY

You don't know what it was.

MOTHER

So, what was it?

JERRY

Well, we would fight a lot, for some reason.

MOTHER	**FATHER**
Oh . . . well.	Oh . . . well.

JERRY

And, there was a little problem with the physical chemistry.

A stunned silence—everyone is uncomfortable.

MOTHER

(FINALLY) Well, I think she's a very attractive girl.

JERRY

Oh, she is . . . she absolutely is.

MOTHER

I can see if there was a weight problem.

JERRY

No, it's not that. It wasn't all one-sided.

MOTHER

You know, you can't be so particular. Nobody's perfect.

JERRY

I know. I know.

FATHER

(GOING FOR THE JOKE) You know, Jerry, it's a good thing I wasn't so particular.

MOTHER

Idiot. (TO JERRY) So, who are you looking for, Sophia Loren?

JERRY

That's got nothing to do with it.

FATHER

How about Loni Anderson?

MOTHER

Where do you get Loni Anderson?

FATHER

Why, what's wrong with Loni Anderson?

MOTHER

I like Elaine more than Loni Anderson.

JERRY

What are you two talking about? Look, Elaine just wasn't the one.

MOTHER

And this other one's the one?

JERRY

I don't know, maybe.

FATHER

So ask Elaine there for the number.

JERRY

I can't. She'll get upset. I never talk about other women with her, especially this one tonight.

MOTHER

How could you still see her if you're not interested?

JERRY

We're friends.

FATHER

Doesn't sound like you're friends to me. If you were friends, you'd . . . you'd ask her for the number. Do you know where this other one works?

JERRY

Oh yeah.

FATHER

So go up to the office.

MOTHER

Up to her office?

FATHER

Go to the building. She goes out to lunch, doesn't she?

JERRY

I guess.

FATHER

So you stand in the lobby by the elevator and wait for her to come down for lunch.

JERRY

You mean stake out the lobby?

MOTHER

Oh, Morty, that's ridiculous. Just ask Elaine for the number.

FATHER

He doesn't want to ask Elaine for the number!

MOTHER

So, you've got him standing by the elevator like a dope. What happens when he sees her?

FATHER

He pretends he bumped into her.

JERRY

You know what? This is not that bad an idea.

FADE OUT:

END OF ACT ONE

ACT TWO

SCENE G

FADE IN:

EXT. OFFICE BUILDING

INT. OFFICE BUILDING—LOBBY—THE NEXT DAY (3)

Angle *on a closed elevator door. After a few beats the door opens and a lunch throng pours out. Then* angle *on Jerry and George watching intently.*

GEORGE

What does she look like?

JERRY

I don't know. Hard to say.

GEORGE

What actress, uh, does she remind you of?

JERRY

Loni Anderson.

GEORGE

Loni Anderson?

JERRY

What? There's something wrong with Loni Anderson? Hey, listen, thanks again for running over here. I appreciate it.

GEORGE

Oh, yeah, sure. I was showing a condo on Forty-eighth Street. Besides, you think I want to miss this? (HE LAUGHS)

A beat.

JERRY

I'm a little nervous.

GEORGE

Yeah, me too.

JERRY

If I see her, what do I say that I'm doing here in the building?

GEORGE

You came to see me. I work in the building.

JERRY

What do you do?

GEORGE

I'm an architect.

JERRY

You're an architect?

GEORGE

I'm not?

JERRY

I don't see architecture coming from you.

GEORGE

I suppose you could be an architect.

JERRY

I never said that I was the architect. Just something else.

GEORGE

Alright, she's not even gonna ask. If we see her, which is remote.

JERRY

Well, what do you want me to say? I just wandered in here?

GEORGE

We're having lunch with a friend, he works in the building.

JERRY

What is his name?

GEORGE

Burt . . . Har . . . bin . . . son. Burt Harbinson.

JERRY

Burt Harbinson. It sounds made up.

GEORGE

No good? Alright, uh . . . Art . . . Core.

JERRY

Art Core.

GEORGE

velay.

JERRY

Corevelay?

GEORGE

Yeah, right.

JERRY

What does he do?

GEORGE

He's an importer.

JERRY

Just imports? No exports?

GEORGE

He's an importer/exporter, okay? Elaine ever call you back?

JERRY

No, I guess she's still mad.

GEORGE

I don't understand. You . . . you never talk to her about other women?

JERRY

Never.

Angle *on elevator. More office workers exit.*

JERRY (CONT'D)

Wait a second. That's her on the right.

GEORGE

(PANICKING) I forgot who I am. Who am I?

JERRY

You're you. We're having lunch with Art Corevelay.

GEORGE

Vandelay.

JERRY

Corevelay.

GEORGE

Let me be the architect. I can do it.

As Vanessa passes:

JERRY

Hey, hey . . . Uh . . . Pamela's birthday party. Didn't I see you there? Jerry.

VANESSA

Sure, hi.

George nudges Jerry to introduce him.

JERRY

Uh, this is George . . . (REACHING FOR HER NAME) I'm sorry.

VANESSA

Vanessa.

GEORGE

Nice to meet you.

JERRY

Oooohhh . . . Sagman, Bennett, Robbins, Oppenheim
and Taff.

VANESSA

(LAUGHS) That's right.

JERRY

Yeah.

VANESSA

What are you doing here?

JERRY & GEORGE

Oh.

JERRY

We're meeting a friend of ours for lunch. Works here in
the building.

GEORGE

Art Vandelay.

VANESSA

Oh, really. Which company?

JERRY	**GEORGE**
I don't know . . . uh.	I don't really know . . . uh. . . .

JERRY

He's an importer.

VANESSA

Importer?

GEORGE

And exporter.

JERRY

He's an importer/exporter.

GEORGE

I'm, uh, I'm an architect.

VANESSA

Really. What do you design?

> **GEORGE**
>
> Uh . . . railroads.

> **VANESSA**
>
> I thought engineers do that.

> **GEORGE**
>
> They can.

> **JERRY**
>
> You know, I'm sorry you had to leave so early the other night.

> **VANESSA**
>
> Oh, me too. My cousin had to go back to Boston.

> **JERRY**
>
> Oh, that guy was your cousin?

> **VANESSA**
>
> Yeah . . . And that woman was your . . .

> **JERRY**
>
> Friend.

> **GEORGE**
>
> I'll just, uh, get a paper.

They watch George leave, then:

> **JERRY**
>
> So . . . uhm, do you, date, uh, immature men?

> **VANESSA**
>
> Almost exclusively.

CUT TO:

ACT TWO
SCENE H

EXT. APARTMENT—NIGHT

INT. JERRY'S APARTMENT—THREE DAYS LATER (4)

Jerry is playing scrabble with his mother while his father is sitting on the couch repairing a pair of shoes. Jerry waits impatiently for his mother to make a move.

THE STAKE OUT

MOTHER

(SHE HUMS, THEN:) I have no letters. (HUMS AGAIN)

JERRY

Ma, will you go already.

Jerry's mother picks up the dictionary.

JERRY (CONT'D)

What are you doing?

MOTHER

Wait, I just want to see something.

JERRY

You can't look in there. We're playing.

She continues looking. Kramer enters.

KRAMER

Hi.

JERRY

Hi.

FATHER

Good evening, Mr. Kramer.

KRAMER

Hey, Morty. (TO JERRY) Salad dressing?

JERRY

Look.

Kramer enters the kitchen.

MOTHER

Quo. Is that a word?

JERRY

Maybe.

MOTHER

Will you challenge it?

JERRY

Ma, you can't look up words in the dictionary . . . Dad,
she's cheating.

KRAMER

(FROM KITCHEN) Quo. That's not a word.

MOTHER

You're such a stickler.

JERRY

Well put something down. You're taking twenty
minutes on this . . . So is Uncle Mac and Artie, they're
all coming over here before the wedding?

MOTHER

They'll be here at two o'clock. Oh, Elaine called. She
said she'd be here at two-thirty and she says
(CONSULTING PAD FOR MESSAGE) ". . . Hope your
meeting went well with Art Vandelay."

JERRY

She said that?

MOTHER

Just what I said. Here.

*She hands Jerry the pad with Jerry's message. Kramer is now standing
over Jerry's mother's shoulder, rearranging the scrabble tiles on her rack.*

JERRY

She knows. Oh, I am such a jackass.

MOTHER

She knows what?

JERRY

She knows the whole stupid thing—Vanessa and the
elevator.

As Kramer fiddles with the mother's letters:

MOTHER

(TO KRAMER) No, no, no. That won't do he might have
the Z.

*Kramer wanders behind Jerry, sneaks a peek at his letters, and shoots
the mother a "be careful" look.*

THE STAKE OUT

FATHER

So, how did she find out?

JERRY

Because Vanessa probably told Pamela and Pamela probably told Elaine.

FATHER

So, what are you afraid of her?

JERRY

Yes. Yes, I am. (TO MOTHER) What else did she say on the phone?

MOTHER

Whatever I wrote down.

JERRY

Yeah, but what was the tone in her voice? How did she sound?

MOTHER

Who am I, Rich Little?

FATHER

Well, she can't be too mad, she's still coming to the wedding.

JERRY

Yeah, but now I'm nervous.

MOTHER

Oh, stop it.

Kramer rearranges the tiles. Mother looks back at him quizzically. He responds with a confident nod. She places letters on the board.

JERRY

Quone?

MOTHER

(ADDING UP) Thirty, thirty-one, thirty-two—

JERRY

"Quone?" No, I'm afraid I'm gonna have to challenge that.

Jerry grabs the dictionary.

> **KRAMER**
>
> No, no, you don't have to challenge that. That's a word.
> That's a definite word.

> **JERRY**
>
> I am challenging.

> **KRAMER**
>
> Quone—to quone something.

> **JERRY**
>
> No. No.

> **MOTHER**
>
> I'm not playing with you anymore.

> **FATHER**
>
> Quone's not a word.

> **JERRY**
>
> (FINDING IT) No good. Sorry, there it is. Get it off.

> **MOTHER**
>
> (TO KRAMER) Why did you make me put that down?

> **KRAMER**
>
> No. We need a medical dictionary. A patient gets
> difficult, you quone him.

CUT TO:

ACT TWO
SCENE J

EXT. APARTMENT—DAY

INT. JERRY'S APARTMENT—DAY (5)

*Jerry's parents and other couples have gathered in Jerry's apartment
before the wedding. They're all on the verge of leaving. Jerry is anxiously
checking his watch.*

THE STAKE OUT

CAROL

You want to get some funny material, you ought to come down to where I work. There's a sitcom.

JERRY

You must have quite a time down there.

Jerry checks his watch again.

CAROL

We got plenty of time.

JERRY

Oh, I'm sorry. I'm just waiting for someone.

Uncle Mac approaches Jerry and Carol.

UNCLE MAC

(TO CAROL) Watch what you say to this guy. He'll put it in his next act.

JERRY

Yeah, yeah.

Jerry turns and, from across the room, sees Elaine enter. She's greeted by Jerry's parents and is introduced to his aunt.

UNCLE MAC

Jerry, did I tell you I'm writing a book? An autobiography.

JERRY

(DISTRACTED) Yeah, Uncle Mac, you mentioned it.

UNCLE MAC

It's based on all my experiences.

JERRY

Perfect. Could you excuse me one second.

Jerry approaches Elaine, who meets him halfway. Jerry sticks out his hand.

JERRY

(AS THEY SHAKE HANDS) How do you do? Jerry Seinfeld.

ELAINE

Oh, how do you do? Elaine Benes.

They both give an uncomfortable sigh.

JERRY

Uh, do you wanna do this now or you wanna wait until we get in the car?

ELAINE

Oh, no. Let's do it now.

JERRY

Alright, the whole elevator business, let me just explain . . .

ELAINE

Okay.

Cousin Artie interrupts from across the room.

ARTIE

Jerry, are you going with us?

JERRY

No, I'm gonna take my car.

ARTIE

That's why I brought the wagon. (TO CAROL) Why the hell did I bring the wagon?

JERRY

(TO ELAINE) Anyway, you know why I didn't ask you. I mean I felt so uncomfortable and you were so annoyed in the cab . . .

ELAINE

Well, Jerry, I never saw you flirt with anyone before. It was quite the spectacle.

MOTHER

(INTERRUPTING) Jerry, we'll see you there. Bye Elaine.

ELAINE

Oh, bye. Good to see you.

The three couples begin to file out. They're all out except Artie.

THE STAKE OUT

ARTIE

(TO ELAINE) We didn't meet.

JERRY

Oh, I'm sorry. Elaine, this is my cousin, Artie Levine.

ARTIE

(CORRECTING) Levine. (AS IN "VINE")

CAROL

Artie, come on.

Carol and Artie leave.

JERRY

Yeah "Levine," and I'm Jerry Cougar Mellencamp.

Elaine laughs, then:

JERRY

Anyway, I admit it was a fairly ridiculous thing to do, but I mean . . . I mean obviously we have a little problem here.

ELAINE

Yeah, obviously.

JERRY

I mean if we're gonna be friends, we gotta be able to talk about other people.

ELAINE

Couldn't agree more.

JERRY

Good.

ELAINE

Good.

JERRY

Good.

ELAINE

Great.

JERRY

Great? Where do you get great?

ELAINE

It's great . . . to talk about . . . other people.

JERRY

Guys.

ELAINE

Yeah.

JERRY

Uh-huh. Yeah, so anybody specific?

ELAINE

No. A general guy.

JERRY

Oh, really. Elaine Marie Benes.

ELAINE

What? No. It's not a big deal.

JERRY

(INTERRUPTING) No. That's great. Terrific.

ELAINE

No, we just met.

JERRY

Doesn't matter. What's the young man's name? I would like to meet him.

ELAINE

Mmm . . . I don't think so.

JERRY

Well, what does he do? Is he an artisan, a craftsman, a laborer of some sort?

ELAINE

Wall Street.

JERRY

Ah, high finance. Bulls, bears, people from Connecticut.

THE STAKE OUT

ELAINE

And he happens to be pretty good looking.

JERRY

Alright, sir.

ELAINE

And, he's hilarious.

JERRY

Now that's not fair . . . So where did you meet this guy?

ELAINE

I staked out his health club.

JERRY

Uh-huh. When you're on a stake out do you find it's better to stand up against the wall—(DEMONSTRATES) or kinda crouch down behind a big plant?

As he closes the door,

CUT TO:

ACT TWO
SCENE K

INT. NIGHTCLUB—NIGHT
(Jerry, Extras)

JERRY

You know, I think that even if you've had a relationship with someone, or let's say, especially if you've had a relationship with someone and you try and become friends afterwards, it's very difficult. Isn't this? It's hard because you know each other so well. You know? You know all each other's tricks. It's like two magicians trying to entertain each other. You know, the one goes,

"Look, a rabbit." The other goes, "So? . . . I believe
that's your card." "Look why don't we just saw each
other in half and call it a night? Okay?"

FADE OUT:

END OF SHOW

THE *Seinfeld* SCRIPTS

THE
ROBBERY

WRITTEN BY

MATT GOLDMAN

DIRECTED BY

TOM CHERONES

AS BROADCAST JUNE 7, 1990

ACT ONE

SCENE A

OPENING CREDITS OVER.

INT. NIGHTCLUB
(*Jerry, Extras*)

JERRY

So, I move into the center lane—now I get ahead of this
woman who felt, for some reason, I guess, that she
thought that I cut her off. So, she pulls up along side of
me—gives me—the finger. It seems like such an
arbitrary, ridiculous thing to just pick a finger and you
show it to the person. It's a finger, what . . . what does
it mean? Someone shows me one of their fingers and
I'm supposed to feel bad. Is that the way it's supposed
to work? I mean, you could just give someone the toe
really, couldn't you? I would feel worse if I got the toe
than if I got the finger, 'cause it's not easy to give
someone the toe. You gotta get the shoe off, the sock
off and drive, get it up in the—"Look at that toe
buddy!" I mean that's really insulting to get the toe, isn't
it?

CUT TO:

ACT ONE
SCENE B

EXT. APARTMENT—DAY

INT. APARTMENT—DAY (1)
(*Jerry, Elaine, George*)

Jerry is finishing packing his garment bag with a masterful flourish. Elaine watches in awe.

JERRY

Is that it? I got the Q-Tips, got the mini-umbrella, something boring to read on the plane. (HE ZIPS UP THE BAG) That's it. Done.

ELAINE

(APPLAUDING LIGHTLY) That is the single greatest packing performance I have ever seen.

JERRY

I am the Master Packer.

ELAINE

(SARCASTICALLY) Yeah, right, you're the Master Packer.

JERRY

What you must understand, Elaine, packing is no different than leading men into battle. You've got to know the strengths and weaknesses of every soldier in that platoon, from a collapsible toothbrush to a pair of ordinary black socks.

ELAINE

Excuse me, Master Packer.

JERRY

Yes?

ELAINE

Just give me your keys.

JERRY

Alright, sir.

He gives her the keys.

SFX: *buzzer*

JERRY

George?

GEORGE (O.S.)

Yeah . . .

Jerry buzzes him in.

ELAINE

Okay. So, now is there anything else I need to know about this place?

JERRY

Uh, yeah, the hot water takes a little while to come on. So the best thing to do is to turn it on, do all your shopping, come back and take a shower.

ELAINE

Okay, this is quite a place.

JERRY

There's more, the refrigerator. (AS A SQUADRON COMMANDER) Deduct a minimum of two days off all expiration dates. No meat, no leftovers, no butter. And I cannot overstate this, no soft cheeses of any kind. Is that clear?

ELAINE

I'll eat out.

JERRY

And one more thing, Benes. Regarding sexual activity. It is strictly prohibited. But if you absolutely must, do us all a big favor, do it in the tub.

George enters.

GEORGE

You ready?

JERRY

Yeah, one sec.

GEORGE

Hey, Elaine.

ELAINE

Hi.

GEORGE

You coming to the airport with us?

ELAINE

No, I'm staying here for the weekend. I'm getting a break from my roommate.

GEORGE

Oh, the actress/waitress?

ELAINE

No, the waitress/actress. She just got some part in some dinner theater production of *A Chorus Line.* So now all day long she's walking around the apartment singing, "God I hope I get it. I hope I get it." Oh, she's gonna get it right in the . . .

GEORGE

Why don't you just kick her out?

ELAINE

She's on the lease. George, you have got to find another place for me.

GEORGE

Yeah, well—a little rough finding something good in your price range. (TO JERRY) Hey, but you, my friend, may be in luck.

JERRY

I'm not looking.

GEORGE

No, no, no, no. This one's different, this one's a beauty.

JERRY

Yeah? What's it like?

GEORGE

I haven't seen it yet but it's a two bedroom, it's on West Eighty-third, about a half block from the park.

JERRY

How much?

GEORGE

About twice what you're paying here but it's a great building, it's two bedrooms.

JERRY

Two bedrooms? What do I need two bedrooms? I got enough trouble maintaining activity in one.

George and Elaine exchange looks.

JERRY (CONT'D)

I saw that.

ELAINE

You ought to at least take a look at it.

JERRY

Really? Why?

ELAINE

'Cause then I could move in here.

JERRY

Aaaaahhhh . . . I know what you're saying now.

ELAINE

Aaaahhhh. (SHE LAUGHS) It's time you got out of here anyway.

GEORGE

Yeah, yeah, tell him. But quickly, I'm double-parked here.

ELAINE

Listen, Jerry, this place is falling apart. You have no hot water, you can't have soft cheese.

GEORGE

And let's not forget the radiator? The steam has been on here for ten years. No human can turn this off.

THE ROBBERY

ELAINE

Jerry, come on, you're doing okay now. You should at
least take a look at this place. You shouldn't have to live
like this.

JERRY

Like this? You just said you wanted to live here.

ELAINE

Well, for me it's a step up, it's like moving from Iceland
to Finland.

GEORGE

Jerry, what do you . . . do you . . . do you want to see
the place or not?

JERRY

I can't think about it now. Come on, I'm going to
Minneapolis. I got four shows this weekend.

DISSOLVE TO:

ACT ONE
SCENE D

EXT. APARTMENT—DAY

INT. APARTMENT—DAY (2)
(*Jerry, Elaine, Kramer*)

Jerry arrives two days later. Elaine's in the bathroom.

JERRY

Elaine (PUTS HIS BAG DOWN) Ugh.

*Jerry sits on the couch and picks up the TV remote, pushes it—there is
no T.V. He looks around.*

JERRY (CONT'D)

Elaine?

She comes out of the bathroom with a plunger. Something is obviously wrong.

> **ELAINE**
>
> Jerry. Jerry. Oh, hi. Welcome back. How were the shows?

> **JERRY**
>
> Great. I had fun. (LOOKING AROUND) Where's the TV? Where's the VCR?

Elaine makes a face.

> **JERRY (CONT'D)**
>
> What?

> **ELAINE**
>
> They were stolen.

> **JERRY**
>
> Stolen? When?

> **ELAINE**
>
> A couple of hours ago. The police are coming right over.

> **JERRY**
>
> Stolen?

Kramer enters.

> **ELAINE**
>
> Someone left the door open.

Kramer's expression tells all. He shrugs apologetically.

> **JERRY**
>
> You left the door open?

> **KRAMER**
>
> Oh . . . just . . . you know . . . I was cooking. And I . . . I, you know, I came to get the spatula. I left the door open 'cause I was going to bring the spatula right back.

> **JERRY**
>
> Wait. You left the lock open or the door open?

THE ROBBERY

KRAMER

The door.

JERRY

The door. You left the door open?

KRAMER

Yeah, well I was gonna bring the spatula right back.

JERRY

Yeah, and?

KRAMER

Well, I got caught up watching a soap opera. *The Bold and the Beautiful.*

JERRY

So the door was wide open.

KRAMER

Wide open.

JERRY

(TO ELAINE) And where were you?

ELAINE

I was at Bloomingdale's . . . waiting for the shower to heat up.

KRAMER

Look, Jerry, I'm sorry. I'm . . . You have insurance, right, buddy?

JERRY

No.

KRAMER

(ADMONISHING) How can you not have insurance?

JERRY

Because I spent my money on the Clapco D-29, it's the most impenetrable lock on the market today. It has only one design flaw, the door must be closed.

KRAMER

Jerry, I'm gonna find your stuff. I'm . . . I'm gonna solve it. I'm on the case, buddy, I'm on the case.

> **JERRY**
>
> Yeah. Don't investigate. Don't pay me back. It was an accident.

> **KRAMER**
>
> I made a mistake.

> **JERRY**
>
> These things happen.

> **KRAMER**
>
> I'm human.

> **JERRY**
>
> In your way.

DISSOLVE TO:

ACT ONE
SCENE E

EXT. APARTMENT—DAY

INT. APARTMENT TEN MINUTES LATER DAY (2)
(Cop, Elaine, Jerry, George)

A cop talks to Jerry and Elaine.

> **COP**
>
> (READING REPORT) Let's see, that's one TV, stereo, one leather jacket, a VCR and a computer. Is that about it?

> **ELAINE**
>
> Answering machine.

> **JERRY**
>
> Answering machine? Boy I hate the idea of somebody out there returning my calls.

> **COP**
>
> What do you mean?

JERRY

It's a joke.

COP

I see. Well, Mr. Seinfeld, uh, we'll look into it, and we'll let you know if we, you know, if we find anything.

JERRY

Do you ever find anything?

COP

(PAUSE) No.

JERRY

Well, thanks anyway.

COP

You bet.

The cop exits *as* George enters.

ELAINE

I didn't get that joke either.

JERRY

The crook has the machine. The messages aren't for him . . . he's the crook. Why would he answer . . . (SPOTTING GEORGE) How'd you get in here?

GEORGE

I walked in. Your lobby door is broken again.

JERRY

Again?

GEORGE

I don't know how you put up with this?

ELAINE

Yeah, tell him, George.

JERRY

(TO ELAINE) You would still want to move in here?

ELAINE

Yes. You don't understand. I'm living with Ethel Merman without the talent.

JERRY

Is that, uh, other apartment still available?

George holds up the keys.

CUT TO:

ACT ONE
SCENE G

INT. NIGHTCLUB—NIGHT
(*Jerry, Extras*)

JERRY

I got ripped off for about the eighteenth time. And, uh, the first couple of times you go through it it's very upsetting. And your first reaction or one of your friends will say, "Call the police. You really should call the police." So you think to yourself, you know, you watch TV, you think, "Yeah, I'm calling the police—stake outs, manhunts, I'm going to see some real action." Right? You think that. So the police come over your house. They fill out the report. They give you . . . your copy. Now, unless they give the crook his copy, I don't really think we're going to crack this case, do you? It's not like Batman where there's three crooks in the city, and everybody pretty much knows who they are. Very few crooks even go to the trouble to come up with a theme for their careers anymore. It makes them a lot tougher to spot. "Did you lose a Sony? It could be the Penguin. I think we can round him up . . . He's dressed like a penguin. We can find him. He's a penguin."

CUT TO:

THE ROBBERY

ACT ONE
SCENE H

EXT. NEW APARTMENT—DAY

INT. NEW APARTMENT—THE NEXT DAY (3)
(*Jerry, George, Elaine*)

Jerry, George and Elaine enter *an empty apartment. They wander around throughout the scene.*

ELAINE
Oh, well, c'mon. This is an apartment. This is a home. This is a place to live . . . (SHE GASPS) . . . A fireplace! Are you kidding me? Does this work?

GEORGE
I didn't know there was a fireplace. A fireplace, that's incredible.

JERRY
How would you get all that wood in here?

ELAINE
They deliver it.

JERRY
They deliver wood?

ELAINE
Yeah.

JERRY
What do you tip a wood guy?

GEORGE
I didn't know there was a fireplace.

ELAINE
Look, look at . . . look at this, there's a garden!

GEORGE
(ANOTHER SHOCK) A garden? I can't believe there's a garden.

They move toward the garden.

JERRY

Would I have to get a gardener?

ELAINE

Yeah. You can get a gardener.

JERRY

Do you tip him?

ELAINE

You can.

GEORGE

You don't tip a gardener!

ELAINE

You can tip a gardener!

GEORGE

You don't need a gardener!

ELAINE

Jerry, you can barbecue back here.

JERRY

They deliver the coal?

ELAINE

Sure, it's the same guy who delivers the wood.

JERRY

Oh, then I gotta tip him.

ELAINE

Oh, man, this place is incredible. Look at all this great light.

JERRY

I don't have any plants.

GEORGE

I have plants!

ELAINE

Jerry, look at this closet, look at this. I'm walking in it.

THE ROBBERY

It's a walk-in. (SHE WALKS INTO THE CLOSET) Can you believe it? I'm nuts about this. What do you think?

JERRY

(CLOSING HER IN THE CLOSET) I like that. (HE OPENS THE CLOSET. SHE WALKS OUT, ANNOYED)

JERRY

What do you think, George?

GEORGE

It's your decision.

Jerry takes it all in—he paces the place, Elaine shadows him.

JERRY

(FINALLY) I'm taking it. I'm taking the place. I'm gonna take it. This is gonna be my new place. I'm living here. I'm moving.

ELAINE

You're moving! That means I'm moving! (SHE LAUGHS) Geee. . . . is that incredible!

GEORGE

Congratulations.

FADE OUT:

END ACT ONE

ACT TWO

SCENE J

Ext. apartment—day

Int. Jerry's apartment—day (4)
(*Jerry, Elaine, George, Kramer*)

Elaine and Jerry are in negotiation.

ELAINE

What about the couch?

JERRY

You like the couch? I'll tell you what I'm gonna do.

ELAINE

What?

JERRY

You're moving in, you're a good friend, I want to start you off on the right foot. Give me a hundred and fifty dollars.

Elaine is outraged.

JERRY (CONT'D)

In fact, get it out of here right now, take it out the door, I don't even want to see it, get it out of here.

ELAINE

Wait a minute, excuse me—a hundred and fifty dollars!
A hundred and fifty dollars? For what? For *this* couch?

JERRY

Yeah.

ELAINE

For this couch?

JERRY

Okay, you tell me. What is it worth?

ELAINE

Okay, uh, I tell you what . . . I could go as high as, I
don't know . . . maybe . . . twenty dollars.

George buzzes the intercom.

SFX: buzzer

JERRY

Yeah?

GEORGE (O.S.)

Yeah, it's George.

JERRY

C'mon up. (TO ELAINE) Alright, forget it, I'm gonna take
it with me then. I'm just gonna pack up the cushions
right now.

Jerry picks up a cushion.

ELAINE

Okay, okay, okay, okay, you win, forty dollars.

JERRY

You wanna get the other end 'cause I wanna get it in
the hall.

ELAINE

Fifty dollars, okay, fifty dollars, is that alright?

JERRY

Fifty dollars?

ELAINE

Um-hum.

JERRY

Thank you very much.

ELAINE

Thank you very much.

George enters.

GEORGE

Hey, what's going on?

ELAINE

I just bought Jerry's couch for fifty dollars.

JERRY

So did you bring the lease?

George hands it to Jerry.

JERRY (CONT'D)

(SCANNING CONTRACT) Okay. Gee, three years, that kind of seems like a long time?

GEORGE

Jerry, Jerry, Jerry, Jerry, Jerry, listen, if you are feeling uncomfortable about this at all, at all, do not feel like you have to take it.

JERRY

Why?

GEORGE

If you're having second thoughts, if you didn't want it, don't worry about it because, uh, you know, I . . . I . . . I could take it, you know.

JERRY

You could take it? You want it?

GEORGE

No, I don't want it. I want it if you don't want it.

JERRY

So, you *do* want it?

GEORGE

No, I want it if you don't want it.

JERRY

You just said you wanted it.

GEORGE

No, I'm saying if a situation arose in which you didn't want it, I might take it.

JERRY

So, take it.

GEORGE

How can I take it?

JERRY

How can *I* take it?

GEORGE

It's your apartment.

JERRY

How can I want it now if you want it?

ELAINE

Excuse me . . . Uh, uh, I don't want to cause any trouble here, but, George, if you take it, can I take your place?

GEORGE

Yes, but I am not taking it.

JERRY

I am not taking it.

ELAINE

Well, one of you better damn well take it.

JERRY

Well what do you wanna do here?

GEORGE

I don't know.

JERRY

You want to flip a coin?

GEORGE

Who flips? You flip. I'll call.

JERRY

Okay. Fine. (TAKES OUT COIN) This is the official flip.
No crying, no guilt. Winner takes all and that's it.
Agreed?

GEORGE

I'm good.

ELAINE

I don't know who to root for, George's place has
carpeting.

JERRY

Alright, now you call it in the air.

GEORGE

No catching.

JERRY

No, no.

GEORGE

Flip it.

Jerry flips the coin.

GEORGE

Heads!

The coin bounces off the counter. On its descent, hits the ground.

JERRY

Tails.

GEORGE

No. It hit the table! It hit the table!

JERRY

So what?

GEORGE

Interference. You can't count that. C'mon. Are you crazy? The coin cannot touch anything. It affects it.

JERRY

You didn't call "no interference."

GEORGE

You don't have to call that, that's a rule.

JERRY

I don't believe this.

GEORGE

Oh, oh, oh, alright, fine, Jerry, you win. Take it, just take it.

JERRY

I don't want to win it like this. Elaine, what do you think?

George scoffs in protest.

ELAINE

(AFTER A BEAT) I better not.

JERRY

Well, I'll tell you what. I'll choose you for it. Straight choose, three takes it. No disputes, that's it. You gotta win three.

GEORGE

Okay. Okay. I'll choose you. What do you want?

George stares intently, trying to figure Jerry's strategy.

JERRY

Odds.

GEORGE

I want evens.

JERRY

Good.

GEORGE

You got odds.

JERRY

You got evens.

GEORGE

Right. Ready?

JERRY

For the apartment.

In unison:

JERRY	**GEORGE**
Once-twice-threee— shoot!	Once-twice-threee— shoot!

JERRY

Mine.

JERRY	**GEORGE**
Once-twice-threee— shoot!	Once-twice-threee— shoot!

JERRY

Mine.

George backs off under the extreme pressure. He's one away from losing. He tries to regain his composure. George returns, psyched. In unison again:

JERRY	**GEORGE**
Once-twice-threee— shoot!	Once-twice-threee— shoot!

GEORGE

Mine.

JERRY	**GEORGE**
Once-twice-threee— shoot!	Once-twice-threee— shoot!

They shake hands.

THE ROBBERY

GEORGE

Congratulations. Congratulations.

JERRY

Thanks . . .

GEORGE

(MUMBLING, ON HIS WAY INTO THE BATHROOM) I'm just gonna wash . . . (EXITING INTO THE BATHROOM) Why did I put out two? Why did I put out two?

Kramer enters.

KRAMER

Jerry, I think I'm onto something. I think I found your stuff. You know the Englishman who lives down the hall?

JERRY

Yeah.

KRAMER

The last couple days he's been acting very strange. I think he's avoiding me.

JERRY

Hard to imagine.

KRAMER

Yeah, get this. I just got off the elevator with him and I tested him. I tested him. Like I . . . this is what I said to him. Like I was like this, (CASUALLY PICKING HIS NAILS TO DEMONSTRATE) "Oh, by the way, I know about the stuff." You know, very casual so he's going to take me into his confidence.

JERRY

Right.

ELAINE

So, what did he say?

KRAMER

"What stuff?"

JERRY

Oooohhhh. Case closed.

KRAMER

You don't understand. You see, he swallowed. See, the guy, he swallowed. Oh, he was nervous about something. Now I'm going to go over there, I'm gonna borrow some tea. You know, if I don't get back in five minutes, maybe you better call the police.

JERRY

(LOOKING AT WATCH) Okay, starting now!

Kramer exits.

DISSOLVE TO:

ACT TWO
SCENE M

INT. NIGHTCLUB—NIGHT

(Jerry, Extras)

JERRY

One of the problems in life is that when you're a kid you have a certain way of working out disagreements and those laws do not work in the adult world. One of the main ways that kids resolve any dispute is by calling it. One of them will say, "I got the front seat." "I wanted the front seat." "I called it." And the other kid knows he's got nothing to say. "He called it, what can I do?" If there was a kid court of law it holds up. "Your honor, my client did ask for the front seat." And the judge would go, "Did he call it?" "Well, no, he didn't call it . . ." Bang. "He has to call it. Case closed. Objection overruled."

CUT TO:

THE ROBBERY

ACT TWO
SCENE K

INT. COFFEE SHOP—DAY (5)
(*Jerry, George, Waitress, Extras*)

George walks towards the table where Jerry is sitting.

GEORGE

I love the mirror in that bathroom. I don't know what
in the hell it is. I look terrific in that mirror. I don't
know if it's the tile or the lighting. I feel like Robert
Wagner in there.

JERRY

It's a good mirror. So, what are you getting?

GEORGE

I don't know, what can you eat? You can't have
anything anymore.
Look at this, look at this.
Eggs, out.
Coffee, out.
French Fries, out.
BLT, out.
I go visit my grandparents, they're eating big brisket
sandwiches, I'm sitting there with a carrot. They're
closing in on a hundred, I'm saying to them, "How can
you eat that stuff?" (BEAT) I'm so sick about losing that
choose, you don't know.

JERRY

Alright, forget it, forget it. I'm not taking the place.

GEORGE

What?

JERRY

How can I live there?

GEORGE

Why not?

JERRY

Look at you. You're still thinking about it. I'll never feel comfortable.

GEORGE

Oh, get out of here.

JERRY

How could I ever have you over? You'll sit there moping.

GEORGE

I won't mope.

JERRY

You're already moping. Would you take the place?

GEORGE

No. Impossible. It's your apartment.

JERRY

You found the place.

GEORGE

You won the choose.

JERRY

Alright, forget it. It's over. I'm not moving.

GEORGE

Well, me neither.

JERRY

Definitely?

GEORGE

Definitely.

JERRY

Alright, well then just get rid of it. You won't have any problem.

GEORGE

No, it's not a problem. I can get rid of the apartment this afternoon.

The waitress approaches.

THE ROBBERY

WAITRESS

What apartment?

GEORGE

Oh, it's a great place. It's a two bedroom, on West Eighty-third, about half a block from the park.

WAITRESS

What's the rent?

DISSOLVE TO:

ACT TWO
SCENE L

INT. NEW APARTMENT—EVENING (6)
(George, Jerry, Elaine, Carolyn, Larry, Diane, Man #1, Man #2, Extras)

We hear the hubbub of a party in progress. Jerry, George and Elaine sit glumly on a couch, centerstage.

GEORGE

I hate housewarmings. I don't know what we're doing here. This is ridiculous.

JERRY

(SNAPPING) She wanted to thank us for the apartment.

ELAINE

I can't believe I lost the deposit on that U-Haul . . . And I threw out my couch.

JERRY

If only the coin hadn't hit the table.

GEORGE

The table is interference and you know it.

JERRY

It is not.

GEORGE

It is too.

ELAINE

My roommate starts rehearsal tonight on "Carousel."

The waitress, Carolyn, comes over with her husband, Larry.

CAROLYN

Hi.

GEORGE

Hi, Carolyn.

CAROLYN

I just wanted to introduce you to my husband, this is Larry. This is George, Elaine and Jerry. These are the guys who got us the apartment.

LARRY

You don't know how grateful I am. If there's anything I can ever do to repay you. I mean we're just so thrilled with this place.

CAROLYN

It's a dream.

LARRY

I'm running in the park now, I've lost weight. We're barbecueing every night. And the rent is unbelievable!

GEORGE

We're really glad for you.

ELAINE

I couldn't be happier.

JERRY

It's wonderful.

CAROLYN

Oh, Diane, Diane, come here.

A very attractive woman approaches.

THE ROBBERY

CAROLYN (CONT'D)

This is my new next door neighbor, Diane. These are
the guys who turned this place down. Can you believe
it? Diane gave me the greatest back rub today, she's a
masseuse.

Jerry and George exchange a look.

DIANE

How . . . how could you guys have turned this place
down? It's such a great location and it's so close to the
park.

GEORGE

We're aware of the proximity to the park.

DIANE

Well it was nice to meet you.

They mumble goodbyes and sit back on the couch. A beat.

JERRY

How late are the stores open? I'm thinking of maybe,
uh, buying a new TV and smashing it over my head.

MAN #1

(BEHIND COUCH) So, I get a call from Gilmore this
morning—now get this—they're restructuring the
organization in Atlanta and I gotta be there on the first
of the month.

MAN #2

Really? What are you gonna do about the apartment?

MAN #1

Well, what can I do? . . . I'll give it up.

The three turn in unison.

JERRY/GEORGE/ELAINE

What's the rent?

FADE OUT:

END OF SHOW

THE *Seinfeld* SCRIPTS

MALE
UNBONDING

WRITTEN BY

LARRY DAVID & JERRY SEINFELD

DIRECTED BY

TOM CHERONES

AS BROADCAST JUNE 14, 1990

ACT ONE

SCENE A

OPENING CREDITS OVER:

INT. NIGHTCLUB—NIGHT
(*Jerry, Extras*)

JERRY

Most men like working on things, tools, objects, fixing things. This is what men enjoy doing. Have you ever noticed if a guy's out in his driveway working on something with tools, how all the other men in the neighborhood are magnetically drawn to this activity. They just come wandering out of the house like zombies. Men, it's true, men hear a drill, it's like a dog whistle. Just . . . You know, they go running up to that living room curtain, "Honey, I think Jim's working on something over there." So they run over to the guy. Now they don't actually help the guy. No. They just want to hang around the area where work is being done. That's what men want to do. We want to watch the guy, we want to talk to him, we want to ask him dumb questions. You know, "What are you using, the Phillips head?" You know, we feel involved. That's why, when they have construction sites, they have to have those wood panel fences around it, that's just to keep the men out. They cut those little holes for us so we

can see what the hell is going on. But if they don't cut those holes—we are climbing those fences. Right over there. "What are you using the steel girders down here? Yeah, that'll hold."

CUT TO:

ACT ONE
SCENE B

EXT. APARTMENT BUILDING—DAY

INT. JERRY'S APT. BLDG. LOBBY—DAY (1)
(*Jerry, George*)

Jerry and George are waiting for the elevator. Jerry's carrying dry cleaning.

GEORGE
(MORE TO HIMSELF) I had to say something. I had to say something. Everything was going so well I had to say something.

JERRY
I don't think you did anything wrong.

GEORGE
I told her I liked her. Why? Why did I tell her I like her? I have this sick compulsion to tell women how I feel. I like you I don't tell you.

JERRY
We can only thank God for that.

The elevator doors open. People exit and enter. George and Jerry enter *elevator.*

GEORGE
I'm outta the picture. I am outta the picture. (LAUGHS) It's only a matter of time now.

JERRY

You're imagining this. Really.

GEORGE

Oh no. No, no, no, no.

Elevator doors close.

CUT TO:

ACT ONE
SCENE C

INT. ELEVATOR—CONTINUOUS
(Jerry, George)

GEORGE

I'll tell you when it happened. When that floss came
flying out of my pocket.

JERRY

What floss? When?

GEORGE

We were in the lobby during the intermission of the
play. I was buying her one of those containers of orange
drink, for five dollars. I reached into my pocket to pay
for it, I look down, there's this piece of green floss
hanging from my fingers.

JERRY

Ah, mint.

GEORGE

Of course. So, I'm looking at it, I look up, I see she's
looking at it. Our eyes lock. It was a horrible moment.
I just . . .

The elevator doors open.

CUT TO:

MALE UNBONDING

ACT ONE
SCENE D

INT. HALLWAY—CONTINUOUS
(*Jerry, George*)

Jerry and George exit *the elevator into the hallway of the apartment building. As they walk towards Jerry's apartment:*

> **JERRY**
> So let me get this straight: she saw the floss, you panicked and you told her you liked her.

> **GEORGE**
> If I didn't put that floss in my pocket, I'd be crawling around her bedroom right now looking for my glasses.

> **JERRY**
> And you're sure the floss was the catalyst?

They stop at Jerry's door.

> **GEORGE**
> Yes. I am.

> **JERRY**
> (STARES AT CARRYING POUCH AROUND GEORGE'S WAIST)
> You don't think it might've had anything to do with that?

> **GEORGE**
> What? You don't like this?

> **JERRY**
> It looks like your belt is digesting a small animal.

Jerry opens the door.

CUT TO:

ACT ONE
SCENE E

INT. JERRY'S APARTMENT—CONTINUOUS
(*Jerry, George, Kramer*)

Kramer is sitting on the couch talking on Jerry's phone.

KRAMER

Oh, they've got a cure for cancer. See, it's all big
business . . .

Jerry and George enter *the apartment.*

KRAMER (CONT'D)

Oh hey, Jerry just walked in. Hi, George.

Kramer signals Jerry that he'll be off in a second.

KRAMER (CONT'D)

Yeah. Yeah, yeah, yeah, take my number—555-8643.
Okay, here he is.

Kramer tries to hand phone to Jerry.

JERRY

(TAKING PHONE, COVERING MOUTH PIECE) Who is it?

KRAMER

Take it.

JERRY

Who is it?

KRAMER

It's for you.

JERRY

(INTO PHONE) Hello? (CAUGHT OFF GUARD) Oh, hi Joel.

Jerry hits Kramer with a magazine.

JERRY (CONT'D)

. . . No. I was out of town. I just got back . . . Kramer
doesn't know anything . . . He's just my next-door
neighbor. Uh . . . nothing much . . . Tuesday? Uh,
Tuesday, no, I'm meeting somebody . . . Uh,
Wednesday? (UNABLE TO THINK OF AN EXCUSE)
Wednesday's okay . . . Alright, uh, I'm a little busy right
now. Can we talk Wednesday morning? . . . Okay . . .
Yeah . . . Right . . . Thanks . . . Bye . . .

Jerry hangs up the phone.

JERRY (CONT'D)

(TO KRAMER) Why did you put me on the phone with him? I hate just being handed a phone.

KRAMER

Well it's your phone. He wanted to talk to you.

JERRY

Maybe I didn't want to talk to him.

KRAMER

Well, why not?

JERRY

He bothers me. I don't even answer the phone anymore because of him. He's turned me into a screener. Now I gotta go see him on Wednesday.

GEORGE

What do you mean Wednesday? I thought we had tickets to the Knick game Wednesday. We got seats behind the bench. What happened, we're not going?

JERRY

We're going. That's next Wednesday.

GEORGE

Oh. Who is this guy?

JERRY

His name is Joel Horneck. He lived like three houses down from me when I grew up. He had a Ping Pong table. We were friends. Should I suffer the rest of my life because I like to play Ping Pong? I was ten. I would've been friends with Stalin if he had a Ping Pong table . . .

JERRY (CONT'D)

He's so self-involved.

SFX: phone rings

Kramer pulls a cordless phone out of his pocket.

KRAMER

That's for me. (ANSWERING PHONE) Kramerica
Industries . . . Oh, hi, Mark . . . No, no, no. Forget that,
I got a better idea. A pizza place where you make your
own pie.

JERRY

Can you conduct your business elsewhere?

KRAMER

(INTO PHONE) No, no, no. I'm talking about a whole
chain of 'em. Yeah.

Kramer exits *on phone.*

GEORGE

I don't know why you even bother with this ping pong
guy, I'll tell you that.

JERRY

I don't bother with him. He's been calling me for seven
years. I've never called him once. He's got the attention
span of a five-year-old. Sometimes I sit there and I make
up things just to see if he's paying attention.

GEORGE

I don't understand why you spend time with this guy.

JERRY

What can I do, break up with him? Tell him "I don't
think we're right for each other . . ." He's a guy. At least
with a woman, there's a precedent. You know, the
relationship goes sour, you end it.

GEORGE

No, no, no, no you have to approach this as if he was a
woman.

JERRY

Just break up with him?

GEORGE

Absolutely. You just tell him the truth.

MALE UNBONDING

JERRY

The truth . . .

They grimace.

DISSOLVE TO:

**ACT ONE
SCENE G**

INT. NIGHTCLUB—NIGHT
(*Jerry, Extras*)

JERRY

As a guy I don't know how I can break up with another
guy. You know what I mean? I don't know how to say,
"Bill, I feel I need to see other men." Do you know
what I mean? There's nothing I can do. I have to wait
for someone to die. I think that's the only way out of
this relationship. It could be a long time. See, the great
thing about guys is that we can become friends based
on almost nothing. Just two guys will just become
friends just because they're two guys. That's almost all
we need to have in common. 'Cause sports—sports and
women—is really all we talk about. If there was no
sports and no women the only thing guys would ever
say is, "So, what's in the refrigerator?"

CUT TO:

**ACT ONE
SCENE H**

INT. COFFEE SHOP—DAY (2)
(*Jerry, Joel, Waitress, Extras*)

Jerry and Joel are sitting at a table. Jerry wishes he was someplace else.

JOEL

. . . so my shrink wants me to bring my mother in for a
session. This guy is a brilliant man. Lenny Bruce used
to go to him . . . and I think, uh, Geraldo.

JERRY

You know, I read the Lenny Bruce biography, I thought
it was really—interesting . . . he would—

JOEL

(INTERRUPTING) Hey, hey, hey, hey we're starving here.
We've been waiting here for ten minutes already.

Joel waves for the waitress.

JERRY

(TESTING HIM) So, I'm thinking about going to Iran this
summer.

JOEL

I have to eat! I mean, I'm hypoglycemic.

JERRY

Anyway, the Hizballah has invited me to perform. You
know, it's their annual terrorist luncheon. I'm gonna do
it in Farsi.

JOEL

Do you think I need a haircut?

The waitress brings two glasses of water.

WAITRESS

Are you ready?

JERRY

Yeah, I'll have the egg salad on whole wheat.

JOEL

Let me ask you a question. This, uh, this turkey
sandwich here, is that real turkey or is it a turkey roll? I
don't want that processed turkey. I hate it.

WAITRESS

I think it's real turkey.

MALE UNBONDING

JOEL

Is there a real bird in the back?

WAITRESS

No, there's no bird but—

JOEL

Well, how do you know for sure? Look, why don't you do me a favor. Why don't you go in the back and find out. Okay?

The waitress exits.

JOEL (CONT'D)

(REFERRING TO WAITRESS) Unbelievable.

JERRY

How can you talk to someone like that?

JOEL

What are you saying? What, you like turkey roll?

JERRY

(WITH GREAT DIFFICULTY) Listen, Joel, there's something I have to tell you.

JOEL

Wait, you'll never guess who I ran into.

JERRY & JOEL

Howard Metro.

JOEL

He asked me if I still saw you. I said, "Sure, I see him all the time, we're still great friends." Anyway, Howard says hello.

JERRY

. . . Listen, Joel . . . I don't think we should see each other anymore.

JOEL

What?

JERRY

This friendship . . . it's not working.

JOEL

Not working? What are you talking about?

JERRY

We're just not suited to be friends.

JOEL

How can you say that?

JERRY

Look, you're a nice guy, it's just that—we don't have anything in common.

JOEL

(GETTING EMOTIONAL) Wait What did I do? Tell me . . . I want to know what I did?

JERRY

You didn't do anything. It's not you, it's me. It's . . . This is very difficult.

JOEL

Look, I know I call you too much. Right? I mean I know you're a very busy guy.

JERRY

No, it's not that.

JOEL

(STARTING TO CRY) You're one of the few people I can talk to.

People are starting to watch.

JERRY

Oh, come on. That's not true.

JOEL

I always tell everybody about you, tell everybody to go see your show. I mean, I'm your biggest fan.

JERRY

I know, I know.

JOEL

I mean, you're my best friend.

JERRY

Best friend, I've never been to your apartment.

JOEL

I cannot believe that this is happening. I can't believe it.

JERRY

Okay, okay. Forget it, it's okay, I didn't mean it.

Jerry turns his head away and hands him a napkin for his tears.

JOEL

Didn't mean what?

JERRY

What I said. I've been under a lot of stress.

JOEL

Oh, you've been under a lot of stress.

JERRY

Just, can we just forget the whole thing ever happened. I'm sorry, I didn't mean it. I took it out on you. We're still friends. We're still friends. Still friends. Okay, look, I'll tell you what. I've got Knick tickets this Wednesday. Great seats behind the bench. You want to come with me? Come on.

JOEL

Tonight?

JERRY

No next Wednesday. If it was tonight, I would've said tonight.

JOEL

Do you really want me to go?

JERRY

(FAKING) Yes.

JOEL

Okay. Yeah, okay, great, that would be, that'd be great . . . So next Wednesday.

JERRY

Next Wednesday.

JOEL

Where is that waitress? Hey . . .

FADE OUT:

END OF ACT ONE

ACT TWO

SCENE J

FADE IN:

Ext. bank—day

Int. bank—day (3)
(*Jerry, George, Customer, Teller, Extras*)

Jerry is at the bank counter filling out a deposit slip. George is carrying a huge cider jug of pennies.

GEORGE

. . . she calls me up at my office she says, "We have to talk."

JERRY

Uh, the four worst words in the English language.

GEORGE

That, or "Whose bra is this?"

JERRY

That is worse.

GEORGE

So we order lunch, and we're talking, finally she blurts out how it's "not working."

JERRY

Really.

They get on line.

GEORGE

So I'm thinking, as she's saying this, I'm thinking, great, the relationship's over, but the egg salad's on the way. So now I have a decision—do I walk or do I eat?

JERRY

Hm? You ate.

GEORGE

We sat there for twenty minutes, chewing, staring at each other in a defunct relationship.

JERRY

Someone says, "Get out of my life," and that doesn't affect your appetite?

GEORGE

Have you ever had their egg salad?

JERRY

It is unbelievable.

GEORGE

It's unbelievable. You know what else is unbelievable? I picked up the check. She didn't even offer. She ended it. The least she could do is send me off with a sandwich.

JERRY

(RE: PENNY JUG) How much could you possibly have in there?

GEORGE

It's my money. What should I do, throw it out the window? I know a guy who took his vacation on his change.

JERRY

Yeah? Where'd he go, to an arcade?

GEORGE

That's funny. You're a funny guy.

Jerry gestures for George to move ahead.

JERRY

C'mon, move up.

George catches up to the line, closes the gap, and overhears:

CUSTOMER

Oh great, Ewing's hurt.

GEORGE

Ewing's hurt? How long is he going to be out?

CUSTOMER

A couple of days at the most but . . .

GEORGE

Geez.

JERRY

Oh God.

GEORGE

(TO JERRY) I got scared there for a second. The Knicks without Ewing.

JERRY

Listen, George, little problem with the game.

GEORGE

What about it?

JERRY

The thing is, yesterday I kind of, uh . . .

GEORGE

What?

JERRY

I gave your ticket to Horneck.

GEORGE

You what?

JERRY

Yeah, I'm sorry. I had to give it to Horneck.

GEORGE

No. My ticket, you gave my ticket to Horneck?

Jerry motions George toward window.

JERRY

C'mon, c'mon, go ahead move up.

As George backs up towards teller:

GEORGE

(CRAZED) Why did you give him *my* ticket for?

JERRY

(FROM HIS PLACE ON LINE) You didn't see him. It was horrible.

GEORGE

Oh, c'mon, Jerry, I can't believe this.

JERRY

I had to do it.

George is at window. Jerry moves to another teller window.

GEORGE

Oh, please. (TO TELLER, RE: JUG) Can you change this into bills?

TELLER

I'm sorry, sir, we can't do that.

JERRY

Do you want to go with him? You go. I don't mind.

GEORGE

I'm not going with him. I don't even know the guy. (TO TELLER) Look, they did this for me before.

TELLER

Look, I can give you these and you can roll them yourself.

MALE UNBONDING

GEORGE

You want me to roll six thousand of these? What, should I quit my job?

DISSOLVE TO:

**ACT TWO
SCENE JJ**

INT. NIGHTCLUB—NIGHT
(*Jerry, Extras*)

JERRY

I do not like the bank. I've heard the expression "Laughing all the way to the bank." I have never seen anyone actually do it. And those bank lines. I hate it when there's nobody on the line at all, you know that part, you go to the bank, it's empty and you still have to go through the little maze. "Can you get a little piece of cheese for me? I'm almost at the front. I'd like a reward for this please."

CUT TO:

**ACT TWO
SCENE K**

INT. JERRY'S APARTMENT—LATE AFTERNOON
(*Jerry, George, Kramer*)

George is sitting in Jerry's apartment, stuffing pennies into rolls. He has piles of pennies in stacks of ten.

GEORGE

(COUNTING) Thirty-two, thirty-three—

JERRY

George.

GEORGE

(RAISES HAND) Not now . . . (COUNTS TO HIMSELF)

JERRY

Could you stop the counting?

GEORGE

Nnnnningaaa (DUMPING OUT ROLL) What?!

JERRY

Can I make it up to you? I'll give you fifty bucks for the jug.

GEORGE

Oh, yeah sure. Keep your money.

JERRY

Well, then I'm not going to the game either. Okay? I'll give him both tickets.

GEORGE

(STICKS IMAGINARY KNIFE IN HEART AND TWISTS) Oh, gheeee . . . Go, go!

JERRY

I . . . No, I don't want to go.

GEORGE

He was really crying?

JERRY

I had to give him a tissue. In fact, let me call his machine now and I'll just make up some excuse why I can't go to the game either.

GEORGE

Wait a minute. Wait a minute. As long as you're going to lie to the guy, why don't you tell him that you lost both of the tickets, then we can go?

JERRY

George, the man wept.

Kramer enters, *upbeat.*

MALE UNBONDING

KRAMER

Oh, hey guys. Man, I'm telling you, this pizza idea, is really gonna happen.

GEORGE

This is the thing where you go and you have to make your own pizza?

KRAMER

Yeah, we give you the dough, you smash it, you pound it, you fling it up in the air, and then you get to put your sauce and you get to sprinkle your cheese, and then—you slide it into the oven.

GEORGE

You know, you have to know how to do that. You can't have people shoving their arms into a six-hundred-degree oven.

KRAMER

It's all supervised.

GEORGE

Oh. Well.

KRAMER

All of it. You want to invest?

GEORGE

My money's tied up in change right now.

KRAMER

No, I'm tellin' ya, people, they really want to make their own pizza pie.

JERRY

I have to say something. With all due respect, I just never . . . I can't imagine anyone, in any walk of life, under any circumstance, wanting to make their own pizza pie . . . But that's me.

KRAMER

That's you.

JERRY

I'm just saying . . .

KRAMER

Okay, okay. I just wanted to check with you guys.

JERRY

Okay.

KRAMER

You know, this business is going to be big. I just wanted
. . . Okay.

Kramer exits *quickly, then immediately sticks his head back in.*

KRAMER (CONT'D)

One day, you'll beg me to make your own pie.

And he's gone. Jerry dials phone and begins to speak to an answering machine.

JERRY

Hi, Joel. This is Jerry. I hope you get this before
you—Oh, hi Joel. . . . Oh, you just came in . . . Listen, I
can't make it to the game tonight. I, uh, have to tutor
my nephew—Yeah, he's got an exam tomorrow . . .
geometry . . . you know, trapezoids, rhombus . . .
Anyway, listen, you take the tickets, they're at the Will-
Call window . . . and I'm really sorry . . . Have a good
time. We'll talk next week. Okay . . . Yeah . . . I don't
. . . Fine . . . Fine . . . Bye.

Jerry hangs up phone.

GEORGE

Trapezoid?

JERRY

I know. I'm really running out of excuses with this guy.
I need some kind of excuse Rolodex.

CUT TO:

ACT TWO
SCENE M

EXT. JERRY'S APARTMENT—NIGHT

INT. JERRY'S APARTMENT—NIGHT

MALE UNBONDING

(Jerry, Elaine, Kramer, Joel)

Jerry and Elaine are standing in the kitchen.

ELAINE
Come on, let's go do something. I don't want to just sit around here.

JERRY
Okay.

ELAINE
Want to go get something to eat?

JERRY
Where do you want to go?

ELAINE
I don't care, I'm not hungry.

JERRY
We could go to one of those cappuccino places? They let you just sit there.

ELAINE
What are we gonna do there—*talk*?

JERRY
We could talk.

ELAINE
I'll go if I don't have to talk.

JERRY
We'll just sit there.

ELAINE
Okay. I'm gonna check my machine first.

Elaine walks to the phone. When she gets there she sees a yellow legal pad and starts reading aloud.

ELAINE (CONT'D)
"Picking someone up at airport." "Jury duty." "Waiting for cable guy."

He moves towards her. She eludes him.

JERRY

(EMBARRASSED) Okay, just hand that over please.

ELAINE

Oh, what is this?

JERRY

It's a list of excuses, it's for that guy Horneck who's at the game tonight with my tickets. I have that list now so in case he calls, I just consult it and I don't have to see him.

Elaine laughs heartily.

JERRY (CONT'D)

I need it.

Elaine starts writing on the list.

JERRY (CONT'D)

What are you doing?

ELAINE

I got some for you.

JERRY

I don't need anymore.

ELAINE

No, no, no, no, no, these are good. Listen, listen, "You ran out of underwear. You can't leave the house."

JERRY

(SARCASTIC) Very funny.

ELAINE

How about, "You've been diagnosed as a multiple personality, you're not even you, you're Dan."

JERRY

I'm Dan. Can I have my list back please?

ELAINE

(SHE HANDS HIM THE LIST) Here, here. Jerry Seinfeld, I cannot believe you're doing this. This is absolutely infantile.

MALE UNBONDING

JERRY

What can I do?

ELAINE

Deal with it. Be a man.

JERRY

Oh, no. That's impossible. I'd rather lie to him for the rest of my life than go through that again. He was crying, tears accompanied by mucus.

ELAINE

You made a man cry? I've never made a man cry. I even kicked a guy in the groin once and he didn't cry . . . I got the cab.

JERRY

A couple of tough monkeys.

Elaine laughs. Kramer enters.

KRAMER

Oh, hi Elaine, hey. (ENTHUSIASTIC) Hey, you missed a great game tonight, buddy.

JERRY

Game?

KRAMER

Knick game. Horneck took me. We were sitting two rows behind the bench. We were getting hit by sweat.

JERRY

Wait. How does Horneck know you?

Kramer wanders into the kitchen for some ketchup.

KRAMER

Last week. When I, you know, gave you the phone. He's really into my pizza place idea.

JERRY

This is too much.

ELAINE

Wait. What pizza place idea?

JERRY

Oh, no.

KRAMER

You make your own pie.

ELAINE

Oh, that sounds like a great idea. It would be fun.

JOEL (O.S.)

Kramer . . .

KRAMER

Yeah.

JERRY

Perfect.

Horneck comes in.

JOEL

Hey . . .

KRAMER

(POINTING TO THE OTHERS) Okay, who wants
meatloaf?

JERRY & ELAINE

No, no thanks.

KRAMER

(TO JOEL) It's gonna be hot in a minute.

He exits.

JOEL

So, I thought you were tutoring your nephew?

JERRY

Oh, we finished early.

JOEL

Uhm, I'll bet. So, are you going to introduce me to
your—nephew?

JERRY

Elaine Benes, this is Joel Horneck.

ELAINE

Hi.

JOEL

Whoa, Nelson. This is Elaine. I thought you guys split
up.

JERRY

We're still friends.

JOEL

(LINGERING OVER ELAINE, THEN:) So, thanks again for
those tickets. But next week I'm going to take you. How
about next Tuesday night? (TO ELAINE) And why don't
you come along?

ELAINE

Oh, no, no. Tuesday's no good because we've got choir
practice.

JERRY

Right, I forgot about choir.

ELAINE

We're doing that evening of Eastern European National
Anthems.

JERRY

Right. You know, the wall being down and everything.

JOEL

(TO JERRY) What about Thursday night? I mean, they're
playing the Sonics.

Jerry shakes his head no.

ELAINE

Huh . . . Thursday is not good because we've got to get
to the hospital to see if we qualify as those organ
donors.

JOEL

You know, I should really try something like that.

JERRY

You really should.

JOEL

(TAKING OUT SCHEDULE) Well, let's just take a look here. Forty-one home games. Saturday night we've got the Mavericks. If you don't like the Mavericks, next Tuesday—Lakers. I mean you gotta like Magic, right? Let's see, on the road, on the road, on the road, on the road, back, back on the fourteenth they play the Bulls. You can't miss Air Jordan . . .

CUT TO:

ACT TWO
SCENE 0

INT. NIGHTCLUB—NIGHT
(*Jerry, Extras*)

JERRY

You know, I really . . . I've come to the conclusion that there are certain friends in your life that they're just always your friends and you have to accept it. You see them, you don't really want to see them. You don't call them, they call you, you don't call back, they call again. The only way to get through talking with people that you don't really have anything in common with is to pretend you're hosting your own little talk show. This is what I do. You pretend there's a little desk around you. There's a little chair over there and you interview them. The only problem with this is there's no way you can say, "Hey, it's been great having you on the show. We're out of time."

FADE OUT:

END OF SHOW

MALE UNBONDING

THE Seinfeld SCRIPTS

THE
STOCK
TIP

WRITTEN BY

LARRY DAVID & JERRY SEINFELD

DIRECTED BY

TOM CHERONES

AS BROADCAST JUNE 21, 1990

ACT ONE

SCENE A

OPENING CREDITS OVER:

INT. NIGHTCLUB—NIGHT
(*Jerry, Extras*)

JERRY

Went out to dinner the other night, check came at the
end of the meal as it always does. Never liked the check
at the end of the meal system. Because money's a very
different thing before and after you eat. Before you eat
money has no value. And you don't care about money
when you're hungry, you sit down in a restaurant,
you're like the ruler of an empire. "More drinks,
appetizers, quickly, quickly. It will be the greatest meal
of our lives." Then after the meal, you know, you've
got the pants open, you've got the napkins destroyed,
cigarette butt in the mashed potatoes. Then the check
comes at that moment. People are always upset, you
know, they're mystified by the check. "What is this?
How could this be?" They start passing it around the
table, "Does this look right to you? We're not hungry
now, why are we buying all this food?"

CUT TO:

127

ACT ONE
SCENE B

INT. COFFEE SHOP—DAY (1)
(Jerry, George, Elaine, Waitress, Extras)

We find Jerry and George in a booth.

JERRY

I think Superman probably has a very good sense of humor.

GEORGE

I never heard him say anything really funny.

JERRY

But it's common sense, he's got super strength, super speed, I'm sure he's got super humor.

GEORGE

You would think that, but either you're born with a sense of humor or you're not. It's not going to change even if you go from the red sun of Krypton all the way to the yellow sun of the Earth.

JERRY

Why? Why would that one area of his mind not be affected by the yellow sun of the Earth?

GEORGE

I don't know but he ain't funny.

Elaine approaches the booth. George and Jerry both check their watches in unison.

ELAINE

I know, I know. I'm sorry I'm late.

JERRY

No problem.

ELAINE

I dropped a grape.

GEORGE

Pardon?

ELAINE

I dropped a grape in the kitchen and it disappeared. I couldn't find it. I was . . . I was literally on my knees for ten minutes looking for this stupid grape. I have no idea where it went.

JERRY

Were you crying? I mean it's just a grape, you'll find it.

ELAINE

No, I'm just getting over an allergy attack. This guy I'm going out with—

JERRY

Robert.

ELAINE

Robert. Yes . . . Thank you. He has two cats and I'm allergic to them. You know, I finally meet a normal man and I can't even go into his apartment, you know. And of course my apartment is the actors studio so we can't go there. It's really causing a lot of problems, you know. He won't even go away for the weekend because of these cats.

GEORGE

Guys with cats . . . I don't know.

JERRY

I've been thinking about asking this girl I'm, uh, seeing—

ELAINE

Vanessa.

JERRY

Vanessa, thank you . . . I been thinking about asking her to go away for a couple of days.

GEORGE

Oh no. No, no, no, no, no. I'd have to advise against

that. What do you know this woman, a month? Let's see, you're going to be with her seventy-two hours, that's a dating decathlon.

ELAINE

(TO JERRY WHILE BALANCING A SPOON ON HER NOSE) Hey, why don't you take her to that place in Vermont I was telling you about. You know, that really charming place with the separate faucets for the hot and cold. She'll love it.

GEORGE

(TO ELAINE) That's exquisite. Listen, uh, if it's not too much trouble could you pass me that paper over there?

She reaches for the paper at the next table.

GEORGE (CONT'D)

Just the business section.

She hands him the paper. He starts flipping through it.

JERRY

You better find that grape before it mutates into another life form.

She laughs.

JERRY (CONT'D)

There was once a mutant grape that terrorized an entire town in the Texas Panhandle. They brought in the army, nobody could stop it. (OFF HER LOOK) Apparently it had a pit of steel.

GEORGE

(TO HIMSELF) Up again? This is incredible. I'm . . . I'm getting it.

ELAINE

You're getting what?

GEORGE

A stock.

JERRY

What stock?

GEORGE

Did you ever meet my friend, Simons?

JERRY

Maybe.

GEORGE

He knows this guy Wilkinson, he made a fortune in the stock market. Now he's got some new thing—you know, there's supposed to be a big merger. He wasn't even supposed to say anything. You guys should think about doing this too.

JERRY

How high's it supposed to go?

GEORGE

I don't know, but Simons said that if I wanted to get involved that Wilkinson would tell me the exact right minute to sell. You wanna do it?

JERRY

Boy . . . I don't know.

ELAINE

I'd do it but I don't have any money.

JERRY

What kind of company is it?

GEORGE

It's Sendrax. They've got some new kind of technique for televising opera.

ELAINE

Televising opera?

GEORGE

Some sort of electronic thingey.

JERRY

Well, how much are you going to invest?

THE STOCK TIP

GEORGE

Five thousand . . . Ten, ten thousand. . . . Five thousand.

JERRY

Boy . . .

GEORGE

C'mon on, Wilkinson's got millions invested in this stock. It's gone up three points since I've been watching it.

JERRY

What if I lose it?

GEORGE

C'mon, go for twenty-five hundred. We'll do it together. Come on, come on, we're in it together.

A beat.

JERRY

All right—twenty-five hundred.

GEORGE

That's it.

The waitress arrives.

WAITRESS

Yeah, can I take your order?

GEORGE

(GESTURING TO JERRY) Check to the raiser.

JERRY

My bet? Alright . . . I'll open with a tuna sandwich.

ELAINE

Tuna?

JERRY

(TORTURED) Oh, the dolphin thing?

ELAINE

They're dying in the nets.

JERRY

Ooohhh, you know the whole concept of lunch is based on tuna.

ELAINE

Jerry, can't you incorporate one unselfish act in your daily routine?

JERRY

Hey, when I'm driving I let people in ahead of me all the time. I'm always waving everybody in. "Go ahead, go ahead, go ahead." (OFF HER LOOK:) . . . Alright. Alright. (WITH CONTEMPT) I'll have the chicken salad.

ELAINE

And I'm going to have an English muffin with margarine on the side and a cup of coffee.

WAITRESS

Okay. (TO GEORGE) What about you?

GEORGE

I'll have the tuna.

CUT TO:

ACT ONE
SCENE C

INT. KOREAN MARKET—NIGHT (2)
(*Jerry, Vanessa, Stock Boy, Extras*)

Jerry and Vanessa are doing some late shopping.

JERRY

I have to say, those people talking behind us really ruined that movie for me.

VANESSA

Why didn't you do something?

THE STOCK TIP

JERRY

What do you want me to do? I gave the guy the half-turn. Then I gave him the full-turn with the eye roll. I mean beyond that I'm risking a punch in the mouth . . . (TO STOCK BOY) Excuse me, do you have these in the puffs?

STOCK BOY

No puffs. Just flakes.

JERRY

Have you thought any more about that trip?

VANESSA

Yeah, I've been thinking about it.

JERRY

You know, my friend told me about this great place in Vermont.

VANESSA

I don't know. I just worry about trips like this. It's a lot of pressure.

JERRY

It's great. It speeds up the intimacy level. It's like putting the relationship in a time compressor. Where we would be six months from now we accomplish (SNAPS HIS FINGERS) three days.

VANESSA

Oh, so you want to move our relationship into Phase Two.

JERRY

Exactly. I love Phase Two. Extra toothbrushes, increased phone call frequency, walking around naked—You know the presents get a lot better in Phase Two.

VANESSA

(BRIGHTENING) Really? Could we go fishing up there?

JERRY

Yeah, we can fish. What—blues, carp, marlin?

> VANESSA

They have marlin in Vermont?

> JERRY

Oh, big fighting marlin.

Jerry picks up a paper in front of the counter.

> VANESSA

Jerry, the stock is the same as when you checked it earlier. There are no changes after the market closes. The stock is still down.

> JERRY

I know, but this is a different paper. I thought maybe they have, uh, different . . . sources.

CUT TO:

ACT ONE
SCENE D

EXT. APARTMENT—DAY

INT. JERRY'S APARTMENT—DAY (3)
(*Jerry, Kramer*)

Jerry has a road map spread out on the table. He's tracing a route with a tiny car. Kramer enters *holding a newspaper, slightly pleased.*

> JERRY

Is that my paper?

> KRAMER

Bad news, my friend.

> JERRY

What? What news?

> KRAMER

Sendrax.

THE STOCK TIP

JERRY

Oh, c'mon. It's down again?

KRAMER

Two and a half points.

JERRY

Oh, I can't believe it. Let me see that.

Kramer hands him the paper.

JERRY (CONT'D)

That's four and a half points in three days. That's almost half my money.

KRAMER

Hey, I told ya.

JERRY

(HEADS FOR PHONE) Yeah, you told me.

KRAMER

It's all manipulated with junk bonds. You can't win.

JERRY

(HOLDING THE PHONE) There's one thing I don't understand. Why does it please you? (INTO PHONE) George Costanza, please.

KRAMER

Hey, I don't care, I'm just telling you to (YELLING) get rid of that stock now.

JERRY

(INTO PHONE) George, what's going on? . . .

KRAMER

Sell it, just say I'm selling!

JERRY

(INTO PHONE) Well, where is the guy? Nothing? Almost half my money's gone . . . Well, call me right back. (HANGS UP) Nobody can reach Wilkinson. He hasn't been home or in his office in the past three days.

KRAMER

You know, I can't believe you put your money in that Sendrax and you could've invested in my roll-out tie dispenser.

JERRY

Roll-out tie dispenser, what was that one?

KRAMER

Okay, you're in a restaurant, you've got a very big meeting coming up.

JERRY

Okay.

KRAMER

Oh man, you got mustard on your tie!

JERRY

Oh no!

KRAMER

You just (MAKES A ROLL NOISE) tear it off and (DEMONSTRATES) you got a new one right here. Then you're gone.

JERRY

You're gone alright.

KRAMER

(NOTICING MAP) Hey, where . . . where are you going? You gonna take a trip? The map . . . what . . .

JERRY

Yeah, I'm going to Vermont with Vanessa for a few days.

KRAMER

Hey, can I use your place? I got a bunch of friends coming over this weekend.

JERRY

What friends?

KRAMER

Well, it's just some people I met at a rock concert.

SFX: phone rings

THE STOCK TIP

KRAMER (CONT'D)

Do you mind if they use your bed?

Jerry gives him a look.

KRAMER (CONT'D)

'Cause they're really good people, Jerry, I'm telling you,
you know they're anarchists. They're . . . they're . . .
they're . . . huge.

Jerry answers the phone.

JERRY

(INTO PHONE) George . . . What? You're kidding . . .
Well what's wrong? . . . So what are we gonna do? . . .
Great . . . Alright, I'll speak to you later. (HE HANGS UP)
Wilkinson, the guy who's supposed to tell us when to
sell the stock, he's in the hospital.

On Kramer's pleased reaction we:

FADE OUT:

END OF ACT ONE

ACT TWO

SCENE E

FADE IN:

EXT. DRY-CLEANING STORE—DAY

INT. DRY-CLEANING STORE—DAY (4)
(Jerry, George, Dry Cleaner, Customers)

Jerry and George are standing by the counter waiting for the owner of Middle East descent to finish up with a customer. Jerry is holding a very small size shirt on a hanger

> **JERRY**
> So you don't know what's wrong with him?

> **GEORGE**
> All Simons was able to find out is that he's in the hospital.

> **JERRY**
> Okay, fine. Has Simons been in touch with him?

> **GEORGE**
> Of course he's been in touch with him. He left two messages. He just hasn't heard back yet, that's all.

> **JERRY**
> Well this is it, I'm selling.

GEORGE

Just give it a little more time.

JERRY

I never should've gotten involved in this. I'm a nervous wreck. I'm not cut out for investing.

GEORGE

Alright, alright, that's it. I'm gonna go down there.

JERRY

Where?

GEORGE

To the hospital.

JERRY

The hospital?

GEORGE

I'm gonna find out what's going on. Alright?

JERRY

Are you nuts? You don't even know the guy.

GEORGE

So what, I'll start talking to him, you know, casual, and I'll work my way around to it.

JERRY

What if he's in an iron lung or something? What are you gonna do? (KNOCKING ON GLASS) "How you feeling, Mr. Wilkinson? (HE MAKES A HISSING SOUND) By the way, what's happening with Sendrax?"

GEORGE

Maybe he's there resting.

JERRY

Who goes to a hospital to rest?

GEORGE

What are you, a doctor?

JERRY

Okay fine, fine. When are you going down there?

GEORGE

Today. I'm going today. Just don't do anything until you hear from me.

JERRY

Alright.

George has turned momentarily and doesn't see Jerry move up to the counter, nor does he see the woman who's moved into Jerry's position.

GEORGE

Boy I have to get to a bathroom.

The woman looks at him incredulously.

DRY CLEANER

May I help you?

JERRY

Yeah. I picked up this shirt here yesterday. It's completely shrunk. There's absolutely no way I can wear it.

DRY CLEANER

When did you bring it in?

JERRY

What's the difference? Look at it. Do you see the size of this shirt?

DRY CLEANER

You got a receipt?

JERRY

I can't find the receipt.

DRY CLEANER

You should get the receipt.

JERRY

Look forget about the receipt, all right? Even if I had the receipt, look at it, it's a hand puppet. What am I gonna do with this?

DRY CLEANER

Yes, but how do I know we did the shirt?

JERRY

What do you think this is a little scam I have? I take this tiny shirt all over the city conning dry cleaners out of money? In fact, forget the money. I don't even want the money. I just once I would like to hear a dry cleaner admit that something was their fault. That's what I want. I want an admission of guilt.

DRY CLEANER

Maybe you asked for it to be washed?

JERRY

No . . . dry-cleaned.

DRY CLEANER

Let me explain to you something. Okay? With certain types of fabrics, different chemicals can react causing . . .

JERRY

(INTERRUPTING) You shrunk it! You know you shrunk it. Just tell me you shrunk it!

DRY CLEANER

I shrunk it.

CUT TO:

ACT TWO
SCENE F

INT. NIGHTCLUB
(*Jerry, Extras*)

JERRY

I think the only reason we go to the dry cleaner is so I can say to the dry cleaner, "Well, it's ruined." And of course, the dry cleaner can respond, "It's not our fault. We're not responsible. We just ruin the clothes, that ends our legal obligation." You see the whole problem with dry cleaning is that we all believe that this is actually possible. Right? They're cleaning our clothes but they're not getting anything wet, it's all dry. I know there's gotta be some liquids back there, some fluids that they're using. There's no such thing as dry cleaning, when you get something on your shirt, ever get something on your shirt and try and get it off like that (BRUSHES HIS SHIRT) that's dry cleaning. I don't think that's what they're doing back there. They don't have eighty guys going, (WITH IMAGINARY BRUSH) "Come on, hurry up. There's a lot of shirts today."

CUT TO:

ACT TWO
SCENE G

EXT. APARTMENT—DAY

INT. JERRY'S APARTMENT—SAME DAY (4)
(Elaine, Jerry, Kramer, George)

Elaine sneezes.

JERRY

Bless you.

ELAINE

Thank you. What evidence is there that cats are so smart anyway, huh? What do they do? Because they're clean. I am sorry. My Uncle Pete showers four times a day and he can't count to ten. So don't give me hygiene.

JERRY

So what are you gonna do?

ELAINE

I don't know. I can't think of any solution, unless of course they should meet with some unfortunate

accident. What do you think a hit man would charge to rub out a couple of cats?

JERRY

Well it couldn't be too expensive, thirteen, fourteen bucks a cat?

ELAINE

What do you think Jerry, you wanna make twenty-eight bucks?

JERRY

I'm no cat killer.

ELAINE

How about we go over there right now and we shave them?

JERRY

I'd really like to go, Elaine, but George is coming back from the hospital. I gotta wait for him. But otherwise I would definitely go.

ELAINE

He actually went to the hospital?

JERRY

Yeah.

ELAINE

Oh man, he's nuts.

JERRY

Yeah, he's nuts. You wanta bump off a couple of cats.

Kramer enters, *holding a newspaper.*

JERRY (CONT'D)

I know, I know, it's down again.

KRAMER

How much are you down altogether?

JERRY

I don't know . . . fifteen hundred dollars.

KRAMER

Wow.

JERRY

You don't have to say "wow." I know it's "wow." And there's that smile again. Well, what is that?

SFX: buzzer rings

JERRY

It's George.

He presses the button to let George in. Elaine goes into the bathroom. Kramer picks up a pair of binoculars and looks out the window.

KRAMER

Oh, look at this one by the bus stop. Jerry, come here, take a look at this.

JERRY

I really don't need to look.

KRAMER

What a body. Yeeaaah . . . that's for me.

JERRY

Yeah and you're just what she's looking for too—a stranger, leering through a pair of binoculars ten floors up.

KRAMER

I'm gonna go down there and try and talk to her.

He leaves. A moment later George enters, *shaken. He's been through an ordeal. He rolls onto the couch.*

JERRY

What? What? Did you go down there?

He nods.

JERRY (CONT'D)

Did he tell you what's gonna happen?

George shakes his head "no."

THE STOCK TIP

JERRY (CONT'D)

How long were you there?

GEORGE

Fifteen seconds.

JERRY

You told him you knew Simons?

GEORGE

Yeah, I mentioned Simons. Next thing I know—I'm in the parking lot. Perhaps they had some sort of a falling out. I'll tell you one thing, I don't know what he's got, but for a sick guy he's very strong.

Elaine exits *the bathroom.*

JERRY

Well, that's it. Look, I'm going to Vermont, I don't want to think about this. I'm selling.

ELAINE

Didn't work, huh?

GEORGE

(LAUGHS) Not quite.

ELAINE

Well, what are you gonna do about the stock?

GEORGE

I'm keeping it, I'm going down with the ship.

DISSOLVE TO:

ACT TWO
SCENE H

INT. COUNTRY INN—DAY (5)
(*Jerry, Vanessa*)

Jerry and Vanessa are seated in the lobby area. It's raining heavily. They're talked out. They clearly have nothing to say.

JERRY

So I know this guy. I'm getting all my sneakers at a
discount now.

VANESSA

I know, you mentioned it.

JERRY

Oh yeah, right.

A beat.

JERRY (V.O.)

Oh God, get me out of here. What a mistake. What
made me think this would work? And I've still got
another day. I've got nothing left to say. Wait . . . wait
. . . got one.

JERRY (CONT'D)

That's a nice watch. Do you wind it?

VANESSA

No, it's got a little battery.

JERRY

Well that's good.

JERRY (V.O.)

Well, the drive home should be a delight. I'm speeding
the whole way, let them throw me in jail, I don't care.

JERRY (CONT'D)

That's the manager? Do you want me to see if we can
get another room?

VANESSA

No. It's okay.

JERRY

So, I guess you don't find the separate faucets for the
hot and the cold—charming?

VANESSA

Not especially.

JERRY

Well, what do you want to do this afternoon?

VANESSA

What can we do, it's raining?

JERRY

We could play "SORRY!" We could play "STEAL THE OLD MAN'S BUNDLE."

JERRY (V.O.)

Maybe I can get an extension cord and hang myself.

JERRY (CONT'D)

What kind of perfume is that you're wearing?

VANESSA

Oh, you've never heard of it.

JERRY

No, what? What kind is it?

VANESSA

I can't tell you.

JERRY (V.O.)

Yeah, that's real normal.

JERRY (CONT'D)

(TO MAN NEARBY) Excuse me, sir, could I have a look at that business section?

VANESSA

That stock? I thought you got out of that.

JERRY

I did. I'm just curious. It's been almost a week. I want to check it out. (HE FINDS THE STOCK) Six points. It's up six points!

VANESSA

I told you not to sell.

JERRY

You did not tell me not to sell.

VANESSA

I said, the market fluctuates. Remember?

JERRY

Look, Vanessa, of course the market fluctuates. Everybody knows that. I just got fluctuated out of four thousand dollars.

VANESSA

That's probably why—(STOPS HERSELF)

JERRY

What?

VANESSA

Forget it.

JERRY

No, what? That's probably why . . .

VANESSA

That's probably why we're staying here, because you lost money on the stock.

JERRY (V.O.)

So, what am I looking at here? Twenty-nine hours to go. Well, at least I got plenty of time to find out the name of that perfume.

CUT TO:

ACT TWO
SCENE J

INT. COFFEE SHOP—DAY (6)
(George, Jerry, Elaine, Waitress, Extras)

George is smoking a large cigar, acting very expansive, laughing, mumbling, enjoying.

GEORGE

Have something else. C'mon, have a little dessert?

THE STOCK TIP

JERRY

I'm good, thanks.

GEORGE

Elaine, get something. It's all taken care of.

ELAINE

I'm kinda full.

GEORGE

So don't finish it.

JERRY

(ACIDLY) She's full.

George puts hands up in "excuse me" gesture.

JERRY (CONT'D)

So, Big Daddy, I'm just curious, how much did you clear
on your little transaction there, all told?

GEORGE

I don't like to discuss figures.

JERRY

How much?

GEORGE

I don't know, what? Eight thousand. It's a Hyundai. Get
out of here . . . I told you not to sell. Simons made
money, Wilkinson cleaned up.

JERRY

So Wilkinson's out of the hospital now?

GEORGE

No. You'd be surprised. You don't recover that quickly
from a nose job.

Elaine sneezes.

JERRY

Is that still from those cats?

ELAINE

No. I just got a cold.

JERRY

So, what ever happened with that?

ELAINE

I gave him an ultimatum.

She shrugs.

GEORGE

He chose the cats?

ELAINE

They're very clean animals.

JERRY

I gotta say that's pretty bad, losing out to a cat.

ELAINE

Almost as bad as losing out to a perfume.

GEORGE

I told you those trips are relationship killers. Too bad you can't get your buddy Superman to fly around the earth at super speed and reverse time. You'd get all the money back, you could have avoided the whole trip to Vermont.

ELAINE

Superman can go back in time?

JERRY

We went over that.

GEORGE

(CALLING THEM IN CLOSE. SOTTO VOCE) Wilkinson's got a bite on a new one. Petramco Corp., out of, uh, Springfield, I think. They're about to introduce some sort of a robot butcher.

JERRY

A robot butcher?

GEORGE

Sh-h-h-h. If you want to get in—there's very little time. (CALLING TO WAITRESS) Sweetheart . . .

THE STOCK TIP

She approaches and tears off the check. George raises his hand, stopping her.

GEORGE (CONT'D)
No, no, no, no. That ought to cover it.

He hands her some money. She turns to leave.

GEORGE (CONT'D)
Just a second. Just a . . . let me . . . (HE TAKES A PEEK AT THE CHECK AND THEN PRIES SOME OF THE MONEY BACK OUT OF HER HAND, THEN URGES JERRY AND ELAINE TO EAT) Come on, come on, come on . . .

CUT TO:

ACT TWO
SCENE K

INT. NIGHTCLUB—NIGHT
(Jerry, Extras)

JERRY
I'm not an investor. People always tell me, you should have your money working for you. I've decided I'll do the work, I'm gonna let the money relax. You know what I mean, 'cause you send your money out there working for you—a lot of times it gets fired. You go back there, "What happened, I had my money, it was here, it was working for me." "Yeah, I remember your money, showing up late, taking time off. We had to let him go."

FADE OUT:

END OF SHOW

SEASON TWO

THE *Seinfeld* SCRIPTS

THE
Ex-Girlfriend

WRITTEN BY

LARRY DAVID & JERRY SEINFELD

DIRECTED BY

TOM CHERONES

AS BROADCAST JANUARY 23, 1991

SHOW OPEN

STAND UP #1

INT. COMEDY CLUB—NIGHT

JERRY

I'm always in traffic with the lane expert. You know this type of person? Constantly, reevaluating their lane choice. Never quite sure "Is this the best lane for me, for my life?" They're always a little bit ahead of you, "Can I get in over there, could I get in over here? Could I get in there?" "Yeah, come on over here, pal, we're zoomin' over here. This is the secret lane, nobody knows about it." The ultimate, I think the ultimate psychological test of traffic is the total dead stop. Not even rolling. And you look out the window, you can see gum clearly. So we know that in the future traffic will get even worse than that. I mean what will happen? Will it start moving backwards I wonder? I mean is that possible? That someday we'll be going "Boy, this is some really bad traffic now, boy. This, is really bad. I'm gonna try to get off and get back on going the other way."

CUT TO:

ACT ONE

SCENE A

INT. JERRY'S CAR—NIGHT

Jerry and George, stopped outside Elaine's building. George is in a state of frenzy.

GEORGE

She can't kill me right?

JERRY

No, of course not.

GEORGE

People break up all the time.

JERRY

Everyday.

GEORGE

It just didn't work out. What can I do? I wanted to love her. I tried to love her. I couldn't.

JERRY

You tried.

GEORGE

I kept looking at her face. I'd go, "C'mon, love her. Love her."

JERRY

Did you tell her you loved her?

GEORGE

Oh, I had no choice, she squeezed it out of me! She'd tell me she loved me. Alright, at first, I just look at her. I'd go "Oh really?" or "Boy, that's, that's, something." But, eventually you have to come back with "Well, I love you." You know, you can only hold out for so long.

JERRY

You're a human being.

GEORGE

And I didn't even ask her out. She asked me out first. She called me up. What was I supposed to do, say no? I can't do that to someone.

JERRY

You're too nice a guy.

GEORGE

I am. I'm a nice guy . . . (THEN SUDDENLY) And she seduced me! We were in my apartment. I'm sitting on the couch. She's on the chair. I get up to go to the bathroom. I come back, she's on the couch. What am I supposed to do, not do anything? I couldn't do that. I would've insulted her.

JERRY

You're flesh and blood.

GEORGE

I had nothing to do with any of this! I met all her friends. I didn't want to meet them. I kept trying to avoid it. I knew it would only get me in deeper. But they were everywhere. They kept popping up, all over the place. "This is Nancy, this is Susan, this is Amy. This is my cousin. This is my brother. This is my father." It's like I'm in quicksand.

JERRY

I told you when I met her . . .

GEORGE

My back is killing me.

JERRY

You gotta go to my chiropractor, he's the best.

GEORGE

Oh yeah, everybody's guy is the best.

JERRY

I'm gonna make an appointment for you. We'll go together.

GEORGE

Please. They don't do anything . . . Look, do I have to break up with her in person? Can't I do it over the phone? I have no stomach for these things.

JERRY

You should just do it like a Band-Aid. One motion. Right off.

At that exact moment the door opens and we see Elaine.

ELAINE

Hi.

JERRY

Hi.

George leans his seat forward to let her squeeze in the back.

ELAINE

Hey, what are you doing?

GEORGE

I'm letting you in.

ELAINE

Oh no, no, I don't want to sit in the back. I'll be left out of the conversation.

GEORGE

No you won't.

ELAINE

Yes, I will George. I'll have to stick my chin on top of the seat.

GEORGE

(RELUCTANTLY) Okay.

George gets out of the car now, so Elaine can slide in the front. He gestures for her to hop in first.

ELAINE

Why can't you sit in the middle?

GEORGE

Please, it doesn't look good—boy, boy, girl.

ELAINE

I think you're afraid to sit next to a man. You're a little homophobic, aren't you?

GEORGE

Is it that obvious?

Elaine gets in the middle.

ELAINE

Hello Jerry.

JERRY

Hello.

ELAINE

Did you get a haircut?

JERRY

No, shower. So, where are we eating?

ELAINE

Tell me if you think this is strange. There's this guy who lives in my building, who I was introduced to a couple of years ago by a friend. He's a teacher or something. Anyway, after we met, whenever we'd run into each other on the street, or in the lobby or whatever, we would stop and we would chat a little. Nothing much. Little pleasantries. He was a nice guy. He's got a family.

Then after a while, I noticed there was no more
stopping. Just saying hello and continuing on our way.
And then the verbal hellos stopped and we just went
into these little sort of nods of recognition. So, fine.
I figure, that's where this relationship is finally gonna
settle, polite nodding. Then one day, he doesn't nod.
Like I don't exist? He went from nods to nothing.

GEORGE

(À LA TONY BENNETT) "You know I'd go from nods to
nothing . . ."

ELAINE

And now there's this intense animosity whenever we
pass. I mean it's like we really hate each other. It's based
on nothing.

JERRY

A relationship is an organism. You created this thing and
then you starved it so it turned against you. Same thing
happened in *The Blob*.

GEORGE

I think you absolutely have to say something to this guy.
Confront him.

ELAINE

Really?

GEORGE

Yes.

ELAINE

Would you do that?

GEORGE

If I was a different person.

CUT TO:

ACT ONE
SCENE B

INT. JERRY'S APARTMENT—DAY

Jerry's on the phone.

JERRY

(INTO PHONE) Hello . . . Hello, is Glenn there? I'm sorry. Is this 805-555-3234? . . . Yes, I know I have the wrong number. But I just want to know if I dialed wrong or if . . .

The caller hangs up on Jerry. He consults his pad and redials.

Kramer enters.

SFX: buzzer
Kramer answers.

KRAMER

Come on up.

JERRY

Oh, it's you again. See? Now if you had answered me, I wouldn't have had to do this. Now that's two long distance calls I made to you why can't you . . . (HE'S HUNG UP ON AGAIN) Why, why do they just hang up like that? Thank you very much.

Kramer, with a quarter of a cantaloupe cut into sections, he spears one with a fork and holds it out for Jerry.

KRAMER

Taste this.

JERRY

No, I just had a sandwich.

KRAMER

No, taste it. Taste it.

JERRY

I don't want cantaloupe now.

KRAMER

You've never had cantaloupe like this before.

JERRY

I only eat cantaloupe at certain times.

KRAMER

Jerry, this is great cantaloupe.

JERRY

(RELUCTANTLY) Alright . . .

KRAMER

Ah, huh. It's good?

JERRY

It's very good.

KRAMER

Good huh?

JERRY

Good.

KRAMER

I got it at Joe's.

JERRY

Uh-huh.

KRAMER

Forty-nine cents a pound. That's practically half than what you're paying at the supermarket. I don't know why you don't go to Joe's.

JERRY

It's too far.

KRAMER

It's three blocks further. You can use my shopping cart.

JERRY

I'm not pulling a shopping cart. What am I supposed to wear a kerchief, put stockings on and roll 'em down below my knee?

KRAMER

See, the other thing is, if you don't like anything, he takes it right back.

JERRY

I don't return fruit. Fruit is a gamble. I know that going in.

George enters. *He's on top of the world. He dances around the room like Zorba, singing the Zorba theme.*

> **GEORGE**
>
> I'm outta there. I did it. It's over.

> **JERRY**
>
> You did it? What happened?

> **GEORGE**
>
> I told her. In the kitchen. Which was risky 'cause it's near all the knives. I started with the word "Listen."

> **JERRY**
>
> Ah ha.

> **GEORGE**
>
> I said "Listen Marlene," and then the next thing I know, I'm in the middle of it. And there's this voice inside of me going "You're doing it! You're doing it!" And then she started to cry, and I weakened a little bit, I almost relented, but the voice, Jerry, the voice, said "Keep going, keep going. You're almost out." It's like I was making a prison break, you know, and I'm heading for the wall and I trip and I twist my ankle and they throw that light on you, you know. So, somehow I get through the crying and I keep running. Then the cursing started. She's firing at me from the guard tower. "Son of a bang, son of a boom." I get to the top of the wall—the front door. I opened it up. I'm one foot away. I took one last look around the penitentiary, and I jumped.

> **JERRY**
>
> See, it's never as bad as you imagine.

> **KRAMER**
>
> I liked that Marlene. What's her number?

> **GEORGE**
>
> No, I, I don't think so.

Kramer is making noise eating the cantaloupe.

THE EX-GIRLFRIEND

JERRY

Could you stop that smacking?

KRAMER

George, I want you to taste this cantaloupe.

GEORGE

Oh no, thank you.

KRAMER

It's the best cantaloupe I ever had.

GEORGE

No, really. No, no, thanks.

KRAMER

Jerry, tell him how good this cantaloupe is.

JERRY

It's very good cantaloupe.

Kramer points to George.

JERRY

So that's it, you're out.

GEORGE

Except for one small problem. I left some books in her apartment.

JERRY

So, go get them.

GEORGE

Oh, no, no I can't go back there. Jerry, it's so awkward and, you know, it could be dangerous, sexually. Something could happen, I'd be right back where I started.

JERRY

So forget about the books. Did you read them?

GEORGE

Well, yeah.

JERRY

What do you need them for?

GEORGE

I don't know. They're books.

JERRY

What is this obsession people have with books? They put them in their houses like they're trophies. What do you need it for after you read it?

GEORGE

They're my books.

JERRY

(AFTER A BEAT) So you want me to get the books? Is that it?

CUT TO:

ACT ONE
SCENE D

INT. COFFEE SHOP—NIGHT

Jerry and George's ex (Marlene) are seated across from each other at a table. Marlene is subtly sensual with a hint of a southern drawl. She has a strong sexual magnetism, but it is well beneath the surface. There's a pile of five or six books on the table.

MARLENE

. . . So, it must've been ninety-five degrees that night and everyone's just standing around the pool with little drinks in their hands. I was wearing my old jeans and T-shirt. And I don't know, I was just in one of those moods so I said to myself, "Marlene, just do it," and I jumped in. And as I'm getting out, I feel all these eyes on me. And I look up and everyone is just staring at me.

THE EX-GIRLFRIEND

JERRY

So what'd you do?

MARLENE

Well, nothing. It's no skin off my hide if people like to look. I just didn't see what the big attraction was.

JERRY

Well, I have a general idea what it was. I could take a guess.

MARLENE

(LAUGHS) Hey, you know, Jerry, just because George and I don't see each other anymore it doesn't mean we shouldn't stay friends.

JERRY

No.

MARLENE

Good enough. I'm really glad we got that settled.

CUT TO:

ACT ONE
SCENE E

INT. CHIROPRACTOR'S WAITING ROOM

Shot of sign—it reads "Prevention is the Cure." Pull back to reveal Jerry and George in chiropractor's waiting room.

JERRY

(IRRITATED) I don't know how this happened.

GEORGE

Jerry, it's not my fault.

JERRY

No, no, it's not your fault. Books, books, I need my books. Have you re-read those books yet by the way?

You know the great thing, when you read *Moby Dick* the second time, Ahab and the whale become good friends. You know it's not like Marlene's a bad person or anything, but, my God, I mean we've had like three lunches and a movie and she never stops calling.

George nods, he's been there.

JERRY (CONT'D)

And it's these meaningless, purposeless, blather calls. She never asks if I'm busy or anything. I just pick up the phone and she's in the middle of a sentence.

GEORGE

That's standard. Has she left you one of those messages where she uses up the whole machine?

JERRY

Oh . . . You know, and sometimes she'll go, "Hello, Jerry?" and I'll go "Oh, hi Marlene." And then it's "Jerry . . ."

JERRY & GEORGE

". . . I don't know sometimes . . ."

GEORGE

What about getting off the phone?

JERRY

Oh-h-h-h, you can't. It's impossible. There's no break in the conversation where you can go, "Alright, then . . ." You know, it just goes on and on and on without a break in the wall. I mean, I gotta put a stop to this.

GEORGE

Just do it like a Band-Aid. One motion, right off. (AFTER A BEAT) She is sexy though. Don't you think?

JERRY

Yeah. Yes, she is.

Receptionist comes out.

RECEPTIONIST

Mr. Costanza?

THE EX-GIRLFRIEND

GEORGE

Yeah.

RECEPTIONIST

The doctor'll see you now.

GEORGE

(TO JERRY, SARCASTICALLY) Yeah, doctor. I'm going to have to wait in that little room by myself, aren't I? (RE: CROSSWORD PUZZLE) I better take this. I hate the little room. "Oh hello, Doctor."

CUT TO:

STAND UP #2

INT. COMEDY CLUB—NIGHT

JERRY

Waiting room. I hate when they make you wait in the room. 'Cause it says "waiting room." There's no chance of not waiting, 'cause they call it the waiting room, they're going to use it. They've got it. It's all set up for you to wait. And you sit there, you know, and you've got your little magazine. You pretend you're reading it but you're really looking at the other people. You know, you're thinking about them things like "I wonder what he's got. As soon as she goes, I'm getting her magazine." And then they finally call you and it's a very exciting moment. They finally call you and you stand up and you kinda look around at the other people in the room. "Well, I guess I've been chosen. I'll see you all later." You know, so you think you're going to see the doctor, but you're not, are you? No. You're going into the next waiting room. The littler waiting room. But if they are, you know, doing some sort of medical thing to you, you want to be in the smallest room that they have, I think. You don't want to be in the largest room that they have. You know what I mean? You ever see these operating theaters, that they have with like stadium seating? You don't want them doing anything to you that makes other doctors go, "I have to see this." "Are you kidding? Are they gonna really do that to him?" "Are there seats? Can we get in?" Do they scalp tickets to these things? "I got two for the Winslow tumor, I got two."

CUT TO:

ACT ONE
SCENE G

INT. WAITING ROOM—LATER

Jerry, still waiting. George returns.

JERRY

So, how was it?

GEORGE

I was in there for two minutes. He didn't do anything. (IMITATING DOCTOR) Touch this, feel that. Seventy-five bucks.

JERRY

Well, it's a first visit.

GEORGE

What's seventy-five bucks? What am I seeing Sinatra in there? Am I being entertained? I don't understand this. I'm only paying half.

JERRY

You can't do that.

GEORGE

Why not?

JERRY

He's a doctor. You gotta pay what he says.

GEORGE

Oh, no, no, no. I pay what I say.

CUT TO:

ACT ONE
SCENE H

INT. JERRY'S CAR—NIGHT

Jerry and Marlene.

MARLENE

Are you feeling weird?

JERRY

No. I'm fine.

MARLENE

Nothing really happened.

JERRY

Yeah, I know.

MARLENE

We just kissed a little. People kiss.

JERRY

Yeah.

MARLENE

Well . . . Night.

She leans in and kisses Jerry lightly on the lips.

JERRY

Good night.

On Jerry's face, we:

FADE OUT:

END ACT ONE

ACT TWO

SCENE J

INT. JERRY'S APARTMENT—DAY

Jerry is in the kitchen slicing a cantaloupe. Kramer enters with a golf club.

KRAMER

Hey.

JERRY

Hey.

KRAMER

I got it! This time I got it!

JERRY

Alright.

KRAMER

Hips! See it's all in the hips.

JERRY

Uh-huh.

KRAMER

You gotta come through with the hips first.

Kramer demonstrates.

                          JERRY

    That is out there.

Kramer notices the cantaloupe. His eyes light up.

                          KRAMER

    Joe's?

                          JERRY

    No. Supermarket.

Jerry tastes it. Kramer awaits the verdict.

                          KRAMER

    Well, is it good?

                          JERRY

    It's okay.

                          KRAMER

    Let me taste it. (STARTS TO TAKE A BITE, QUICKLY SPITS
    IT OUT) See, that stinks. You can't eat that. You should
    take that back.

                          JERRY

    I'm not taking it back.

                          KRAMER

    Alright, I'll take it back. I'm going by there.

                          JERRY

    I don't care about it.

                          KRAMER

    Jerry, you should care. Cantaloupe like this should be
    taken out of circulation.

                          JERRY

    Alright. Take it back.

Phone rings. Jerry freezes.

                       JERRY'S VOICE

    (ANSWERING MACHINE) Leave a message. I'll call you
    back.

MARLENE'S VOICE

Jerry, have you ever taken a bath in the dark? If I'm not
talking into the soap right now. Call me back.

KRAMER

Well?

JERRY

Marlene.

Kramer smiles putting two and two together.

KRAMER

Oh. Oh, Marlene.

JERRY

Yeah, I took her home one night we kinda started up a
little bit in the car.

KRAMER

I thought you were trying to get rid of her.

JERRY

I was. She's got me like hypnotized.

KRAMER

Does George know?

JERRY

No, he'd go nuts.

KRAMER

Yeah. No kidding.

JERRY

I feel terrible.

Kramer smiles.

JERRY (CONT'D)

I mean I've seen her a couple of times since then and I
know I can't go any further but, I've just got like this
psycho-sexual hold over me. I just want her, I can't
breathe. It's like a drug.

THE EX-GIRLFRIEND

KRAMER

Whoa, psycho-sexual.

JERRY

I don't know how I'm going to tell him.

KRAMER

Man. I don't understand people. I mean why would George want to deprive you of pleasure? Is it just me?

JERRY

It's partially you, yeah.

KRAMER

You're his friend. Better that she should sleep with someone else. Some jerk that he doesn't even know.

JERRY

Well he can't kill me, right?

KRAMER

You're a human being.

JERRY

I mean, she called me. I haven't called her. She started it.

KRAMER

You're flesh and blood.

JERRY

I'm a nice guy.

Elaine enters *carrying a small lamp.*

ELAINE

Hi. (THEY AD-LIB HELLOS AS SHE HANDS JERRY THE LAMP)

JERRY

Oh, my little airplane lamp.

ELAINE

You know you have the slowest elevator in the entire city? That's hard to get used to when you're in so many other fast ones.

JERRY

Well the apartment elevators are always slower than the offices, because you don't have to be home on time.

ELAINE

Unless you're married to a dictator . . .

JERRY

Yeah . . . because they would be very demanding people.

ELAINE

Right. Exactly. So I imagine at some point, somebody's going to offer me some cantaloupe.

KRAMER

Nope. No good.

JERRY

Well you know what they say, lucky in love, unlucky with fruit.

KRAMER

Well I'm taking this back.

He exits.

ELAINE

So, I had what you might call a little encounter this morning.

JERRY

Really? That guy who stopped saying hello?

ELAINE

Yep.

JERRY

You talked to him?.

ELAINE

Yep. I spotted him getting his mail. And at first I was just going to walk on by but then I thought no, no, no, no. Do not be afraid of this man.

JERRY

Right.

THE EX-GIRLFRIEND

ELAINE

So I walked up behind him and I tapped him on the shoulder. And I said, "Hi, remember me?" And he furrows his brow as if he's really trying to figure it out. So I said to him, I said, "You little phony. You know exactly who I am."

JERRY

"You little phony"?

ELAINE

I did. I most certainly did. And he said, he goes "Oh yeah, you're Jeanette's friend. We did meet once." And I said, "Well, how do you go from that to totally ignoring a person when they walk by?"

JERRY

Amazing.

ELAINE

And he says, he says, "Look, I just didn't want to say hello anymore, alright?" And I said, "Fine. Fine. I didn't want to say hello anymore either, but I just wanted you to know that I'm aware of it."

As Jerry speaks, Elaine tastes a piece of cantaloupe.

JERRY

You are the Queen of Confrontation. You're my new hero. In fact, you've inspired me. I'm gonna call George about something right now.

ELAINE

This cantaloupe stinks.

She finds it inedible and spits it into a napkin.

CUT TO:

ACT TWO
SCENE K

INT. COFFEE SHOP

(ECU—George)

GEORGE

I don't care.

JERRY

You're kidding.

Cam pulls back to reveal Jerry and George sitting across from each other.

GEORGE

No. I don't care.

JERRY

You mean that?

GEORGE

Absolutely.

JERRY

You don't care?

GEORGE

No.

JERRY

How could you not care?

GEORGE

I don't know. But I don't. I'm actually almost happy to hear it.

JERRY

I thought you'd be upset.

GEORGE

I guess I should be but I'm not.

JERRY

Am I a bad person? Did I do something terrible?

GEORGE

No, you're a fine person. You're a humanitarian. She's very sexy.

JERRY

That voice. That voice. She's driving me crazy.

THE EX-GIRLFRIEND

GEORGE

I know. I know.

JERRY

So I can see her tonight and you don't care?

GEORGE

See her tonight. See her tomorrow. Go, knock yourself out. She's too crazy for me.

JERRY

Alright, as long as you're okay. Because I can't stop thinking about her.

GEORGE

I'm okay. I'm fine. I'm wonderful. I never felt better in my whole life.

JERRY

Good. And I'll tell you what. You don't have to pay me back the thirty-five I gave to the chiropractor for the rest of your bill.

GEORGE

(NOW HE'S MAD) You paid that crook?!

JERRY

I had to.

GEORGE

He didn't do anything, Jerry. It's a scam. Who told you to do that?

JERRY

It was embarrassing to me.

GEORGE

I was trying to make a point.

JERRY

Why don't you make a point with your own doctor?

Suddenly George gulps.

JERRY (CONT'D)

What's wrong?

GEORGE

(GASPING) I think I swallowed a fly! . . . I swallowed a fly. What do I do? What can happen?

As he continues ranting, we:

CUT TO:

ACT TWO
SCENE L

EXT./INT. CAR—STOPPED. NIGHT

A beat, then:

JERRY

. . . So, you want to come up for a few minutes?

MARLENE

. . . I'm sorry, Jerry. I just don't think this is going to work.

JERRY

Really? I thought—

MARLENE

I know. I'm sorry.

JERRY

I guess I just didn't expect it from the way you've been acting.

MARLENE

You sure you want to talk about this? 'Cause I sure don't.

JERRY

Of course I want to talk about it.

MARLENE

Well, okay. I guess things changed for me on Tuesday night.

JERRY

Tuesday night? What happened Tuesday night?

MARLENE

. . . I saw your act.

JERRY

My act? What does that have to do with anything?

MARLENE

Well, to be honest, it just didn't make it for me. It's just so much fluff.

JERRY

I can't believe this. So what are you saying, you didn't like my act so that's it?

MARLENE

I can't be with someone if I don't respect what they do.

JERRY

You're a cashier!

MARLENE

Look Jerry, it's just not my kind of humor.

JERRY

You can't go by the audience that night. It was late. They were terrible.

MARLENE

I heard the material.

JERRY

I have other stuff. You should come see me on the weekend.

FADE OUT:

END OF ACT TWO

SHOW CLOSE

STAND-UP #3

INT. COMEDY CLUB—NIGHT

JERRY

Women need to like the job of the guy they're with. If they don't like the job, they don't like the guy. Men know this. Which is why we make up the phony bogus names for the jobs that we have. "Well right now I'm the regional management supervisor." "I'm in development, research, consulting." Men on the other hand, if they are physically attracted to a woman are not that concerned with her job. Are we? Men don't really care. Men'll just go, "Really? Slaughterhouse? Is that where you work. That sounds interesting. So whatdya got a big cleaver there, you're just lopping their heads off? That sounds great. Listen, why don't you shower up, and we'll get some burgers and catch a movie."

END OF SHOW

THE SEINFELD SCRIPTS

THE
PONY
REMARK

WRITTEN BY
LARRY DAVID & JERRY SEINFELD

DIRECTED BY
TOM CHERONES

AS BROADCAST JANUARY 30, 1991

SHOW OPEN

STAND-UP #1

INT. COMEDY CLUB—NIGHT

JERRY

My parents live in Florida now. They moved there last
year. They didn't want to move to Florida but they're
in their sixties, and that's the law. You know how it
works. They got the leisure police. They pull up in front
of the old people's house with a golf cart, jump out,
"Let's go Pop, white belt, white pants, white shoes, get
in the back. Drop the snow shovel right there, drop it."
I am not much for the family gathering. You know you
sit there and the conversation's so boring. It's so dull.
And you start to fantasize. You know, you think, what
if I just got up and jumped out that window? What
would it be like? Just crashed right through the glass.
You know. Come back in, there's broken glass,
everybody's all upset. "No I'm alright, I was just a little
bored, there. No, I'm fine. I came back. I wanted to hear
a little about that Hummel collection, Aunt Rose, let's
pick it up right there."

ACT ONE

SCENE A

INT. JERRY'S APARTMENT—LATE AFTERNOON

Jerry's parents are in town. His father (Morty) is sitting on the couch watching television with the sound adjusted for the hard-of-hearing. The mother (Helen) is ironing a loud plaid sport jacket.

HELEN

You have so many nice jackets. I don't know why you had to bring this jacket. Who wears a jacket like this? (HE DOESN'T RESPOND) What's wrong with that nice gray one? You have beautiful clothes. They sit in your closet. Morty, you can't wear—this!

She enters the bathroom, leaving the door open. The phone rings. No one responds. It rings a second time.

MORTY

Are you getting that?

HELEN

I thought you were getting it.

And a third.

MORTY

Should I pick up?

HELEN

You want me to get that?

Rings again.

MORTY

I'll get it!

HELEN

I'll get it!

They both go for the phone on the fifth.

HELEN

(SHE PICKS UP) Hello? . . . Hello?

She hangs up. Jerry enters *wearing sweatpants, a softball jersey, and carrying a bat with a glove on the end of it.*

JERRY

(RE: THE T.V.) Would you make this thing lower! I can hear it on the street!

Jerry turns it off.

MORTY

So how'd you do?

JERRY

We won. I made an incredible play in the field! There was a tag-up at third base and I threw the guy out from left field on a fly! We'll be in the championship game Wednesday because of me. It was the single greatest moment in my life.

HELEN

This is your greatest moment? A game?

JERRY

Well, no, Sharon Besser, of course.

MORTY

You know what my greatest moment was, don't you? 1946 I went to work for Harry Flemming and I came up with the idea for the beltless trench coat.

THE PONY REMARK

HELEN

Jerry look at this sport jacket. Is this a jacket to wear to an anniversary party?

JERRY

Well, the man's an individualist. He worked for Harry Flemming. He knows what he's doing.

HELEN

But it's their 50th anniversary.

MORTY

Your mother doesn't like my taste in clothing.

HELEN

You know I spoke to Manya and Isaac on the phone today. They invited you again. I think you should go.

JERRY

First of all, I made plans with Elaine.

HELEN

So bring her.

JERRY

I don't even know them. What is she, your second cousin? I mean I've met them three times in my life.

MORTY

I don't know her either. (GESTURING TO HELEN) She makes me fly all the way from Florida for this and then she criticizes my jacket.

HELEN

At least come and say hello, have a cup of coffee, then you'll leave.

MORTY

How come he gets to leave?

JERRY

If I wind up sitting next to Uncle Leo, I am leaving. He's always grabbing my arm when he talks to me. I guess it's because so many people have left in the middle of his conversation.

MORTY

And it's always about Jeffrey, right?

JERRY

Yeah, he talks about him like he split the atom. The kid works for the Parks Department.

Kramer enters.

KRAMER

Morty, are you coming in?

MORTY

Oh, yeah. I forgot all about it.

KRAMER

(TO JERRY) Hey, how'd you do?

JERRY

We won. We're in the finals on Wednesday . . .

KRAMER

Yeah!

JERRY

(RE: KRAMER AND MORTY) What is this about?

KRAMER

I'm completely changing the configuration of the apartment. You're not gonna believe it when you see it. A whole new lifestyle.

JERRY

What are you doing?

KRAMER

Levels.

JERRY

Levels?

KRAMER

Yeah, I'm getting rid of all my furniture. All of it. And I'm going to build these different levels, with steps, and it'll all be carpeted with a lot of pillows. You know, like ancient Egypt.

JERRY

You drew up plans for this?

KRAMER

No, no, it's all in my head.

MORTY

I don't know how you're going to be comfortable like that.

KRAMER

Oh I'll be comfortable.

JERRY

When do you intend to do this?

KRAMER

Ohh, should be done by the end of the month.

JERRY

You're doing this yourself?

KRAMER

It's a simple job. Why, you don't think I can?

JERRY

Oh no, it's not that I don't think you can. I know that you can't and I'm positive that you won't.

KRAMER

Well, I got the tools, I got the pillows, all I need is the lumber.

MORTY

Hey, that's some big job.

JERRY

I don't see it happening.

KRAMER

Well, this time, this time you're wrong. C'mon I'll even bet you.

JERRY

Seriously?

HELEN

I don't want you betting. Morty, don't let them bet.

KRAMER

A big dinner with dessert. But I've got till the end of the
month.

JERRY

I'll give you a year.

KRAMER

No, no, no. End of the month.

JERRY

It's a bet.

Kramer sticks his pinky out, and they lock pinkies.

CUT TO:

ACT ONE
SCENE B

INT. MANYA'S APARTMENT—EARLY EVENING

*They've put all the leaves on the dining room table to accommodate the
guests. Jerry sits between Elaine and Uncle Leo. Leo grabs his shoulder.*

JERRY

Seriously, do you want to switch chairs?

ELAINE

No, no, I'm fine.

UNCLE LEO

Jerry, you listening to this?

JERRY

Yeah, Uncle Leo.

UNCLE LEO

So, so, now the parks commissioner is recommending
Jeffrey for a citation.

THE PONY REMARK

JERRY

Right, for the reducing of the pond scum?

UNCLE LEO

No, for the walking tours.

JERRY

Oh, yeah, where the people eat the plant life—the edible foliage tour.

UNCLE LEO

That's exactly right. He knows the whole history of the park. For two hours he's talking and answering questions. But you want to know something? Whenever he has a problem with one of these high-powered big shots in the Parks Department, you know who he calls?

JERRY

Mickey Mantle?

ELAINE

(SENSING HE'S IN TROUBLE) Jerry, Jerry, did you taste these peas? These peas are great.

JERRY

(EATING A FORKFUL) These peas are bursting with country-fresh flavor.

ELAINE

Mmm . . . phenomenal peas . . .

MORTY

Are you ready for dessert?

JERRY

Well, actually we do have to kind of get going.

MANYA

(SURPRISED) You're going?

ELAINE

I don't really eat dessert. I'm dieting.

JERRY

Yeah, I can't eat dessert either. The sugar makes my ankles swell up, and I can't dance.

MANYA

Can't dance?

HELEN

He's kidding, Manya.

MANYA

Is that a joke?

HELEN

(CHANGING THE SUBJECT, TO MANYA) So, did you hear Claire's getting married?

MANYA

Yeah, yeah.

HELEN

I hear the fella owns a couple of racehorses. You know trotters like at Yonkers.

JERRY

Horses. They're like big riding dogs.

ELAINE

What about ponies? What kind of abnormal animal is that? And those kids who had their own ponies . . .

JERRY

I know. I hated those kids. In fact I hate anyone that ever had a pony when they were growing up.

MANYA

. . . I had a pony.

The room falls deadly silent.

JERRY

. . . Well, I didn't really mean a pony per se.

MANYA

(UPSET) When I was a little girl in Poland, we all had ponies. My sister had pony, my cousin had pony . . . So, what's wrong with that?

JERRY

Nothing. Nothing at all. I was just merely expressing . . .

HELEN

Should we have coffee? Who's having coffee?

MANYA

He was a beautiful pony! And I loved him.

JERRY

Well, I'm sure you did. Who wouldn't love a pony?
Who wouldn't love a person that had a pony?

MANYA

You! You said so!

JERRY

No, see we didn't have ponies. I'm sure at that time in
Poland they were very common, they were probably
like compact cars . . .

MANYA

That's it! I've had enough!

Manya's had enough. She leaves *the room. Everyone's silent.*

ISAAC

Have your coffee everyone. She's a little upset. It's been
an emotional day.

He leaves. *All eyes fall on Jerry.*

JERRY

I didn't know she had a pony. How was I to know she
had a pony? Who figures an immigrant's going to have
a pony? Do you know what the odds are on that? I mean
in all the pictures I saw of immigrants on boats coming
into New York harbor, I never saw one of them sitting
on a pony. Why would anybody come here if they had
a pony? Who leaves a country packed with ponies to
come to a non-pony country? It doesn't make sense . . .
Am I wrong?

CUT TO:

**ACT ONE
SCENE D**

INT. JERRY'S APARTMENT

Morty and Helen are ready to leave for Florida. Their bags are packed.

JERRY

I'll drive you to the airport.

HELEN

No, we're taking a cab.

JERRY

I just hope that whole pony incident didn't put a damper on the trip.

HELEN

Don't be ridiculous. It was a misunderstanding.

MORTY

Hey I agree with him. Nobody likes a kid with a pony.

JERRY

Well, if you ever talk to her, tell her I'm sorry, Elaine too. She feels terrible.

HELEN

You know, you should give Manya a call.

JERRY

Maybe I will.

Jerry opens the door—Kramer is there.

KRAMER

Oh, hi. I just came to say goodbye. (RE: THE BAGS)
. . . Need any help with those?

MORTY

It's nothing. I got it. So, how are your levels coming along?

KRAMER

Oh, well, I decided I'm not gonna do it.

JERRY

Really? What a shock.

Parents start to exit.

HELEN

Goodbye Jerry.

THE PONY REMARK

JERRY

Take care.

HELEN

We'll call you.

She kisses him, then Kramer, and leaves.

MORTY

Bye Jer.

JERRY

Bye Dad. Take it easy.

MORTY

Bye Mr. Kramer.

KRAMER

Yeah. So long, Morty.

Morty leaves.

JERRY

So, when do I get my dinner?

KRAMER

There's no dinner. The bet's off. I'm not gonna do it.

JERRY

Yes. I know you're not gonna do it. That's why I bet.

KRAMER

There's no bet if I'm not doing it.

JERRY

That's the bet! That you're not doing it.

KRAMER

Yeah well, I could do it. I don't want to do it.

JERRY

We didn't bet on if you wanted to. We bet on if it would be done.

KRAMER

And it could be done.

JERRY

Well of course it could be done! Anything could be done, but it only is done if it's done. Show me the levels. The bet is the levels.

KRAMER

But I don't want the levels!

JERRY

That's the bet!

SFX: phone rings

Jerry picks up.

JERRY (CONT'D)

(INTO PHONE) Hello . . . No, oh, hi . . . No, they just left . . . Oh my God . . . Hang on a second, maybe I can still catch them. (JERRY GOES TO THE WINDOW AND OPENS IT. SCREAMS) Ma . . . Ma . . . up here. Don't get in the cab . . . Manya died . . . Manya died!!!

FADE OUT:

END OF ACT ONE

ACT TWO

SCENE E

INT. JERRY'S APARTMENT

The parents have returned with their bags.

HELEN

Who did you talk to?

JERRY

Uncle Leo.

HELEN

And when's the funeral?

JERRY

I don't know. He said he'd call back.

MORTY

You know what this means don't you? We lost the
supersaver. Those tickets are non-refundable.

HELEN

She just had a check-up. The doctor said she was fine.
Unless . . .

JERRY

What?

HELEN

What? Nothing.

JERRY

You don't think . . . What the pony remark? . . .

HELEN

Oh, don't be ridiculous. She was an old woman.

JERRY

You don't think I killed her?

MORTY

You know what that flight back'll cost us?

JERRY

It was just an innocent comment! I didn't know she had a pony!

MORTY

Maybe we can get an army transport flight. They got a base in Sarasota, I think.

JERRY

The whole thing was taken out of context. It was a joke.

SFX: phone rings

JERRY (CONT'D)

That's probably Uncle Leo.

Helen picks up.

HELEN

Hello? . . . Yes, I know . . . Well it's just one of those things . . . Sure, sure we'll see you then.

She hangs up.

HELEN (CONT'D)

The funeral's Wednesday.

JERRY

Wednesday? What, what Wednesday?

HELEN

Two o'clock, Wednesday.

Jerry shrugs.

THE PONY REMARK

HELEN (CONT'D)

What?

JERRY

I've got the softball game on Wednesday. It's the championship.

HELEN

So you're not obligated. Go play in your game.

JERRY

I didn't even know the woman.

HELEN

So don't go.

JERRY

I mean I met her three times. I don't even know her last name.

HELEN

Jerry, no one's forcing you.

JERRY

I mean who has a funeral on a Wednesday? That's what I want to know. I mean it's the championship. I'm hitting everything.

He assumes a batting stance.

HELEN

I don't have a dress to wear. (TO MORTY) And you, you don't have anything.

MORTY

I got my sport jacket.

HELEN

You're not wearing that to a funeral.

MORTY

What's wrong with it?

HELEN

It looks ridiculous.

MORTY
What I'm gonna buy a new jacket now?

JERRY
I don't know what to do.

MORTY
. . . You know what this funeral's gonna wind up costing me? Oh boy!

CUT TO:

STAND-UP #2

INT. COMEDY CLUB—NIGHT

JERRY
We don't understand death. And the proof of this is that we give dead people a pillow. And uh, I mean hey, you know. I think if you can't stretch out and get some solid rest at that point, I don't see how bedding accessories really make the difference. I mean they got the guy in a suit, with a pillow. Now is he going to a meeting, or is he catching forty winks? I mean let's make up our mind where we think they're going.

ACT TWO
SCENE G

INT. COFFEE SHOP—DAY

We join Elaine, Jerry and George in mid-conversation.

ELAINE
I actually like ponies. I was just trying to make conversation. What time's your game?

THE PONY REMARK

JERRY

Two forty-five.

ELAINE

And what time's the funeral?

JERRY

Two o'clock.

ELAINE

How long does a funeral take?

JERRY

Depends on how nice the person was. But you gotta figure, even Oswald took forty-five minutes.

ELAINE

So you can't do both.

JERRY

You know, if the situation were reversed and Manya had some mah-jongg championship or something, I wouldn't expect her to go to my funeral. I would understand.

ELAINE

How can you even consider not going?

GEORGE

You know, I've been thinking. I cannot envision any circumstances in which I'll ever have the opportunity to have sex again. How's it gonna happen? I just don't see how it could occur.

ELAINE

You know, funerals always make me think about my own mortality and how I'm actually going to die someday. Me, dead. Imagine that.

GEORGE

They always make me take stock of my life and how I've pretty much wasted all of it, and how I plan to continue wasting it.

JERRY

I know, and then you say to yourself, "From this moment on, I'm not going to waste any more of it." But then you go "How? What can I do that's not wasting it?"

ELAINE

Is this a waste of time? What should we be doing? Can't you have coffee with people?

GEORGE

You know, I can't believe you're even considering not playing. We need you. You're hitting everything.

ELAINE

He has to go. He may have killed her.

JERRY

Me? What about you? You brought up the pony.

ELAINE

Oh, yeah, but I didn't say I hated anyone who had one.

GEORGE

(TO JERRY) Who's going to play left field?

JERRY

Bender.

GEORGE

Bender? He can't play left. He stinks. I just don't see what purpose is it going to serve your going? I mean you think dead people care who's at their funeral? They don't even know they're having a funeral. It's not like she's hanging out in the back going, "I can't believe Jerry didn't show up."

ELAINE

Maybe she's there in spirit. How about that?

GEORGE

If you're a spirit and you can travel to other dimensions and galaxies, and find out the mysteries of the universe,

you think she's going to want to hang around Drexler's
funeral home on Ocean Parkway?

ELAINE

George, I met this woman! She is not traveling to any
other dimensions.

GEORGE

You know how easy it is for dead people to travel? It's
not like getting on a bus. One second. It's all mental.

JERRY

Fifty years they were married. Now he's moving to
Phoenix.

ELAINE

(EYES LIGHT UP) Phoenix? What's happening with his
apartment?

JERRY

I don't know. They've been in there since like World
War II. The rent's three hundred a month.

ELAINE

Three hundred a month. Oh my God.

CUT TO:

ACT TWO
SCENE H

INT. FUNERAL HOME—DAY

*A eulogy is in progress, delivered by a man in his forties. We pan the
faces: First, Morty in his new jacket, then Helen, Elaine, then Jerry
staring out—this is the last place in the world he wants to be.*

MAN

Although this may seem like a sad event, it should not
be a day of mourning . . . for Manya had a rich, fulfilling

life. She grew up in a different world, a simpler world, with loving parents, a beautiful home in the country, and from what I understand, she even had a pony . . . (JERRY THROWS HIS HANDS UP) Oh, how she loved that pony. Even in her declining years, whenever she would speak of it, her eyes would light up. Its lustrous coat, its flowing mane. It was the pride of Krakow.

As Jerry lowers himself under his seat . . .

DISSOLVE TO:

ACT TWO
SCENE J

INT. ANTEROOM OF FUNERAL PARLOR—DAY

The service is over. Guests are milling about. We find Jerry, Elaine, and Helen talking.

JERRY
(LOOKING AT HIS WATCH) Well, the game's starting just about now.

HELEN
It was good that the two of you came. It was a nice gesture.

CUT TO:

Morty and a man in his mid-20's.

INTERN
I'm not a doctor yet, Uncle Morty. I'm just an intern. I can't write a note to an airline.

MORTY
You've got your degree. They don't care. They just want to see something.

THE PONY REMARK

Back to:

Jerry and Elaine approach the widower, Isaac.

JERRY

I just wanted to say how sorry I was . . .

He's interrupted by a hand on his shoulder: Uncle Leo.

UNCLE LEO

Jerry, you wanna hear something? Your cousin, Jeffrey, is switching parks. They're transferring him to Riverside so he'll completely revamp that operation, you understand? He'll do in Riverside now what he did in Central Park. It's more money. So, that's your cousin.

Back to: Morty and intern.

MORTY

You don't understand. I've never paid full fare.

Back to: Jerry turns from Uncle Leo, back to Isaac.

JERRY

Once again, I just want to say how sorry I am about the other night.

ELAINE

Oh, me too.

ISAAC

Oh no, no, no. She forgot all about that. She was much more upset about the potato salad.

ELAINE

So I understand you're moving to Phoenix?

Jerry shakes his head and walks away.

ISAAC

Yeah, my brother lives there. I think Manya would've liked Phoenix.

ELAINE

Mmm, gorgeous, exquisite town. So what's happening with your apartment?

ISAAC

Of course it's very hot there. I'll have to get an air-conditioner.

ELAINE

Oh, you can have mine. I'll ship it out to you . . . But what about that big apartment on West End Avenue?

ISAAC

Although they say it's a dry heat.

ELAINE

Dry, wet . . . What's happening with your apartment?

ISAAC

I don't even know if I should take my winter clothing.

ELAINE

I have an idea. Leave the winter clothing in the apartment and I'll watch it for you and I'll live there and I'll make sure that nothing happens to it.

Jerry returns.

ISAAC

Oh the apartment. Jeffrey's taking the apartment.

ELAINE

(TO JERRY) Oh Jeffrey.

JERRY

(TO ELAINE) You know Jeffrey.

ELAINE

Yeah. From what I understand he works for the Parks Department.

Helen approaches and taps Jerry on the shoulder.

SFX: clap of thunder

HELEN

It's raining.

Jerry goes to the window.

THE PONY REMARK

JERRY

It's raining? It's raining. The game will be postponed. We'll play tomorrow.

Back to: Morty and intern.

MORTY

Believe me, I wouldn't bother you if the army hadn't closed that base in Sarasota. Here, scribble a little something here.

INTERN

I can't. I'll get in trouble.

MORTY

Oh, for God's sakes.

CUT TO:

ACT TWO
SCENE K

INT. COFFEE SHOP—DAY

Jerry, George, Elaine at a booth. Jerry and George are wearing their softball uniforms. Elaine is wearing sunglasses.

GEORGE

Who gets picked off in softball? It's unheard of.

JERRY

It's never happened to me before.

ELAINE

I remember saying to myself "Why is Jerry so far off the base?"

JERRY

I'll have to live with this shame for the rest of my life.

GEORGE

And then in the fifth inning why did you take off on the pop fly?

JERRY

I thought there were two outs.

ELAINE

I couldn't believe it when I saw you running. I thought maybe they had changed the rules or something.

JERRY

It was the single worst moment of my life.

GEORGE

What about Sharon Besser?

JERRY

Oh, well, of course, 1973.

ELAINE

Makes you wonder though, doesn't it?

JERRY

Wonder about what?

ELAINE

You know . . . the spirit world.

JERRY

You think Manya showed up during the game and put a hex on me?

ELAINE

I never saw anyone play like that.

JERRY

But I went to the funeral.

ELAINE

Yeah but that doesn't make up for killing her.

GEORGE

Maybe Manya missed the funeral because she was off visiting another galaxy that day.

THE PONY REMARK

JERRY

Don't you think she would've heard I was there?

GEORGE

Not necessarily.

Elaine laughs.

JERRY

Who figures an immigrant's gonna have a pony?

CUT TO:

END OF ACT TWO

SHOW CLOSE

STAND-UP #3

INT. COMEDY CLUB—NIGHT

JERRY

What is the pony? What is the point of the pony? Why
do we have these animals, these ponies? What do we do
with them? Besides the pony ride. Why ponies? What
are we doing with them? I mean police don't use them
for, you know, crowd control. "Hey, uh, you wanna get
back behind the barricades. Hey! Hey, little boy. Yeah,
I'm talking to you. Behind the barricades." So
somebody, I assume, genetically engineered these
ponies. Do you think they could make them any size? I
mean, could they make them like the size of a quarter,
if they wanted? That would be fun for Monopoly
though wouldn't it? Just have a little pony and you put
him on the, "Baltic, that's two down, go ahead. Hold it,
right there, Baltic. Yeah, that's it. Fine. Right there, hold
it right here."

END OF SHOW

THE Seinfeld SCRIPTS

THE JACKET

WRITTEN BY

LARRY DAVID & JERRY SEINFELD

DIRECTED BY

TOM CHERONES

AS BROADCAST FEBRUARY 6, 1991

SHOW OPEN

STAND-UP #1

INT. COMEDY CLUB—NIGHT

JERRY

I hate clothes, okay? I hate buying them. I hate picking them out of my closet. I can't stand every day trying to come up with little outfits for myself. I think eventually fashion won't even exist. It won't. I think eventually we'll all be wearing the same thing. 'Cause anytime I see a movie or a TV show where there's people from the future or another planet, they're all wearing the same thing. Somehow they decided. "This is going to be our outfit. One-piece silver jumpsuit, V-stripe, and boots. That's it." We should come up for an outfit for earth. An earth outfit. We should vote on it. Candidates propose different outfits, no speeches. They walk out, twirl, walk off. We just sit in the audience and go, "That was nice, I could wear that."

CUT TO:

ACT ONE

SCENE A

INT. CLOTHING STORE—UPSCALE COLUMBUS AVE. TYPE—DAY

Jerry and Elaine are browsing. Along with her purse, Elaine holds a wallet and a book.

JERRY

I think I've seen enough.

SALESMAN

Well, I might have something in the back.

ELAINE

The back? They never find anything in the back. If they had anything good in the back, they'd put it out in the front.

JERRY

Why don't they open up an entire store for the back? Call it, "Just Back." All back, no front. You walk in the front, you're immediately in the back. (PICKS UP TIE DISPLAY) Look, Elaine, tie car wash.

CUSTOMER

(RE: ELAINE'S BOOK) Oh, I just read that. That's terrific.

JERRY

(POINTING TO ELAINE) Her father wrote that.

CUSTOMER

Alton Benes is your father?

ELAINE

Yeah.

CUSTOMER

I always felt he deserved a wider audience.

ELAINE

I'm not so sure he wants one.

She leaves.

ELAINE (CONT'D)

Hey don't forget Sunday, okay. You and George are coming right? Hotel Westbury, eight o'clock.

JERRY

. . . I guess I'm coming. I mean . . .

ELAINE

What? What you don't want to go now?

JERRY

No, I'll go. I'm going.

ELAINE

No Jerry, you have to. I need a buffer. You know, I haven't seen my father in a while and . . . you know.

JERRY

I'm worried I won't be able to talk to him. He's such a great writer. Frankly I prefer the company of nitwits.

ELAINE

So that's why we're not together anymore.

Jerry examines a jacket.

JERRY

What is this?

Jerry holds up a suede jacket.

JERRY (CONT'D)

This is beautiful, but these jackets never fit me right.

THE JACKET

ELAINE

Try it on. (FEELS THE SUEDE) Wow, this is soft suede.

JERRY

This may be the most perfect jacket I have ever put on.

Elaine grabs the tag.

JERRY (CONT'D)

How much is it?

ELAINE

(SHOCKED) Oh my God.

JERRY

Bad? (ELAINE NODS) . . . Very bad?

ELAINE

You have no idea.

JERRY

I have some idea.

ELAINE

No idea.

JERRY

I've got a ballpark.

ELAINE

There is no park and the team has relocated.

JERRY

(HE GLANCES AT THE TAG) . . . That is high.

ELAINE

Oh man, that is a beautiful jacket though.

JERRY

What's with the pink lining and the candy stripes?

ELAINE

Well, it's just a lining. You can always have it changed.

JERRY

Should I get it?

Elaine shrugs. It's his decision.

JERRY (CONT'D)

I hate these moments. I'm hearing the dual voices now, you know, "What about the money?" "What's money?"

SALESMAN

It looks wonderful on you.

DISSOLVE TO:

ACT ONE
SCENE B

INT. JERRY'S APARTMENT—NIGHT

Jerry is sitting on the couch wearing slippers, worn-out Scotch plaid pajama bottoms, a long T-shirt and the jacket. He gets up to admire himself in the mirror. Kramer enters.

JERRY

Hey.

KRAMER

Hey. New jacket.

JERRY

What do you think?

KRAMER

It's beautiful.

JERRY

Is it me?

KRAMER

That's definitely you.

JERRY

Really?

KRAMER

That's more you than you've ever been. (HE STARTS TO INSPECT IT) What is with the pink lining?

THE JACKET

JERRY

I don't know. It's got a pink lining.

KRAMER

Oh . . . So, what did you pay for this?

JERRY

I paid what it costs.

KRAMER

How much?

JERRY

What's the difference?

KRAMER

What, you're not gonna tell me?

JERRY

I'd rather not say it out loud. It's embarrassing.

KRAMER

Over three hundred?

JERRY

Yes, but let's just stop it right there.

KRAMER

It's over four hundred.

JERRY

Really, I'm not answering anymore.

KRAMER

Is it over four hundred?

JERRY

Would you?

Kramer finds the tag.

KRAMER

Whoa Nelson.

JERRY

I know, I know.

> KRAMER

What are you gonna do with the leather one?

> JERRY

I don't know.

> KRAMER

Well, are you gonna wear it?

> JERRY

Maybe.

> KRAMER

You're not going to wear this.

> JERRY

Do you want it?

> KRAMER

Well, yeah. Okay, I'll take it . . . I like the jacket.

Jerry takes one last look at the jacket.

> JERRY

. . . Okay. Take it.

> KRAMER

Good karma for you.

Kramer tries it on. They stand there looking in the mirror, admiring their jackets.

> KRAMER (CONT'D)

Oh baby.

DISSOLVE TO:

ACT ONE
SCENE C

INT. JERRY'S APARTMENT—NIGHT

Jerry is putting on a tie. George has already buzzed and is on his way up. George enters singing "Master of the House" from Les Miserables.

THE JACKET

GEORGE

"Master of the House . . .
doling out the charm,
ready with a handshake
and an open palm.
Tells a saucy tale,
loves to make a stir
everyone appreciates a . . ."

JERRY

What is that song?

GEORGE

Oh, it's from *Les Miserables*. I went to see it last week. I can't get it out of my head. I just keep singing it over and over. It just comes out. I have no control over it. I'm singing it on elevators, buses, I sing it in front of clients, it's taking over my life.

JERRY

You know, Schumann went mad from that.

GEORGE

Artie Schumann, from Camp Hatchapee?

JERRY

No, you idiot.

GEORGE

What are you, Bud Abbott? What, are you calling me an idiot?

JERRY

You don't know Robert Schumann, the composer?

GEORGE

Oh Schumann, of course.

JERRY

(SCARING HIM) He went crazy from one note. He couldn't get it out of his head. I think it was an A. He kept repeating it over and over again. He had to be institutionalized.

GEORGE

Really? . . . Well, what if it doesn't stop?

Jerry gestures "that's the breaks." George takes a deep breath.

GEORGE (CONT'D)

Oh, that I really needed to hear. That helps a lot.
Alright, just say something. Just start talking, change the
subject . . . Let's just go, alright? I can't believe we're
having dinner with Alton Benes.

JERRY

I know exactly what's going to happen tonight. I'm
gonna try and act like I'm not impressed, he's gonna see
right through it.

GEORGE

Yeah. He'll be looking at us like he's backstage at a
puppet show.

JERRY

Let me just get my jacket.

Jerry heads to bedroom.

GEORGE

"Master of the house,
Keeper of the inn . . ."

*Jerry, with great care, dons his prized jacket and models it proudly to
George, waiting for the reaction. George stands back for a second in
admiration. He then approaches Jerry, carefully feels the material.*

GEORGE (CONT'D)

This is huge. When did this happen?

JERRY

Wednesday. This jacket has completely changed my life.
When I leave the house in this, it's with a whole
different confidence. Like tonight I might've been a little
nervous. But inside this jacket, I am composed,
grounded, secure that I can meet any social challenge.

GEORGE

(NODS APPROVINGLY) Can I say one thing to you? And I

THE JACKET

say this with an unblemished record of staunch
heterosexuality.

JERRY

Absolutely.

GEORGE

. . . It's fabulous.

JERRY

I know.

GEORGE

And I'll tell you something else. I'm not even going to
ask you. I want to know. But I'm not gonna ask. You'll
tell me when you feel comfortable . . . So what was it
four hundred? Five hundred? Did you pay five hundred
for this? Over six? Can't be seven. Don't tell me you
paid seven hundred dollars for this jacket. Did you pay
seven hundred dollars for this jacket? Is that what you're
saying to me? You are sick. Is that what you paid for this
jacket? Over seven hundred? What did you pay for this
jacket? I won't say anything. I wanna know what you
paid for this jacket. Oh my God! A thousand dollars?
You paid a thousand dollars for this jacket. Alright, fine.
I'm walking out of here right now thinking you paid a
thousand dollars for this jacket unless you tell me
different.

Jerry doesn't answer.

GEORGE (CONT'D)

Oh, ho! Alright, I'll tell you what, if you don't say
anything in the next five seconds, I'll know it was over
a thousand . . .

Kramer enters.

KRAMER

Hey. Hey, would you do me a solid?

JERRY

Well, what kind of solid?

KRAMER

I need you to sit in the car for two minutes while it's double-parked. I gotta pick up some birds.

JERRY

Birds?

KRAMER

Yeah. A friend of mine, he's a magician, he's going away on vacation. He asked me to take care of his doves.

JERRY

So take a cab.

KRAMER

They won't take a cage full of birds.

JERRY

I can't. I'm on my way out. There's no way I can do it.

KRAMER

George, do me a solid? Two minutes.

GEORGE

Well, I'm going with him. I'd like to, I've never done a solid before.

KRAMER

Alright . . . Yeah . . . Alright, have a good one.

He leaves.

JERRY

Two minutes. Believe me, I know his two minutes. By his conception of time, his life will last over two thousand years.

DISSOLVE TO:

ACT ONE
SCENE D

INT. HOTEL LOBBY—NIGHT

It's a venerable New York hotel, for people who like leather couches and leather patches on their elbows. Jerry and George enter through a revolving door. George is in the middle of "Master of the House."

THE JACKET

GEORGE

"Master of the House. Quick to catch your eye, never wants a passerby to pass him by."

Jerry taps him.

JERRY

(POINTING TO HIS HEAD) Schumann. (GEORGE IS SCARED OF THE REMINDER) Where are they?

GEORGE

Maybe he didn't show up.

JERRY

What, you don't want to do this?

GEORGE

I don't think there's ever been an appointment in my life where I wanted the other guy to show up.

They walk into the hotel lobby.

GEORGE

Wait a second, is that him?

JERRY

Yeah, I think it is.

They start walking toward him.

JERRY (CONT'D)

Where's Elaine?

GEORGE

I'm nervous.

They approach him. He's an imposing figure, not so much in size, as personality. He resembles Hemingway and probably wouldn't be afraid to take a poke at him. He has a smoker's cough. An irritable, unhealthy specimen.

JERRY

Excuse me . . . Mr. Benes?

BENES

Yeah?

JERRY

I'm Jerry, Elaine's friend, and this is George.

GEORGE

It's a great thrill to meet you sir.

Benes erupts in a hacking, tubercular cough. George withdraws his hand.

BENES

Sit down. Want a drink?

JERRY

Sure.

He summons the waiter.

BENES

What do you have?

JERRY

(TO WAITER) I'll have a cranberry juice with two limes.

GEORGE

(TO WAITER) And, I'll have a club soda with no ice.

Benes shoots them a look.

BENES

(TO WAITER) I'll have another Scotch with plenty of ice.

GEORGE

You like ice?

BENES

Huh?

GEORGE

I said, do you like ice?

BENES

Like it?

GEORGE

Don't you think you get more without it?

After a beat:

THE JACKET

BENES

Where's Elaine?

JERRY

Well, we thought she was meeting you earlier. She's usually pretty punctual. (JERRY GETS NO ANSWER) . . . Don't you find that George?

GEORGE

Yeah, yeah. She's punctual . . . and she's been late sometimes.

JERRY

Yeah, yeah. Sometimes she's on time and sometimes she's late.

GEORGE

I guess today she's late.

JERRY

It appears that way.

GEORGE

(UNCOMFORTABLY) Yup.

JERRY

Yup.

They both turn to look at the door to see if she's coming. He coughs again. When he's done:

BENES

Looks like rain.

GEORGE

(PERKS UP) I know, I know, that's what they said.

BENES

Who said?

GEORGE

The weather guy, Dr. Waldo.

BENES

I don't need anybody to tell me it's gonna rain.

GEORGE

No, of course not. I didn't . . .

BENES

All I have to do is stick my head out the window.

They turn to the door. The waiter shows up with the drinks.

BENES (CONT'D)

Which one's suppose to be the funny guy?

GEORGE

(POINTING AT JERRY) Oh, he's the comedian.

JERRY

I'm just a regular person.

GEORGE

No, no, he's just being modest.

BENES

We had a funny guy with us in Korea. A tailgunner.
They blew his brains out all over the Pacific. (A LONG
PAUSE, STUNNED SILENCE) There's nothing funny about
that.

*That renders everyone speechless. Jerry and George turn again to the
door.*

JERRY

Would you excuse me a minute? I'm gonna go to the
bathroom. I'll be right back.

Jerry leaves. *George swallows hard.*

GEORGE

I just wanted to tell you that I really enjoyed *Fairgame.* I
thought it was just brilliant.

BENES

Drivel.

GEORGE

Maybe some parts.

THE JACKET

BENES

What parts?

GEORGE

The drivel parts . . . Oh my gosh, I just realized, I have to make a phone call. I can't believe. . . . would you . . .

CUT TO:

ACT ONE
SCENE E

INT. HOTEL BATHROOM

George enters. *Jerry's splashing water on his face.*

GEORGE

Thank you for leaving me alone with him!

JERRY

That was brutal. I can't go back out there.

GEORGE

Well let's just leave.

JERRY

Elaine'll kill me.

GEORGE

Where is she?

JERRY

She's gotta be here soon.

GEORGE

How could she leave us alone with this lunatic? Ten more minutes and that's it. I'm leaving. I have to tell you, this guy scares me.

JERRY

The waiter was trembling.

GEORGE

If she doesn't show up we can't possibly have dinner with him alone.

JERRY

How are we gonna get out of it?

GEORGE

We'll say we're frightened and we have to go home.

JERRY

Yeah, that's good. He'd clunk our heads together like Moe.

GEORGE

I don't know. Just start scratching. Tell him you have the crabs. He was in the military. He'll understand that.

CUT TO:

STAND-UP #2

INT. COMEDY CLUB—NIGHT

JERRY

All fathers are intimidating. They're intimidating because they are fathers. Once a man has children, for the rest of his life, his attitude is, "To hell with the world, I can make my own people. I'll eat whatever I want, I'll wear whatever I want and I'll create whoever I want."

ACT ONE
SCENE F

INT. LOBBY—NIGHT

Jerry and George return *from the bathroom.*

THE JACKET

> **BENES**

Who'd you call?

> **GEORGE**

(CAUGHT OFF GUARD) My uncle is having an operation.
I just wanted to see how he was.

> **BENES**

What kind of an operation?

> **GEORGE**

Bone marrow.

Manager approaches.

> **MANAGER**

Mr. Benes.

> **BENES**

Yes?

> **MANAGER**

A message for you.

He hands him a message.

> **BENES**

From Elaine. She got tied up. She'll be here in thirty
minutes.

On Jerry's and George's frozen faces, we:

FADE OUT:

END OF ACT ONE

ACT TWO

SCENE G

INT. HOTEL LOBBY—NIGHT

Two shot of Jerry and George looking years older. Benes is holding forth.

BENES
Yeah, they should've taken care of Castro when they
had the chance. (ANGLE) Like we did in Guatamala in
'fifty-three.

JERRY
Well, Guatamala.

GEORGE
Sure, Guatamala.

Benes gets up.

BENES
Alright, you boys get yourselves together. We'll head up
to the restaurant. I'll leave a note for Elaine. I'm going
to the bathroom.

He leaves.

GEORGE
Come on, let's go!

JERRY
What about Elaine?

GEORGE

To hell with Elaine!

JERRY

She'll be furious.

GEORGE

We're dying here!

Jerry turns to the door.

JERRY

That's her! She's here!

She approaches them.

ELAINE

I'm sorry. I'm so sorry. Where is Dad?

GEORGE

(À LA BENES) He's in the bathroom.

JERRY

Where have you been?

ELAINE

(LIVID) Kramer, that Kramer. I'm just about to leave, he calls me up. He begs me to sit in his car for two minutes, so he can pick up these birds . . .

JERRY

Oh you didn't . . .

ELAINE

Well, he said he'd drive me here right after. So I am sitting in his car twenty minutes. He doesn't come down. I am freezing. Then a cop comes by, tells me to get out of the car. He's a city marshal. He's towing the car away. Kramer owes thousands of dollars in back tickets. He was going to tow it with me in the car! So they tow the car. Now I am standing outside, and I am freezing, but I cannot leave because I have to tell him what happened to the car . . . so finally, he finally comes down with this giant cage filled with doves. He said he was getting special instructions, that each dove has a different diet. So we're wandering around trying to get a cab when two of these doves fly out. Now we're running down the street after these doves. I almost got hit by a bus.

She sits.

ELAINE (CONT'D)
(TAKES A DEEP BREATH) . . . So how's everything going over here?

JERRY
(SINCERELY) Great.

GEORGE
Couldn't be better.

ELAINE
Good. 'Cause Dad can make some people a little uncomfortable.

JERRY	GEORGE
Oh no, no.	Get outta here . . .

ELAINE
Man, Kramer, I could kill him.

JERRY
I can't believe it. You know better than to get involved with Kramer.

ELAINE
He said he'd give me a lift.

JERRY
Ah, the lift. Like the lure of the siren's song, never what it seems to be, yet who among us can resist?

GEORGE
Where do you come up with this stuff?

Benes returns.

BENES
Well look who's here.

ELAINE

Oh, hi Dad.

He kisses her.

BENES

Hello, dear. Who's the lipstick for?

ELAINE

No one.

BENES

. . . How's your mother?

ELAINE

Fine.

BENES

How about you, are you working?

ELAINE

Yeah, I'm reading manuscripts for Pendant Publishing. I told you ten times.

BENES

Pendant, those bastards. . . . Alright boys, we'll go to that Pakistani restaurant on 46th Street. (TO THE BOYS) You're not afraid of a little spice, are you?

They head towards the revolving door. Elaine and Benes in front. Jerry and George trailing.

GEORGE

"Master of the House, doling out the charm ready with a handshake and an open . . ."

BENES

Pipe down, chorus boy.

Benes turns sharply and glares, George freezes, embarrassed. Suddenly Elaine stops.

ELAINE

(TAKEN) Ooh, it's snowing.

Angle. Ext. shot of snow falling.

ELAINE (CONT'D)

It's beautiful.

Jerry looks at the snow, looks at the jacket and turns to George.

JERRY

Snow . . . snow, that can't be good for suede, can it?

GEORGE

I wouldn't think so.

JERRY

What should I do? (TO BENES AND ELAINE) We're taking a cab—aren't we?

BENES

Cab? It's only five blocks.

GEORGE

(TO JERRY) Why don't you turn it inside out?

JERRY

Inside out! Great.

Jerry quickly takes his jacket off, turns it inside out, revealing a Pepto Bismol pink with white stripes. He looks ridiculous. Benes waits by the revolving door. Elaine goes through and as Jerry starts to go through Benes sticks his arm out, barring the door.

BENES

Wait a minute. What the hell do you call this?

JERRY

Oh, I turned my jacket inside out.

BENES

Well, you look like a damn fool!

JERRY

(LIKE A KID) Well, it's a new suede jacket. It might get ruined.

BENES

Well you're not going to walk down the street with me and my daughter dressed like that! That's for damn sure!

Jerry throughly intimidated, looks to George.

THE JACKET

GEORGE

It's only a few blocks.

Jerry looks at Benes—a brick wall.

DISSOLVE TO:

ACT TWO
SCENE K

INT. JERRY'S APARTMENT—NEXT NIGHT

Jerry is getting ready to go out. He puts his keys in his pocket and dons an old raggy jacket.

SFX: buzzer

JERRY

Elaine?

ELAINE

Yeah.

JERRY

Come on up.

Kramer enters.

KRAMER

Hey.

JERRY

Hey.

KRAMER

I've gotta feed the birds.

JERRY

So? . . .

KRAMER

You got any of those mini Ritzes?

Jerry reaches for box.

JERRY

I can't believe that I do.

KRAMER

(ENTHUSIASTICALLY) Yeah . . . Well, are you going out?

JERRY

Yeah.

KRAMER

Hey, where's your new jacket?

Jerry points to bathroom.

KRAMER (CONT'D)

What?

Kramer enters bathroom and emits a sound of surprise.

KRAMER (CONT'D)

(RE: JACKET) Ohh . . . What did you do to it?

JERRY

I was out in the snow last night.

KRAMER

Don't you know what that does to suede?

JERRY

I have an idea.

Elaine enters.

JERRY

(TO ELAINE) We can make the nine-thirty at Cinema III.

ELAINE

Okay . . . (TO KRAMER) Hello. (TO JERRY) Listen, thanks again for coming last night. Dad said he had a great time.

JERRY

Is he still in town?

ELAINE

No he's driving back to Maryland tonight.

KRAMER

(TO JERRY RE: THE JACKET) So uh, what are you gonna do with that one now?

JERRY

I don't know.

KRAMER

Well? . . .

ELAINE

(TO JERRY) I didn't want to tell you this, but usually he hates everyone.

JERRY

Really?

KRAMER

(RE: THE JACKET) You gonna throw this out?

JERRY

Well I can't wear it.

ELAINE

(TO JERRY) Yeah, he liked you though. Said you reminded him of somebody he knew in Korea.

KRAMER

Well, if you're just gonna throw it out you know I could take it.

JERRY

Yeah, go ahead, take it.

ELAINE

Dad thinks George is gay.

JERRY

Oh, because of all that singing.

ELAINE

No, he pretty much thinks everyone is gay.

Kramer returns from the bathroom wearing the suede jacket and holding the tan one.

KRAMER
Hey, see, I like it like this.

ELAINE
(POINTING AT KRAMER) Isn't that . . . ?

Jerry nods.

ELAINE (CONT'D)
(RE: CONDITION OF JACKET) Oh, is this from the snow last night?

Jerry nods.

ELAINE (CONT'D)
Ugh . . . You know what you should've done. You should've turned it inside out.

JERRY
I'll try and remember that.

KRAMER
Boy, it's too bad you gave me this one too.

JERRY
Yeah, too bad.

KRAMER
I'm gonna have to do something about this lining.

Kramer exits.

DISSOLVE TO:

ACT TWO
SCENE L

EXT. CAR—NIGHT

We slowly zoom in on the man behind the wheel. It is Alton Benes.

THE JACKET

BENES

(SINGING) "Master of the house
doling out the charm
ready with a handshake
and an open palm . . ."

FADE OUT:

END OF ACT TWO

SHOW CLOSE

STAND-UP #3

INT. COMEDY CLUB   NIGHT

JERRY

I had a leather jacket that got ruined. Now why does moisture ruin leather? I don't get this. Aren't cows outside most of the time? I don't understand it. When it's raining do cows go up to the farmhouse, "Let us in, we're all wearing leather . . . Open the door, we're gonna ruin the whole outfit here . . ." "Is it suede?" "I am suede, the whole thing is suede, I can't have this cleaned, it's all I got."

END OF SHOW

THE *Seinfeld* SCRIPTS

THE
PHONE
MESSAGE

WRITTEN BY

LARRY DAVID & JERRY SEINFELD

DIRECTED BY

TOM CHERONES

AS BROADCAST FEBRUARY 13, 1991

SHOW OPEN

STAND-UP #1

INT. COMEDY CLUB—NIGHT

JERRY

The bad thing about television is that everybody you
see on television is doing something better than what
you're doing. You never see anybody on TV like just
sliding off the front of the sofa with potato chip crumbs
on their face. Some people have a little too much fun
on television. The soda commercial people—where do
they summon this enthusiasm? Have you seen them,
"We have soda, we have soda, we have soda!" Jumping,
laughing, flying through the air. It's a can of soda. Have
you ever been standing there and you're watching TV
and you're drinking the exact product that they're
advertising right there on TV? And it's like, you know,
they're spiking volleyballs, jet skiing, girls in bikinis . . .
And I'm standing there, "Maybe I'm putting too much
ice in mine."

CUT TO:

ACT ONE

SCENE A

INT. COFFEE SHOP—DAY

Jerry and George. George is in the middle of a story . . .

GEORGE

So then, as we were leaving we're just kind of standing there. And she was sort of smiling at me and I wasn't sure if she wanted me to ask her out. Because when women smile at me I don't know what it means. Sometimes I interpret it as like they're psychotic or something. And I don't know if I'm supposed to smile back. I don't know what to do. So I just stood there like, remember how Quayle looked when Bentsen gave him that Kennedy line—that's what I looked like.

JERRY

So you didn't ask.

GEORGE

No, I froze.

JERRY

Counter.

GEORGE

So wait, wait. Half hour later I'm back in my office and I tell Lloyd the whole story and he says "So why don't you call her?" I said "I can't." . . . I couldn't. I couldn't do it right then. For me to ask a woman out I've got to get into a mental state like the karate guys before they break the bricks. So then, Lloyd calls me a wuss.

JERRY

He said "wuss"?

GEORGE

Yeah. Anyway he shamed me into it.

JERRY

So you called?

GEORGE

Right. And to cover my nervousness I started eating an apple. Because I think if they hear you chewing on the other end of the phone, it makes you sound casual.

JERRY

Yeah, like a farm boy.

GEORGE

So I call her up, I tell her it's me. She gives me an enthusiastic "hi."

JERRY

Oh, an enthusiastic "hi" that's beautiful.

GEORGE

Oh, if I don't get the enthusiastic "hi" I'm out of there.

JERRY

Alright, so you're chewing your apple, you got your enthusiastic "hi," go ahead.

GEORGE

So we start talking and I don't like to go too long before I ask them out. I want to get it over with right away so I just blurt out, "What are you doing Saturday night?"

JERRY

And?

GEORGE

She bought.

JERRY

Great day in the morning.

GEORGE

Then I got off the phone right away.

JERRY

Sure, it's like robbing a bank. You don't loiter around in front of the teller holding that big bag of money. You make your hit and you get out.

GEORGE

It's amazing we both have dates the same night, I can't remember the last time that happened.

CUT TO:

ACT ONE
SCENE B

INT. GEORGE'S CAR—NIGHT

George and Carol are parked in front of her building.

GEORGE

I can't stand doing laundry. That's why I have forty pairs of underwear.

CAROL

You do not.

GEORGE

Absolutely. Because instead of doing a wash I just keep buying underwear. My goal is to get to over three hundred and sixty pair, that way I only have to do wash once a year.

She laughs, he's a hit.

CUT TO:

ACT ONE
SCENE C

INT. JERRY'S CAR—NIGHT

Jerry and Donna.

> **JERRY**
> (IN SCOTTISH BROGUE) Come on try it. Let me hear you
> try a Scottish accent.

> **DONNA**
> That's Irish.

> **JERRY**
> Irish, Scottish, what's the difference, Lassie?

BACK TO:

ACT ONE
SCENE D

INT. GEORGE'S CAR—NIGHT

> **CAROL**
> So, thanks a lot for dinner. It was great.

> **GEORGE**
> Yeah. We should do this again.

> **CAROL**
> Would you like to come upstairs for some coffee?

> **GEORGE**
> Oh no, I can't drink coffee late at night. It keeps me up.

> **CAROL**
> Oh, so . . . okay.

THE PHONE MESSAGE

GEORGE

Okay.

He hesitates and doesn't kiss her.

CAROL

Good night.

GEORGE

Yeah, take it easy.

BACK TO:

**ACT ONE
SCENE E**

INT. JERRY'S CAR—NIGHT

DONNA

Thanks again for the movie.

JERRY

You're welcome.

A beat, then:

DONNA

I'd invite you up but the place is being painted.

JERRY

Oh, that's okay.

DONNA

Unless you want to go to your place?

JERRY

Okay, but there's no cake or anything if that's what
you're looking for.

BACK TO:

ACT ONE
SCENE F

INT. GEORGE'S CAR—NIGHT

Driving, shaking his head thoroughly disgusted with himself—maybe even smacking his forehead.

GEORGE
Take it easy. Take it easy . . .

George clunks head on steering wheel.

CUT TO:

ACT ONE
SCENE G

INT. JERRY'S APARTMENT—SATURDAY NIGHT

Jerry and Donna are on the couch.

JERRY
I think if one's going to kill oneself, the least you could do is leave a note. It's common courtesy. I don't know. That's just the way I was brought up.

DONNA
Values are important.

JERRY
Oh, so important . . . So, what are you doing Thursday night? You want to have dinner?

DONNA
Thursday's great.

JERRY
(RE: HIS PANTS) Tan pants. Why do I buy tan pants, Donna? I don't feel comfortable in them.

THE PHONE MESSAGE

DONNA

Are those cotton Dockers?

JERRY

I can't begin to tell you how much I hate that
commercial.

DONNA

Really? I like that commercial.

A beat.

JERRY

(STUNNED) You *like* that commercial?

DONNA

Yeah, it's clever.

JERRY

Now wait a second. You mean the one where those
guys are all standing around, supposedly being very
casual and witty?

DONNA

Yeah, that's the one.

JERRY

What could you possibly like about that?

DONNA

I don't know, I like the guys.

JERRY

Yeah, they're so funny and so comfortable with each
other. And I could be comfortable too if I had pants like
that. I could sit on a porch and wrestle around and
maybe even be part of a real bull session.

DONNA

I know guys like that. To me, the dialogue rings true.

JERRY

Even if the dialogue did ring true. Even if somehow,
somewhere, men actually talked like that, what does

that have anything to do with the pants?! Doesn't that bother you?

DONNA

That's the idea. That is what is clever about it. That they're not talking about the pants!

JERRY

But they're talking about nothing!

DONNA

That's the point!

JERRY

I know the point!

DONNA

No one's telling you to like it.

A long, long pause. Jerry is still stewing.

JERRY

I mean all those quick shots of the pants. Just pants, pants, pants, pants, pants, pants. What is that supposed to be?

CUT TO:

STAND-UP #2

INT. COMEDY CLUB—NIGHT

JERRY

What's brutal about the date is the scrutiny that you put each other through. Because whenever you think about this person in terms of the future, you have to magnify everything about them. Like the guy will be like, "I don't think her eyebrows are even. Could I look at uneven eyebrows for the rest of my life?" And of course, the woman's looking at the guy thinking, "What is he

looking at? Do I want someone looking at me like this for the rest of my life?"

CUT TO:

ACT ONE
SCENE H

INT. JERRY'S APARTMENT—LATE MONDAY AFTERNOON

Jerry and Elaine.

JERRY
I'm supposed to see her again on Thursday but can I go out with somebody who actually likes this commercial?

ELAINE
I once broke up with a guy because he didn't keep his bathroom clean enough.

JERRY
No kidding? Did you tell him that was the reason?

ELAINE
Oh yeah, I told him all the time. You would not have believed his tub. Germs were building a town in there. They were constructing offices, houses near the drain were going for one hundred fifty thousand dollars.

George enters.

ELAINE
Hi.

George is preoccupied.

JERRY
You're still thinking about this?

GEORGE
(VENTING, TO ELAINE) She invites me up at twelve

o'clock at night for coffee, and I don't go up. "No thank you, I don't want coffee. It keeps me up—it's too late for me to drink coffee." I said this to her. People this stupid shouldn't be allowed to live. I can't imagine what she must think of me.

JERRY

She thinks you're a guy that doesn't like coffee.

GEORGE

(TO ELAINE) She invited me up! Coffee's not coffee. Coffee is sex.

ELAINE

Maybe coffee was coffee.

GEORGE

Coffee's coffee in the morning. It's not coffee at twelve o'clock at night.

ELAINE

Some people drink coffee that late.

GEORGE

Yeah, people who work at NORAD who are on twenty-four-hour missile watch . . . And everything was going along so great. She was laughing, I was funny. I kept saying to myself, "Keep it up. Don't blow it. You're doing great."

ELAINE

It's all in your head. All she knows is she had a good time. I think you should call her.

GEORGE

I can't call her now. It's too soon. I'm planning a Wednesday call.

ELAINE

Why? I love it when guys call me the next day.

GEORGE

Of course, but you're imagining a guy you like, not a guy who goes "Uh . . . I don't drink coffee late at

night . . ." If I call her now she's gonna think I'm too needy. Women don't want to see need. They want a take-charge guy, a colonel, a kaiser, a czar.

ELAINE
All she'll think is that you like her.

GEORGE
That's exactly what I'm trying to avoid!

ELAINE
She wants you to like her!

GEORGE
Yes, she wants me to like her . . . if she likes me! . . . But she doesn't like me.

ELAINE
I don't know what your parents did to you.

Kramer bursts in.

KRAMER
(ENTHUSED) Hey, I just thought of a really funny thing for your act. Alright, you're up and you're on the stage and you go, "Hey did you ever notice how cars here in New York, they never get out of the way of ambulances anymore? Someone's in a life and death situation and we're thinking, 'Well, sorry buddy you should've thought of that when you were eating cheese omelettes and sausages for breakfast every morning for the last thirty years.'"

Elaine laughs hard.

KRAMER (CONT'D)
(TO JERRY) So, you gonna use it?

JERRY
I don't think so.

KRAMER
What, it's funny.

ELAINE

It's funny.

JERRY

I like to do my own material.

KRAMER

That's as good as anything you do.

GEORGE

Alright, I gotta make a call. Everybody out. C'mon.

JERRY

Why do we have to leave?

GEORGE

Because I can't call a woman with other people in the room.

ELAINE

Oh see. This is the problem.

JERRY

You're kicking me out of my house?

GEORGE

Yes.

ELAINE

(EXITING) Don't forget. (SHE MAKES TWO FISTS IN A "BE STRONG" GESTURE)

GEORGE

(TO JERRY, REMEMBERING) Oh, Jerry, do you have any apples?

JERRY

Don't do the apples. It's enough already with the apples.

They all exit. *As soon as the door closes George goes to the phone. He coughs. Smooths his hair. He sits. He stands. He dials.*

CAROL'S VOICE

Hi, it's Carol. I'll get back to you.

THE PHONE MESSAGE

GEORGE

(TO HER PHONE MACHINE) Um . . . hi. It's George, George Costanza, remember me? The guy that didn't come up for coffee. You see, I didn't realize that coffee didn't really mean . . . Well, whatever. Anyway, it was fun. It was fun. So, so, you call me back, if you want. It's up to you. You know, whatever you want to do. Either way, the ball's in your court. So uh, take it easy.

He hangs up . . . the horror, the horror.

Jerry peeks his head in.

JERRY

I'm just going to get my jacket. I'll meet you downstairs . . . What's the matter? Did you call?

GEORGE

I got her machine. I'm dead. I'm a dead man. That's it. I'm dead. I'm a dead man. Dead man.

JERRY

What did you say?

Elaine peeks her head in.

GEORGE

I don't know what the hell I said. I gave her an ultimatum. And there's nothing I can do. It's a machine! The little light is blinking right now. "Come and listen to the idiot! Hey everybody, the idiot's on! . . ."

JERRY

After one date you try and improvise on a machine?

GEORGE

Now I'm in the worst position of all.

ELAINE

You know my brother-in-law once left a message on this guy's machine, and he blurted out some business information he wasn't supposed to, and it would've cost him fifteen thousand dollars, so he waited outside the guy's house and when the guy came home he went upstairs with him and switched the tape.

GEORGE

He did that?

ELAINE

Yeah.

GEORGE

Somebody did that?

JERRY

She'll call you back. You're overreacting.

A beat then:

GEORGE

I left a ball in her court.

FADE OUT:

END OF ACT ONE

ACT TWO

SCENE J

INT. JERRY'S APARTMENT—THURSDAY NIGHT

Jerry and Donna.

JERRY

Not once.

DONNA

Never?

JERRY

I have never seen one episode of *I Love Lucy* in my life.
Ever.

DONNA

That's amazing.

JERRY

Thank you.

DONNA

Is there anything else about you I should know?

JERRY

Yes, I'm lactose intolerant.

DONNA

Really?

JERRY

I have no patience for lactose. And I won't stand for it. I'll be right back.

Jerry goes into the bathroom. *A moment later* George enters.

GEORGE

Wait till you hear this.

Now he notices a woman and feels very much the intruder.

GEORGE (CONT'D)

Oh I'm sorry, I didn't . . . I had no idea.

He starts to back out.

DONNA

Wait, wait. He's in the bathroom.

GEORGE

Oh . . . well I just wanted to talk to him for a minute, but I'll come back.

DONNA

You don't have to leave.

GEORGE

You sure?

DONNA

Yes . . . I'm Donna.

GEORGE

Donna. Oh, you're the one who likes that commercial.

DONNA

(OFFENDED) . . . He told you that?

GEORGE

(TRYING TO SQUIRM OUT) . . . No, he didn't actually tell me that. We were talking about that commercial. In fact, I think I brought it up. Because I like the commercial . . . No, he would never actually tell me anything like that. He never discusses anything. He's like a clam. You're not gonna mention this to him . . .

Jerry emerges from the bathroom.

THE PHONE MESSAGE

DONNA

So you go around telling your friends I'm not hip because I like that commercial?

JERRY

(TO GEORGE) What? What did you say?

GEORGE

Say? What? Nothing. I didn't . . .

DONNA

(TO JERRY) You told him how I like the commercial.

JERRY

Well so what if I said that?

DONNA

So you didn't have to tell your friends.

JERRY

No, I had to tell my friends. My friends didn't have to tell you.

GEORGE

(TO DONNA) Why'd you have to get me in trouble?

DONNA

(TO JERRY) I don't like you talking about me with your friends behind my back.

GEORGE

Boy oh boy . . .

JERRY

I said I couldn't believe you like that commercial, so what?

DONNA

I asked some friends of mine this week and all of them liked the commercial.

JERRY

Boy, I'll bet you got a regular Algonquin Round Table there.

Kramer enters.

KRAMER

Hi.

JERRY

Kramer, this is Donna.

KRAMER

Oh . . . cotton Dockers.

GEORGE

"Hello." (TO KRAMER) Alright, we should be going.
Come on.

KRAMER

What? What's going on?

DONNA

Don't bother. Don't bother. I'm leaving.

Jerry, following her to the door.

JERRY

Donna, really, you're making too much of this.

KRAMER

One hundred percent cotton Dockers. If they're not
Dockers, they're just pants.

JERRY

Kramer please . . . Donna.

DONNA

I don't want to hear it.

And she's gone.

GEORGE

I can't believe I said that. You know me. I'm a vault.

JERRY

Don't worry about it. It wasn't working anyway.

KRAMER

What happened there?

JERRY

I'll tell you later.

THE PHONE MESSAGE

GEORGE

You are not gonna believe what's going on with this woman.

DISSOLVE TO:

**ACT TWO
SCENE K**

INT. COFFEE SHOP—DAY

Jerry and George.

GEORGE

Okay. So, you remember I made the initial call on Sunday. She doesn't call back. I call again Monday. I leave another message. I call Tuesday. I get the machine again, "I know you're there, I don't know what your story is." Yesterday, I'm a volcano. I try one more call, the machine comes on and I let fly like Mussolini from the balcony. "Where the hell do you get the nerve? You invite me up for coffee and then you don't call me back for four days? I don't like coffee! I don't have to come up! I'd like to get one more shot at the coffee just so I can spit it in your face!"

JERRY

You said that?

He nods.

GEORGE

I lost it.

JERRY

I can't blame you. I can't believe she never called you back.

GEORGE

She did . . . today.

JERRY

. . . What?!

GEORGE

She called my office. She said she's been in the Hampton's since Sunday. She didn't know if I was trying to get in touch with her. Her machine broke and she's using her old machine and doesn't have the beeper for it.

JERRY

So she didn't get the messages.

GEORGE

Exactly. But they're on there, waiting . . . She said she can't wait to see me. We're having dinner tonight. She's supposed to call me as soon as she gets home.

JERRY

But what about the messages?

He slowly holds up a standard cassette.

JERRY (CONT'D)

Elaine's thing. How are you going to get in?

GEORGE

I'll meet her outside the building.

JERRY

But you know as soon as she gets in the apartment she's going right for that machine.

GEORGE

Unless she goes for the bathroom. That's my only chance . . . Who am I kidding? I can't do this. I can't do this. I don't even know how to work those stupid machines.

JERRY

There's nothing to it, you lift the lid, it comes right out.

GEORGE

You do it for me.

JERRY

What?

GEORGE

Come on, it'll be so much easier.

JERRY

How are you going to get me up there?

GEORGE

I'll tell her I bumped into you and I'm giving you a ride uptown.

JERRY

And who makes the switch?

GEORGE

You do.

JERRY

I do?

GEORGE

I can't do it. I'll keep her busy.

JERRY

I can't get involved in this.

GEORGE

I think I may be in love with this woman.

JERRY

What if she sees me?

GEORGE

Oh you are such a wuss.

JERRY

. . . A wuss? Did you call me a wuss?

CUT TO:

ACT TWO
SCENE L

EXT. CAROL'S BUILDING—EARLY EVENING

George and Jerry are sitting on a three-foot brick ledge in front of the building.

GEORGE
(LOOKING AT HIS WATCH) Well, there is traffic, it might take her till eight-fifteen.

JERRY
I got one problem: You're going to keep her busy in the other room. Now what if she somehow gets away from you and is coming in? You have to signal me that she's coming.

GEORGE
A signal, right. Okay, okay, the signal is . . . I'll call out "tippy toe."

JERRY
"Tippy toe"? . . . I don't think so.

GEORGE
You don't like "tippy toe"?

JERRY
. . . No "tippy toe."

GEORGE
Alright. Okay, I got it . . . I'll sing.

JERRY
What song?

GEORGE
Um . . . (NOT SINGING) "How do you solve a problem like Maria?"

JERRY
What is that?

GEORGE

Oh it's a lovely song. (SINGING) "How do you solve a problem like Maria? . . ."

JERRY

You got anything else?

GEORGE

You pick it.

JERRY

"Lemon Tree."

GEORGE

Peter, Paul and Mary.

JERRY

No, Trini Lopez.

JERRY AND GEORGE

(SINGING) "Lemon tree very pretty and the lemon flower is sweet . . ."

GEORGE

You got the tapes?

JERRY

(HOLDS UP TWO TAPES) Standard, micro.

GEORGE

How do you feel . . . confident?

JERRY

I feel good.

GEORGE

You nervous?

JERRY

Not at all.

GEORGE

Get up! Get up! That's her. Oh, the hell with this! I'm scared to death! Just walk away! It's off. Cancel everything!

Carol approaches.

CAROL

(SURPRISED) Hi. What are you doing here? I thought I was supposed to call you when I got home.

GEORGE

I couldn't wait. I was too anxious to see you.

CAROL

Oh that's so sweet.

GEORGE

Oh, this is my friend, Jerry Seinfeld. I just bumped into him right around the corner. Isn't that a coincidence? Funny thing is I see him all the time.

JERRY

All the time.

CAROL

It's nice to meet you.

JERRY

Hi.

CAROL

(TO GEORGE) So, I'm starving. Where are we gonna eat?

GEORGE

You know we could go uptown, and that way we could give Jerry a ride.

CAROL

Okay, let's go, I'm ready. Where'd you park?

GEORGE

. . . Don't you want to go upstairs first?

CAROL

No, what for? . . . I'll just give my bag to the doorman.

George looks to Jerry for help, then:

JERRY

You know, I really need to use the bathroom.

THE PHONE MESSAGE

CAROL

Oh well there's a bathroom in the coffee shop just next door.

GEORGE

Yes, yes, but . . . I have to make a call, so . . .

CAROL

Well, they have a phone.

GEORGE

(PRIVATELY, TO CAROL) I know Jerry. He has this phobia about public toilets. I think we really should go upstairs.

CAROL

(COVERING FOR GEORGE) You know, I think I will go upstairs. I can check my machine.

GEORGE

Right, right . . .

CUT TO:

ACT TWO
SCENE M

INT. CAROL'S APARTMENT—EARLY EVENING

They enter.

CAROL

(TO JERRY) The bathroom's down the hall and to the right.

George shakes his head "no" to Jerry.

JERRY

You know, why don't you go first? You just had a long trip.

CAROL

No. I'm fine.

JERRY

You know it's the damnedest thing . . . it went away.

CAROL

Well, that's weird.

GEORGE

No, no. That can happen. I've read about that in medical journals. It's a freak thing.

CAROL

Well then let me just check my messages and we'll go.

GEORGE

Carol, could I talk to you for a second?

She's still heading for the machine.

GEORGE (CONT'D)

(A LITTLE TOO LOUD) Right now. Please, this is very important.

He leads her to the bedroom. Jerry rushes to the machine, examines it—lifts up the lid, then hears:

GEORGE (CONT'D, O.C.)

Tippy toe, tippy toe. Uh, Lemon Tree.

Jerry slams it shut and moves away. Carol enters, followed by George. She walks right up to Jerry.

CAROL

(POINTING AT JERRY) Now I know who you are. You're a comedian. I've seen you. It's been driving me crazy.

JERRY

Right. I am.

GEORGE

Carol, that's so rude. Please, I'm serious, just for a moment, if you wouldn't mind . . . And then we'll talk to Jerry.

They go back to the bedroom. Jerry goes back to the machine, lifts the lid, and makes the switch.

THE PHONE MESSAGE

> **JERRY**
>
> Hey you two, I'm ready to go.

George bursts out of the room. Carol follows.

> **CAROL**
>
> That's what you had to tell me? Your father wears sneakers in the pool?

> **GEORGE**
>
> Don't you find that strange?

> **JERRY**
>
> Yes.

> **CAROL**
>
> Well, I'll just check my machine and we'll go.

The machine comes on, but it's blank.

> **CAROL (CONT'D)**
>
> Nope, nothing here. Let's go.

They walk towards the door.

> **CAROL (CONT'D)**
>
> (TO GEORGE) Oh I forgot to tell you. After I talked to you today my neighbor called me and played all my messages for me over the phone.

> **GEORGE**
>
> Oh, I . . .

> **CAROL**
>
> Yours were hilarious. We were both cracking up. I just love jokes like that.

Carol leaves *as George turns to Jerry, we:*

FADE OUT:

END OF ACT TWO

SHOW CLOSE

STAND-UP #3

INT. COMEDY CLUB—NIGHT

JERRY

I love my phone machine. I wish I was a phone
machine. I wish if I saw somebody on the street I didn't
want to talk to I could go, "Excuse me, I'm not in right
now. If you could just leave a message, I could walk
away." I also have a cordless phone but I don't like that
as much. Because you can't slam down a cordless
phone. You get mad at somebody on a real phone, "You
can't talk to me like that, 'BANG' " You know, cordless
phone, "You can't talk to me like that . . . I told her."

END OF SHOW

THE *Seinfeld* SCRIPTS

THE
APARTMENT

WRITTEN BY
PETER MEHLMAN

AS BROADCAST APRIL 4, 1991

SHOW OPEN

STAND-UP #1

INT. COMEDY CLUB—NIGHT

JERRY

Well I painted my apartment again. I've been living in this apartment for years and years and every time I paint it, it kinda gets me down. I look around and I think, well, it's a little bit smaller now. You know, I realize it's just the thickness of the paint, but I'm aware of it. It keeps coming in and coming in. Every time I paint it, it's closer and closer. I don't even know where the wall outlets are anymore. I just look for like a lump with two slots in it. Kinda looks like a pig is trying to push his way through from the other side. That's where I plug in. My idea of the perfect living room would be the bridge on the Starship Enterprise. You know what I mean? Big chair, nice screen, remote control . . . That's why *Star Trek* really was the ultimate male fantasy, just hurling through space, in your living room, watching TV. That's why all the aliens were always dropping in, because Kirk was the only one that had the big screen. They came over Friday night, Klingon boxing, gotta be there.

ACT ONE

SCENE A

INT. JERRY'S APARTMENT—DUSK

Jerry, Elaine and Kramer. Kramer, his hair slicked back, is standing in front of Jerry and Elaine, who study him with arms folded.

JERRY

What did you do?

KRAMER

Mousse. I moussed up.

ELAINE

(TO JERRY) I guess it was just a matter of time.

KRAMER

You know, I should've done this years ago. I mean I feel like I've had two lives. My pre-mousse and now I begin my post-mousse. Hey, tell me the truth, have you ever seen a better looking guy?

JERRY

Oh look, its so subjective.

ELAINE

I don't mean to interrupt or anything, but on Sunday, my friend is having a brunch for the New York Marathon.

KRAMER

Oh, I keep forgetting to enter that.

ELAINE

She lives right above First Avenue and says she has a perfect view of the race. And she said I can invite some friends.

JERRY

Maybe.

Suddenly they are distracted by an argument in the hall. It's Harold and Manny, the building supers.

HAROLD (O.C.)

No, I'm not going up there.

MANNY (O.C.)

(SCREAMING IN SPANISH)

JERRY

Harold and Manny.

HAROLD (O.C.)

I'm not going.

MANNY

(SPANISH LINE)

Jerry goes into the hall.

CUT TO:

ACT ONE
SCENE B

INT. APARTMENT HALLWAY—CONTINUOUS—DUSK

JERRY

Boys, boys.

HAROLD

Oh Jerry.

THE APARTMENT

JERRY

I slid the rent under your door, Harold. Did you get it?

HAROLD

Yeah, yeah. (KIDDING) Hey Jerry, would you like anything from Mrs. Hudwalker's apartment?

MANNY

(REPRIMANDS HAROLD IN SPANISH)

HAROLD

(TO MANNY) I was only joking. (TO JERRY) He thinks I'm going to give you Mrs. Hudwalker's things . . .

MANNY

(MORE SPANISH)

HAROLD

We have to go up there now and clean the apartment. It's a good thing her rent was overdue. She'd be rotting up there for a month.

JERRY

She died? . . . Mrs. Hudwalker died?

HAROLD

Ninety-four years old. I found her yesterday. She didn't have her wig on. It was horrifying.

MANNY

Harold, (Then, in Spanish: "Come on, hurry up.")

HAROLD

(TO MANNY) What's the matter with you?! I'm talking . . . So Jerry, you know anyone who needs an apartment?

JERRY

Are you kidding? You know my friend Elaine?

HAROLD

Oh yeah, I like her. She always says hello to me.

JERRY

It's not promised to anybody? 'Cause she would take it in a second.

> **HAROLD**
>
> Well, Manny wanted it for his brother but he got deported.

> **MANNY**
>
> (PROTESTING)

> **HAROLD**
>
> (TO MANNY) What's the difference, it's true.

> **JERRY**
>
> So, it's okay? I could just tell her she can have it?

> **HAROLD**
>
> Sure, sure. She's getting a bargain too. It's only four hundred dollars a month.

> **MANNY**
>
> (YELLS SOMETHING IN SPANISH)

> **HAROLD**
>
> Okay . . .

> **MANNY**
>
> (MORE SPANISH)

> **HAROLD**
>
> Okay.

Jerry heads back to the apartment. He passes Kramer in the hall.

> **KRAMER**
>
> Hey Harold, what do you think?

> **HAROLD (O.C.)**
>
> Manny, look, Kramer put mousse in his hair.

> **MANNY**
>
> (IN SPANISH: "It looks worse.")

> **KRAMER**
>
> Thanks.

Jerry enters his apartment.

CUT TO:

THE APARTMENT

ACT ONE
SCENE C

INT. JERRY'S APARTMENT—CONTINUOUS—DUSK

Jerry enters, *milking the moment for all it's worth.*

ELAINE

What was that all about?

JERRY

Oh, nothing important.

ELAINE

What's going on? What is that look?

JERRY

What look? Nothing.

ELAINE

Something's going on here.

JERRY

I don't know if you should sit for this or not. Sitting is good if you faint, but standing is good for jumping up and down. I can't decide.

ELAINE

Jumping up and down? What are you talking about? C'mon, cough it up.

JERRY

Oh, Elaine, you know the way I am, rarely ever thinking of myself. My only concern is the welfare and happiness of those close to me. Sure, it hurts sometimes to give and give and give . . .

ELAINE

Would you please?

JERRY

What would you say if I told you that . . .

ELAINE

Told me what?!

JERRY

. . . I got you an apartment in this building.

ELAINE

(SHE'S DUMBFOUNDED) No.

JERRY

Yes.

ELAINE

No.

JERRY

Yes.

ELAINE

You didn't.

JERRY

I did.

ELAINE

You got me an apartment in the building?!

JERRY

I got you an apartment in the building.

ELAINE

How did you . . .

JERRY

Remember Mrs. Hudwalker, the ninety-four-year-old
woman who lived above me?

ELAINE

No.

JERRY

She died.

ELAINE

(THRILLED) She died?!

JERRY

She died.

ELAINE

She died!

JERRY

And the rent's only four hundred dollars a month.

ELAINE

Get out. Four hundred a month? Only four hundred a month?

JERRY

Four hundred a month.

ELAINE

And I'll be right upstairs?

JERRY

Right upstairs.

ELAINE

Right above you.

JERRY

Right above me.

ELAINE

Oh, we're neighbors. I'll be here all the time.

JERRY

(SUDDENLY HAVING SECOND THOUGHTS) All the time.

We stay on Jerry's expression as we hear:

ELAINE

We can exchange keys so we can come in and out. Oh this is gonna be great.

JERRY

. . . All the time . . .

CUT TO:

STAND-UP #2

INT. COMEDY CLUB—NIGHT

JERRY

The problem with talking is that nobody stops you from saying the wrong thing. I think life would be a lot better if it was like you're always making a movie. You mess up, somebody just walks on the set and stops the whole shot. You know what I mean? Think of the things you wish you could take back. You're out somewhere with people, "Gee you look pregnant . . . are ya?" "Cut, cut, cut, cut, cut, that's not gonna work at all. Walk out the door, come back in, let's take this whole scene again. People, think about what you're saying."

CUT TO:

ACT ONE
SCENE D

INT. COFFEE SHOP—NIGHT

George pays his bill.

GEORGE

(TO CASHIER) Thanks, See ya later, Donna.

George exits.

CUT TO:

ACT ONE
SCENE E

EXT. COFFEE SHOP—CONTINUOUS—NIGHT

George runs into Jerry outside the coffee shop window.

GEORGE

What happened to you?

JERRY

You can't believe what I just did.

GEORGE

What? What did you do?

JERRY

I could tell you what I did but you won't believe it. It's not believable.

GEORGE

What did you do?

JERRY

How could I have done that?

GEORGE

Done what?

JERRY

I told Elaine about an apartment opening up in my building. She's going to move in.

GEORGE

(STUNNED) Elaine's moving into your building?

JERRY

Yes, right above me.

GEORGE

Right above you?

JERRY

Yes.

GEORGE

You're gonna be neighbors.

JERRY

I know, neighbors.

GEORGE

She's right above you.

JERRY

Right above me.

GEORGE

How could you do that?

JERRY

'Cause I'm an idiot! You may think you're an idiot.
But with all due respect I'm a much bigger idiot than
you are.

GEORGE

Don't insult me, my friend. Remember who you're
talking to. No one's a bigger idiot than me.

JERRY

Did you ever ask an ex-girlfriend to move into your
building?

GEORGE

Did you ever go to a singles weekend in the Poconos?

JERRY

She's right in my building! Right above me! Every time
I come in the building I'm gonna have to sneak around
like a cat burglar.

GEORGE

You're doomed. You're gonna have to have all your sex
at women's apartments. It'll be like a permanent road
trip. Forget about the home bed advantage.

JERRY

But I need the home bed advantage.

GEORGE

Of course, we all do.

JERRY

Come in for two minutes and sit with me.

GEORGE

I was just in there. It's embarrassing.

JERRY

Oh, who's gonna know?

THE APARTMENT

GEORGE

They all saw me walk out.

JERRY

Two minutes.

CUT TO:

**ACT ONE
SCENE F**

INT. COFFEE SHOP—NIGHT

Jerry and George.

JERRY

My censoring system broke down. You know that little
guy in your head who watches everything you say,
makes sure you don't make a mistake, he went for a cup
of coffee and in that second ruined my life.

GEORGE

My censor quit two years ago. He checked into a clinic.
Emotionally exhausted.

JERRY

. . . So, is there any way out of this Elaine thing?

GEORGE

Tough.

JERRY

You know, the water pressure's terrible in my building
and she loves a good shower.

GEORGE

I don't think anyone's turned down an apartment
because of a weak shower spray.

JERRY

If they were fanatic about showers they might.

GEORGE

For that rent, she'd take a bath in the toilet tank if she had to . . .

JERRY

Look at that woman feeding her baby greasy, disgusting, coffee shop corned beef hash. Isn't that child abuse?

GEORGE

I'd like to have a kid. Of course, you have to have a date first . . . Remember my friend Adam from Detroit?

JERRY

Yeah, the guy with the flat head?

GEORGE

He's a cube . . . Anyway, he got married six months ago. He told me ever since he's been wearing a wedding band, women have been coming on to him everywhere he goes.

JERRY

Yeah, I've heard that about wedding bands.

GEORGE

(HALF-KIDDING) I wonder if that's really true.

JERRY

That would be an interesting sociological experiment. You know Kramer has his father's band, he'd loan it to you.

CUT TO:

ACT ONE
SCENE G

INT. APARTMENT HALLWAY—DAY

George is trying on Kramer's wedding band. They are in the hallway between the two apartments.

THE APARTMENT

GEORGE

Thanks a lot. I'll give it back to you in a week.

KRAMER

You know, I don't even know why you're fooling around with this ring. I've been telling you, get yourself some plugs or a piece.

GEORGE

I'm not doing that.

KRAMER

Oh, man. You know you're crazy, you're a good looking guy. What do you want to walk around like that for?

GEORGE

No, I'll put half a can of mousse in my head like you.

We hear Manny and Harold yelling down the hall.

MANNY (O.C.)

(SPANISH SCREAMING)

HAROLD (O.C.)

I told you I don't like these sponges they're too small! I want a big sponge!

MANNY (O.C.)

(YELLS BACK)

HAROLD (O.C.)

You can't pick up anything with these! There's no absorption!

MANNY

(SPANISH LINE)

Jerry exits into hall.

CUT TO:

ACT ONE
SCENE H

INT. APARTMENT HALLWAY—CONTINUOUS—DAY

Jerry enters hallway *from apartment.*

JERRY

Boys, boys.

HAROLD

Hi Jerry.

MANNY

Hello, Jerry. (SAYS SOMETHING IN SPANISH TO HAROLD)

HAROLD

(TO MANNY) Okay.

MANNY

(SPANISH LINE)

HAROLD

Okay . . . Your friend can't have the apartment, Jerry.

JERRY

What?

HAROLD

Because somebody offered Manny five thousand dollars
for the apartment. I don't want to do it. Manny wants
to do it.

MANNY

(YELLS IN SPANISH)

HAROLD

Because it's true, why shouldn't I tell him?

JERRY

Hey, hey, I understand, you're businessmen.

MANNY

(SPANISH)

HAROLD

Oh now he says that if your friend has five thousand
dollars we'll give it to her.

JERRY

Well, that's a lot of money, but if that's the way it's
gotta be, that's the way it's gotta be.

Jerry heads back to apartment.

CUT TO:

THE APARTMENT

ACT ONE
SCENE J

INT. JERRY'S APARTMENT—DAY

Jerry enters.

JERRY
You know, I used to think that the universe is a random, chaotic, sequence of meaningless events, but I see now that there is reason and purpose to all things.

GEORGE
What happened to you?

JERRY
Religion, my friend, that's what's happened to me. Because I have just been informed that it's going to cost Elaine the sum of five thousand dollars to get the apartment upstairs.

GEORGE
Five thousand dollars. She doesn't have five thousand dollars.

JERRY
Of course she doesn't have five thousand dollars!

GEORGE
So, she can't get the apartment.

JERRY
Can't get it.

GEORGE
So, she doesn't move in.

JERRY
No move. So you see, it's all part of a divine plan.

GEORGE
And how does the baldness fit into that plan?

SFX: *door buzzes*

JERRY

Elaine.

ELAINE (O.S.)

Yeah.

JERRY

Alright, this is going to require some great acting now. I have to pretend I'm disappointed. You're going to really see me being a phony, now. I hope you can take this. Maybe you should go in the other room.

GEORGE

Are you kidding? I lie every second of the day. My whole life is a sham.

JERRY

'Cause you know, I love Elaine.

GEORGE

Of course you do.

JERRY

But you know, not in the building. Really, I feel terrible about this. My intentions were good. What can I do? Tell me . . .

Elaine enters. *She's on top of the world.*

ELAINE

(TO PERSON IN THE HALLWAY) No, I'll be seeing you. (STARTS TO SING) "Good morning, good morning . . ." Have you ever gotten up in the morning and felt it's great to be alive? That every breath is a gift of sweet life from above?

George exits to other room.

ELAINE

Oh, and before I forget, I have the checks for first month, last month, security deposit. I have seventy-five dollars left in my account.

Jerry looks at the checks.

THE APARTMENT

JERRY

Well, there's a little bit of a problem.

ELAINE

Oh, I know. There's a weak shower spray, I know. I've already thought about it and I'm switching to baths. As Winston Churchill said, "Why stand when you can sit?" Maybe I'll get some rubber duckies . . .

JERRY

No, someone offered Harold and Manny five thousand for the apartment. I'm sure they'd just as soon give it to you, but you'd have to come up with that money.

ELAINE

Five thousand dollars? I don't have five thousand dollars.

JERRY

I know.

ELAINE

How am I going to get five thousand dollars?

JERRY

I have no idea.

Kramer enters.

KRAMER

(SPOTTING ELAINE) Hey, my new neighbor!

ELAINE

I'm not moving in.

KRAMER

What?

ELAINE

They want five thousand dollars now.

KRAMER

So, okay. What's the problem?

ELAINE

I don't have five thousand dollars.

KRAMER

C'mon, you can come up with five thousand dollars . . . Jerry, you don't have five thousand dollars you can lend her? Come on.

JERRY

Yeah, well, I didn't . . . (TO ELAINE) Is that something you want to borrow?

ELAINE

No, that's too much money to borrow.

KRAMER

Loan her the money. You can afford it.

JERRY

She doesn't want to borrow the money.

KRAMER

Oh, c'mon she'll pay you back. What's five grand between friends?

ELAINE

Of course I'd pay you back.

KRAMER

Yeah, so what's the problem?

JERRY

Who said there's a problem?

KRAMER

(TO ELAINE) He said he'd loan you the money.

ELAINE

Well Jerry, it might take a while for me to pay you back. Maybe a few years. How do you feel about that?

KRAMER

That's okay, he doesn't care.

ELAINE

You know money can sometimes come between friends.

KRAMER

Get out of here.

ELAINE

Let me think about it.

KRAMER

What's to think about?

ELAINE

I don't know. I don't know, five thousand . . . Let me just take one more look at it.

Elaine leaves.

JERRY

It was all over. Taken care of. Done. Finished. Five thousand. Where's she gonna get five thousand? She doesn't have five thousand. Clean. Goodbye. She's gone, then you come in, "Why don't you loan her five thousand? What do you care? You've got five thousand. Give her five thousand."

KRAMER

You didn't want her in the building?

JERRY

No I didn't.

KRAMER

Well, then what did you loan her the five thousand for? Oh look, maybe she won't take it. I mean, she did say that she was going to think about it.

JERRY

People don't turn down money, it's what separates us from the animals.

KRAMER

I still don't understand what the problem is having her in the building.

JERRY

Let me explain something to you. You see, you're not normal. You're a great guy. I love you, but you're a pod. I, on the other hand, am a human being. I sometimes feel awkward, uncomfortable, even inhibited in certain situations with the other human beings. You wouldn't understand.

KRAMER

Because I'm a pod.

George returns from bedroom *just as* Elaine returns.

ELAINE

I'll take it!

George *turns on his heel and* leaves.

FADE OUT:

END OF ACT ONE

ACT TWO

SCENE L

INT. ROXANNE'S APARTMENT—MORNING

A spacious East Side living room. Guests mill around eating. Elaine enters with Jerry and George. An attractive girl, Roxanne, hugs Elaine at the door.

ROXANNE

Hi, Elaine . . .

ELAINE

Oh, hi, Roxanne, nice to be here. These are my friends. This is George and this is Jerry. (THEY EXCHANGE HELLOS) Jerry's the one who got me my new apartment!

ROXANNE

So, you're Elaine's hero.

JERRY

Yes. It's my life's work.

ROXANNE

There are so few true heros left in this world.

Jerry likes what he sees in Roxanne. Elaine notices.

GEORGE

(UNSUBTLY REVEALING HIS RING) Yeah, my wife couldn't

make it today. She's got some thing with her mother. Who knows what's going on with her. Don't let any one kid you, it's tough.

George goes off to mingle. *Jerry walks over to the food.*

JERRY
Well, better load up on some carbos before the race.

ROXANNE
Oh, the marathon is great, isn't it?

JERRY
Oh yes, particularily if you're not in it.

ROXANNE
I wish we had a view of the finish line.

JERRY
What's to see? A woman from Norway, a guy from Kenya and twenty thousand losers.

Roxanne makes a face.

George is standing at a table talking to an attractive woman.

GEORGE
. . . Yeah, my wife started getting on me about the lawn today. I'm tellin' ya, it's one thing after another.

RITA
Is she here?

GEORGE
No, she's working.

RITA
What does she do?

GEORGE
She's an . . . entymologist—you know, bees, flies, gnats. What about you?

RITA
I work for the Director of Madison Square Garden. It's

great, I can get free tickets to any sporting event in New
York.

George, speechless.

RITA (CONT'D)
Anyway, she's a very lucky woman.

GEORGE
But . . .

*She bolts looking for other prospects, leaving George hanging. Angle on:
Jerry, Roxanne, and Elaine. A woman and a man enter.*

ROXANNE
Hi Stan, Joanne.

ELAINE
Jerry, this is Joanne and this is Stan. They're in my short
story class with Roxanne and me. Hey, Jerry just got me
a great apartment in his building!

Jerry stifles another groan.

JOANNE
Well Jerry, it'll be nice having a close friend nearby?

JERRY
Fantastic.

STAN
She can pop in whenever she wants.

JERRY
I know.

JOANNE
She doesn't even need to knock.

JERRY
It's tremendous.

STAN
Anytime of day.

JERRY
I'm in heaven.

ELAINE

Oh Rita come here. This is Jerry. He's the one who got me the apartment.

RITA

Oh hi . . . (CALLING TO SOMEONE) Bob, this is the guy who got Elaine the apartment.

Angle on:

George talking with another woman.

GEORGE

I'm sorry I don't see the big deal about being a matador. The bull charges, you move the cape, what's so hard?

They laugh. They're clearly flirting.

SUSIE

So, are you really married? Because I've actually heard of single guys who wear wedding bands to attract women.

GEORGE

You'd have to be a real loser to try something like that.

SUSIE

That's too bad because I really have a thing for bald guys with glasses.

She shrugs, smiles and leaves George dazed.

RITA

Hey everybody! Here come the runners!

Everyone rushes toward the windows. Jerry and Elaine stay put.

ELAINE

So you and Roxanne are hitting it off huh?

JERRY

Oh, I wouldn't quite say that.

ELAINE

Really. From a distance, you seemed to be coming on to her.

JERRY
I'm a guy . . . It always looks like that.

ELAINE
Because I was thinking, are you at all concerned that living in the same building will, y'know, cramp our styles?

JERRY
Na . . .

ELAINE
Because, I was worried that there might be a situation in which one of us came home with somebody, it could get a little uncomfortable. But, as long as you're okay with it, it's fine with me.

Angle on:

George, listening to another woman talk to him.

JANICE
I've never been able to be with just one person. I can, however, carry on strictly physical relationships which can last for years and years. It's a shame you're married . . .

George tries to remove the ring.

GEORGE
I'm not. It's just a sociological experiment.

JANICE
Please . . .

Jerry walks over to George.

JERRY
You have no idea what an idiot is. Elaine just gave me a chance to get out and I didn't take it. (POINTS TO HIMSELF) This is an idiot.

GEORGE
Is that right? I just threw away a lifetime of guilt-free sex and floor seats for every sporting event in Madison

Square Garden. So please, a little respect. For I am
Costanza, Lord of the Idiots.

ROXANNE
(YELLING OUT A WINDOW) You're all winners!

GEORGE
But suddenly a new contender has emerged.

DISSOLVE TO:

**ACT TWO
SCENE M**

INT. JERRY'S APARTMENT—DAY

Jerry is talking on the phone.

JERRY
George, I didn't sleep at all last night . . . I decided I
have to tell her . . . I'm just going to be honest, that's
all . . . Yes, I'm nervous . . . Are you listening to me? . . .
Just put some soap on your finger. It'll slide right off . . .
Then try axle grease.

Kramer enters.

JERRY (CONT'D)
I'll call you back after I talk to her. Bye.

KRAMER
Well, it's all taken care of. Everything's cool.

JERRY
What? What's cool?

KRAMER
Elaine.

JERRY
What are you talking about?

KRAMER

I just found a guy who's willing to pay ten thousand dollars for the apartment.

JERRY

You what? Get out! Ten thousand?

KRAMER

(NODS) Cash.

JERRY

Who would pay that much?

KRAMER

He's in the music business.

JERRY

Elaine would never borrow that much money. (HUGGING KRAMER, THEN GRABBING HIM BY CHEEKS) Kramer, my God, man! This is beautiful. I think I'm in the clear here. (RAPID FIRE): Elaine's not moving in, I don't have to confront her. She has no idea I never wanted her to move in . . . I'm golden.

KRAMER

Well, occasionally I like to help the humans.

CUT TO:

**ACT TWO
SCENE N**

INT. JERRY'S APARTMENT—A FEW WEEKS LATER—DAY

Jerry, Elaine, Harold and Manny. There's a pulsing music coming through the walls.

ELAINE

Wow, you're right, that is loud.

JERRY

It's just unbelievable.

ELAINE

They rehearse all the time?

JERRY

All the time. I've been up there six times. They refuse to stop. I can't live like this. I don't know what I'm gonna do. I'm heading for a breakdown. (TO HAROLD) Can't you do something?

HAROLD

I'm not going up, it stinks up there.

JERRY

Manny . . .

MANNY

(IN SPANISH: "They're allowed to play until eleven o'clock.")

HAROLD

I'm not the one who said eleven o'clock. He makes up his own rules.

ELAINE

Boy, too bad. If I was up there you'd never hear a peep out of me. I'm as quiet as a mouse.

Kramer enters, *hears the band, considers it for a moment.*

KRAMER

Hey. (RE: MUSIC) Oh, love the one they do right after this one.

END OF ACT TWO

CUT TO:

SHOW CLOSE

STAND-UP #3

INT. COMEDY CLUB—NIGHT

JERRY

I don't know. What do you do when a neighbor is making, like, a lot of noise at three o'clock in the morning? I mean, can you knock on someone's door and tell them to keep it down? You're really altering your whole self-image, I mean, what am I Fred Mertz now? What's happening to me? Can I do this? Am I a shusher? I used to be a shushee. There's a lot of shushing going on in movie theaters. People are always shushing. SHHH . . . SHHH . . . SHHH . . . SHHH . . . Doesn't work, 'cause nobody knows where a shush is coming from. They just hear a SHH, "Was that a shush? I think somebody just shushed me." Some people you can't shush in a movie theater. There's always that certain group of people, isn't it? They're talking and talking and everyone around them is shushing 'em and shushing 'em, they won't shush. They're the unshushables.

FADE OUT:

END OF SHOW

THE *Seinfeld* SCRIPTS

THE
STATUE

WRITTEN BY
LARRY CHARLES

DIRECTED BY
TOM CHERONES

AS BROADCAST APRIL 11, 1991

SHOW OPEN

STAND-UP #1

INT. COMEDY CLUB—NIGHT

JERRY

I have to tell you that I did get some very exciting news recently and I don't know if I should really tell you exactly what it is because it's really not a definite thing yet. Well, I will tell you what I do know so far. According to the information that I have in the envelope that I've received, it seems that I may have already won some very valuable prizes. Well, thank you, thank you very much, well thank you. It's very nice to hear that. But in all honesty, I have to say, I didn't even know I was in this thing. But according to the readout, it looks like I am among the top people that they are considering. You know, that's what annoys me about the sweepstakes companies, they always tease you with that, "You may have already won." I'd like once for a sweepstakes company to have some guts, come out with the truth, just tell people the truth one time, send out envelopes, "You have definitely lost!" You turn it over, giant printing, "Not even Close!" You open it up, there's this whole letter of explanation, "Even we cannot believe how badly you've done in this contest."

ACT ONE

SCENE A

INT. JERRY'S APARTMENT—DUSK

George sits reading the paper. There are papers and magazines scattered over the coffee table and floor. For Jerry's apartment, the place is in kind of a disheveled state. Kramer and Jerry enter, *carrying a large carton with the name Seinfeld scribbled on it.*

JERRY

(STRUGGLING TO GET BOX THROUGH DOOR, TO KRAMER) To the right.

GEORGE

That took awhile.

JERRY

(SARCASTIC) Don't get up.

GEORGE

I'd like to help. But my neck . . .

They set the box on the table.

GEORGE

So how long has it been in the basement?

JERRY

Since my grandfather died. I was supposed to send it down to my parents in Florida, but they didn't want it.

They told me to get rid of it, but I felt funny and then I sort of forgot about it. And it's been sitting down there for three years . . . until he saw it. (TO KRAMER) Alright, so just take what you want and let's get it out of here.

They open box and begin to examine the contents.

GEORGE

What's in it?

JERRY

Grandpa clothes. I can't wear them.

Kramer lifts out some socks.

KRAMER

You want these? Knee socks. You don't wear knee socks.

JERRY

No, go ahead. (LAMENTING THE CONDITION OF HIS APARTMENT) Look at this place. I can't wait to get it cleaned.

GEORGE

I know someone who'll do it. She's good, she's honest.

JERRY

No, Elaine's got this writer friend from Finland, Rava, her boyfriend goes to Columbia grad school and he's supposed to do it.

GEORGE

Students can't clean. It's anathema.

Jerry's puzzled.

GEORGE (CONT'D)

. . . They don't like it.

JERRY

How long have you been waiting to squeeze that into a conversation?

Kramer has pulled a statue out of the box, a fifties objet d'art. Not a priceless antique, but an interesting piece. It is wrapped in a towel.

THE STATUE

KRAMER

Now this I like.

George's eyes light up at the sight of the statue.

GEORGE

Wait a second. I can't believe this. Let me see this.

KRAMER

Wait, wait, wait . . .

Kramer gets possessive.

GEORGE

Let me just see it.

KRAMER

Come on.

They both grab it.

GEORGE

(FORCEFUL) Let me just see it for a second. Oh my God, it's exactly the same.

JERRY

What?

GEORGE

When I was ten years old my parents had this very same statue on the mantle of our apartment. Exactly. And one day, I grabbed it and I was using it as a microphone. I was singing, "MacArthur Park" and I got to the part about "I'll never have that recipe again," and it slipped out of my hand and it broke. My parents looked at me like I smashed the ten commandments. To this day, they bring it up. It was the single most damaging experience in my life, aside from seeing my father naked.

He grips statue but Kramer will not let go. They begin to tug back and forth for possession of statue.

KRAMER

C'mon George, I saw it first.

GEORGE

No, Kramer, I have to have this statue.

KRAMER

No, I got dibs!

GEORGE

What? No dibs! I need this statue. C'mon give it.

Jerry steps in to restore order.

JERRY

(À LA MOE) Spread out; spread out you numbskulls.
Why don't you just settle it like mature adults?

KRAMER

Potato man!

GEORGE

No, no, no potato man . . . Inka-dink.

Kramer and George do some fancy addition in their heads, then:

KRAMER

(SUPER-SERIOUS) Okay . . . start with me.

GEORGE

Yeah, good, good.

*Jerry begins the child's choosing game of Inka-dink, pointing alternately
to Kramer and George as he completes rhyme.*

JERRY

Inka-dink, a bottle of ink. The cork fell out. And you
stink. Not because you're dirty, not because you're
clean, just because you kissed the girl behind the
magazine. . . .

Jerry lands on Kramer, who brightens, but Jerry completes rhyme.

JERRY	**KRAMER**
. . . And you are it!	What? Wait a minute.
	No, no, no. What are
	you doing?

George wins.

THE STATUE

KRAMER

No, no, oh, oh, okay, he's out. I get it.

GEORGE

No, no, no, no . . . I'm it. I win.

JERRY

(LIKE A FIRST GRADE TEACHER) No, he's it. He wins. It is good.

KRAMER

Do over . . . Start with him.

JERRY

No, no, no, come on, Kramer. Now you got the socks.

Kramer tosses the statue to George.

KRAMER

Alright, you can have it. Okay, I'm gonna take the suit and the shoes and the hat.

JERRY

Alright, c'mon let's go.

KRAMER

Hey, I'll look like Joe Friday in *Dragnet*. Dum-de-dum-dum.

GEORGE

(IN SHOCK) I can't believe I won at Inka-dink.

JERRY

Come on, let's go.

They cross to the door. George sets the statue down.

JERRY (CONT'D)

(TO GEORGE) Aren't you gonna take it?

GEORGE

No, no, no, I don't want to carry it around all night. I'll pick it up later.

JERRY

(TO KRAMER) What about your stuff?

KRAMER

Oh uh, well okay.

He *balls up all his new acquisitions and flings them into his apartment, and* leaves.

JERRY

Alright, let's go. Hey, you know you owe me one.

GEORGE

What?

JERRY

The Inka-dink . . . you were "it."

GEORGE

"It" 's bad?

JERRY

"It" very bad.

DISSOLVE TO:

ACT ONE
SCENE B

INT. JERRY'S APARTMENT—DAY

Elaine, Elaine's friend—Rava. She is attractive, exotic, and "Finnish." She holds up a manuscript.

RAVA

Well, if they don't let you be my editor on this book, I'll go to another publisher. It's that simple.

ELAINE

You told them that?

RAVA

Of course.

THE STATUE

ELAINE

Oh this is so fantastic. I don't know how to thank you.

Jerry enters *from bedroom carrying luggage.*

JERRY

(FRANTIC) So, where's this boyfriend of yours? I can't wait much longer. I've got a flight.

ELAINE

Oh, probably caught in traffic.

RAVA

(MOCK-SERIOUS) Or maybe he's dead.

JERRY

So what do you write, children's books?

SFX: door knock

RAVA

That's Ray.

Ray enters *with cleaning equipment. Although he carries cleaning equipment, he also carries the air of a pretentious, mannerly, affected actor.*

RAY

Ah, greetings, greetings, and salutations, I beg your forgiveness. My tardiness was unavoidable. Rava, my love. Elaine, dear friend . . . And, you must be Jerry. Lord of the manor. Ah, my liege. A pleasure to serve you.

He bows.

JERRY

(SLIGHTLY TAKEN ABACK) . . . Alright.

RAVA

And we have to get back to work.

Rava and Elaine exit.

JERRY

(RUSHED) I gotta get to the airport.

RAY

Your palace shall sparkle like the stars in heaven upon your safe arrival, Sire.

JERRY

The toilet brush is under the sink . . .

Jerry exits.

DISSOLVE TO:

STAND-UP #2

INT. COMEDY CLUB—NIGHT

JERRY

I don't really feel that comfortable with a maid either, because there's that guilt when you have someone cleaning your house. You know, you're sitting there on your sofa and they go by with the vacuum, "I'm really sorry about this, I don't know why I left that stuff over there." And that's why I could never be a maid, because I'd have that attitude. I'd find them, wherever they are in the house, "Oh, I suppose you couldn't do this? . . . No, don't get up, let me clean up your filth. No, you couldn't dust, no this is too tough isn't it?"

CUT TO:

ACT ONE
SCENE C

INT. JERRY'S APARTMENT—TWO WEEKS LATER—DAY

Jerry and Elaine.

JERRY

He really did an amazing job. Look, he uncoagulated the top of the dishwashing liquid.

Jerry opens refrigerator.

JERRY (CONT'D)

He cleaned out the bottom of the little egg cups. Come here. Look at this.

Jerry gets on his knees.

JERRY (CONT'D)

He cleaned in the little one-inch area between the refrigerator and the counter. How did he get in there? He must be like Rubber Man.

ELAINE

There's no Rubber Man.

JERRY

. . . Why did I think there was a Rubber Man? There's Elastic Man and Plastic Man.

ELAINE

I'm leaving.

She starts to go.

JERRY

Where you going?

ELAINE

To Rava's house. I've gotta pick up her manuscript.

JERRY

Wait. I'll go with you.

They head for the door.

JERRY (CONT'D)

(OPENING THE DOOR) Elaine, he Windexed the little peep hole.

They exit.

DISSOLVE TO:

ACT ONE
SCENE D

INT. RAVA'S APARTMENT—EARLY EVENING

Jerry, Elaine and Rava sit around. It is a house crammed with knick-knacks, bric-a-brac, etc.

ELAINE

(TO RAVA) So the meeting with Lippman is all set. He's the editor-in-chief! I think because of your request . . .

RAVA

Demand.

ELAINE

. . . they're going to promote me to editor.

RAVA

Darn tootin' . . .

We hear locks opening.

RAVA (CONT'D)

There's Ray . . . Late as usual.

Rays enters. At first, he seems slightly taken aback, but then he shifts into his charming, gregarious persona.

RAY

Well, this is an unexpected surprise. And delight! The once and future king of comedy, "Jerry the First," gracing our humble abode. Rava, we're in the presence of royalty.

THE STATUE

JERRY

Hey, Ray, listen, you really did a tremendous job cleaning that apartment.

RAY

But I didn't just clean your apartment. It was a ritual, a ceremony, a celebration of life.

JERRY

Shouldn't you be out on a ledge somewhere?

They all laugh, Ray a little too hard and a little too long. Jerry leans back, savoring his snappy retort. His eyes cross to the other side of the room where, much to his surprise, "the statue," sits on the mantle piece, crowded in amongst a clutter of other bric-a-brac. He is completely stunned.

RAVA

(AS SHE LEAVES) The water is boiling. Are you all having tea?

ELAINE/RAY

Yes.

Jerry is not listening.

ELAINE

Jerry . . . Jerry!

SFX: teapot

JERRY

(SUDDENLY) What?

RAVA (O.C.)

Ray, would you give me a hand?

RAY

(BREAKING CHARACTER) Yeah, I'm coming!

They exit into the kitchen. As soon as they enter the kitchen Jerry and Elaine begin talking in exaggerated stage whispers.

JERRY

(POINTING TO STATUE, ANGRILY WHISPERING) I think

that's the statue from my house. That looks like the statue from my house.

                    ELAINE

What statue?

                    JERRY

I had a statue!

                    ELAINE

You have a statue? I never saw a statue.

                    JERRY

My grandfather gave me a statue!

                    ELAINE

Since when?

                    JERRY

What's the difference?! That's the one! He ripped me off. This guy ripped me off!

Ray suddenly pops his head out.

                    RAY

Do you take sugar?

                    JERRY/ELAINE

Uh . . . no.

He returns to the kitchen.

                    JERRY

I can't believe it! This guy ripped me off!

                    ELAINE

Do you realize what you're saying?

                    JERRY

Yes! This guy ripped me off! He stole that statue right out of my house!

Ray pops in again, *surprising Jerry and Elaine.*

                    RAY

Lemon?

THE STATUE

JERRY/ELAINE

(CASUAL) Uh . . . sure, yeah . . .

He returns to kitchen. *Back to whispers.*

ELAINE

Are you sure?

JERRY

Pretty sure! Ninety-nine percent sure.

ELAINE

Ninety-nine percent sure?!

Rava and Ray re-enter, *carrying tray of tea.*

RAY

Ah, sweet elixir. Its fragrant nectar, a soothing balm for the soul.

Jerry smells it suspiciously. We hear a ding from the kitchen.

RAVA

Oh, those are the pastries. Ray, take care of that. I'm gonna get Elaine the manuscript.

RAY

The pastries!

They both exit *in different directions.*

ELAINE

Maybe it just looks the same. Maybe it's just a coincidence.

JERRY

Coincidence? This guy's in my apartment and then, just by coincidence, he has the exact same statue in his apartment?

ELAINE

I never saw any statue.

JERRY

I had a statue! What should I do?

ELAINE

I don't know.

JERRY

. . . I'll call Kramer. He can check my house.

He grabs phone to dial.

ELAINE

Oh Jerry, don't blow this for me.

JERRY

Don't worry. (WITH SAME INTENSE WHISPER) Kramer!
. . . Kramer! . . . It's Jerry! Jerry! . . . from next door! . . .
Never mind where I am! . . . Yes, Jerry Seinfeld . . .

*Rava re-enters carrying manuscript. Jerry assumes a casual "normal"
tone of voice.*

JERRY (CONT'D)

Ma, I told ya, just dip the bread in the batter and put it
right in the pan. Okay bye.

He hangs up.

JERRY (CONT'D)

My mother . . . She forgot how to make French Toast.
You know how mothers are.

RAVA

My mother left us when I was six years old. All seven of
us. We never heard from her again. I hope she's rotting
in an alley somewhere.

A long beat, then:

JERRY

My mom's down in Florida . . . She's got one of those
condos . . . Hot down there in the summer. You ever
been down there?

Ray re-enters with a tray of pastries.

RAY

I love these pastries. You know, in Scandinavian
mythology, the pastries were the food of the gods.

THE STATUE

JERRY

. . . Listen, I just remembered . . . I'm . . . uh . . . getting a facial.

Elaine takes the manuscript.

ELAINE

Oh, see you tomorrow morning.

As they leave:

RAY

Oh, how about dinner?

JERRY

No, I don't eat dinner. Dinner's for suckers.

He and Elaine exit, *awkwardly.*

DISSOLVE TO:

**ACT ONE
SCENE E**

INT. JERRY'S APARTMENT—EVENING

Jerry, George, Kramer and Elaine. Jerry is hanging up the phone.

JERRY

Uh huh . . . Yeah . . . Okay, thanks anyway. Bye.

He hangs up.

JERRY (CONT'D)

Nope, the cop says it's my word against his. There's nothing they can do.

KRAMER

Let's go get him.

JERRY

Yeah, right.

GEORGE

We can't just let him get away with this.

JERRY

Do you realize how crazy he had to be to do something like this? He knew I was gonna know it's missing, and that he took it. And of all things to take—I left my watch, tape recorder, stereo. He's crazy.

KRAMER

You wanta go get him?

ELAINE

Well, then, if he's crazy you should just forget it.

GEORGE

Forget it? I already called my parents. I told them to expect the surprise of a lifetime. My mother's makin' her roasted potatoes!

ELAINE

George, do you realize that Rava's asked me to edit her book?

GEORGE

Who is this Rava?

KRAMER

I say we get him.

ELAINE

No!

GEORGE

Let me just call him.

JERRY

I'll call him.

Jerry crosses to the phone. Jerry picks up the cordless phone. Kramer, Elaine, and George struggle for control of the other phone during the conversation. As Jerry talks, Kramer, Elaine, and George ad-lib whispers to get control of the phone.

THE STATUE

JERRY

Hello, Ray? . . . Hi, Ray, this is Rava's friend, Elaine's
friend, Jerry . . . The King of Comedy . . . Right. Listen,
you know that statue on your mantle, the one with the
blue lady? (TO KRAMER AND GEORGE) Will you shut up?!
(TO RAY) Yeah, you don't want to talk about it over the
phone . . . You don't want Rava to hear . . . Yeah, I
understand . . . You know that coffee shop near my
house, Monk's? . . . Alright, tomorrow, one o'clock.
Great, okay, bye.

They hang up with anticipation.

ELAINE

(SCRAMBLING) Alright, look, look, look . . . Let's say he
stole it.

GEORGE

Oh, he stole it?

ELAINE

C'mon. You can't do anything about it. The cops won't
do anything. What, are you going to fight him? Why
don't you just . . . forget it.

JERRY/GEORGE

(PAUSE, CALMLY) No . . .

FADE OUT:

END OF ACT ONE

ACT TWO

SCENE F

INT. COFFEE SHOP—DAY

Jerry sits alone at the booth. Behind him, unbeknownst to us, in the next booth, with his back to Jerry's, sits George trying to look inconspicuous.

GEORGE

(TO JERRY WITHOUT TURNING HIS HEAD) I thought you said one o'clock.

JERRY

Relax, he's late. He's always late. It's part of his "M.O."

GEORGE

Remember, don't take any crap.

JERRY

Yeah, yeah . . . don't worry about it.

GEORGE

I'll be right here.

JERRY

That's comforting. . . . Shh. He's here. Ray?

RAY

Oh, Jerry.

Ray stands over table.

RAY (CONT'D)

I can't believe you asked me about that statue. Do you
know how much trouble you could've got me into?

He slides into the booth.

JERRY

. . . Well, I didn't . . .

RAY

Rava was standing right next to me. I never told her
where I got the statue.

GEORGE

(TO HIMSELF) I wonder why.

JERRY

Well, just give it back and I won't say anything.

RAY

Give it back?

JERRY

Yeah.

RAY

What are you talking about?

JERRY

What are you talking about?

GEORGE

(MUTTERING) What is he talking about . . .

RAY

I'm talking about the statue.

JERRY

Yeah, me too.

RAY

Give it back to whom?

JERRY

Me.

GEORGE

Yeah him.

RAY

You?

JERRY

Yeah. Me.

RAY

I'm not getting this.

GEORGE

You already got it.

JERRY

Ray, I had a statue in my house, you were in my house, and then I saw it in your house.

RAY

What are you saying?

JERRY

What am I saying?

GEORGE

Take a wild guess.

RAY

Are you saying I stole your statue?

GEORGE

What a mind.

JERRY

Well, I . . .

RAY

I can't believe what I'm hearing.

JERRY

I can't believe what I'm hearing.

GEORGE

I can't believe what I'm hearing.

RAY

For your information, I got that statue in a pawn shop.

GEORGE

A pawn shop?

JERRY

A pawn shop?

RAY

Yes, in Chinatown with the money I earned cleaning people's apartments.

GEORGE

And cleaning 'em out.

Jerry elbows George.

JERRY

Oh, excuse me . . . Look Ray, you were the only person in my house.

RAY

What's behind this? It's Rava isn't it?

GEORGE

Again with the Rava.

RAY

You want her.

JERRY

No, she's a little too cheery for me.

RAY

(LOSING IT) She's from Finland for crying out loud. Finland! Do you understand!

JERRY

I know Finland. They're neutral.

RAY

Is it me? Do I rub you the wrong way?

JERRY

No, I actually find you quite charming . . . a bit verbose at times.

GEORGE

(MOCKING) "Oh I find you so charming" . . . You wuss.

JERRY

(TO GEORGE) Did you call me a wuss?

RAY

What did you say?

JERRY

I said luss . . . I'm at a luss . . .

RAY

I would just love to take you down to the shop where I got it.

JERRY

That's not necessary.

George slams his menu on the table.

JERRY (CONT'D)

You know, maybe it's not that bad an idea.

RAY

And I would love to. Nothing would please me more. But unfortunately the guy retired and moved to Singapore.

GEORGE

Singapore? Do you hear this?

RAY

If you really want maybe I can contact the guy in Singapore and have him make a photostat of the receipt and send it over.

GEORGE

That's it! That's it! I can't take it. I can't take it anymore!

George gets up from the chair, turns around, and confronts Ray.

GEORGE (CONT'D)

You stole the statue! You're a thief! You're a liar!

JERRY

George.

THE STATUE

RAY

(TO JERRY) Who is this?

GEORGE

I'm the judge and the jury, Pal. And the verdict is . . . *guilty!*

RAY

What's going on here?

GEORGE

Guilty!!!

RAY

Your friend is crazy.

GEORGE

Oh, I'm crazy!!!

JERRY

George, George.

RAY

I've got to get going. I have a class.

GEORGE

Oh ho! Class huh? A class? At Columbia? Let me tell you something, pal. I called the registrar's office. I checked you out. They have no record of a Ray Thomas at that school. You liar.

RAY

Well that's because I'm registered under my full legal name, Raymond Thomas Wochinski. Ray Thomas is my professional name.

GEORGE

You mean alias.

RAY

You are starting to make me angry.

GEORGE

Well, that was bound to happen.

RAY

(TO JERRY) I hope you think about what you've done here today. And if you want to call and apologize. You know where to reach me.

Ray turns to go, then:

JERRY

Hey Ray.

RAY

(TURNING) Yes.

JERRY

How did you get the goop out of the top of the dishwashing liquid? It was like a brand-new nozzle.

CUT TO:

ACT TWO
SCENE G

INT. ELEVATOR—ELAINE'S OFFICE BUILDING—DAY

Elaine and Rava wait for the elevator.

ELAINE

Nervous?

RAVA

Why should I be?

ELAINE

Yeah. Right.

RAVA

Your notes were very insightful.

ELAINE

The book is great. Did you go out last night?

> ###### RAVA
>
> No. We made love on the floor like two animals. Ray is insatiable.
>
> ###### ELAINE
>
> They all are . . .
>
> ###### RAVA
>
> Was Jerry?
>
> ###### ELAINE
>
> I can't remember . . .

The doors open. They step in.

> ###### RAVA
>
> You know Ray is very upset over these accusations.
>
> ###### ELAINE
>
> Oh well I'm staying out of this one. This is between them. I am not getting involved.

Elevator doors close.

CUT TO: Elevator doors open.

> ###### RAVA
>
> (ANNOYED) So you think he stole it?
>
> ###### ELAINE
>
> Well, you have to admit the circumstantial evidence.
>
> ###### RAVA
>
> I admit nothing!

Elevator doors close.

CUT TO: Int. elevator.

> ###### MAN (JOHN)
>
> Will you put that cigarette out please?

Rava ignores him.

> ###### ELAINE
>
> Well I mean he was in the apartment and then it's gone and it's in your apartment.

RAVA

Maybe you think we're in cahoots.

ELAINE

No, no . . . but it is quite a coincidence.

RAVA

Yes, that's all, a coincidence.

ELAINE

A *big* coincidence.

RAVA

Not a *big* coincidence. A coincidence!

ELAINE

No, that's a big coincidence.

RAVA

That's what a coincidence is! There are no small coincidences and big coincidences!

ELAINE

No, there are degrees of coincidences.

RAVA

No, there are only coincidences! . . . Ask anyone! (ENRAGED) Are there big coincidences and small coincidences or just coincidences? , , , Well?! Well?!

They shrug their shoulders and murmur. The doors open.

MAN (JOHN)

Will you put that cigarette out!

RAVA

(POINTING LIT END AT HIM) Maybe I put it out on your face! (TO ELAINE) It's just like Ray said—you and Jerry. You're jealous of our love. You're trying to destroy us.

ELAINE

Shouldn't you be out on a ledge somewhere?

And the doors close.

CUT TO: Floor fifty.

THE STATUE

The doors open. The elevator is empty except for Elaine. There's a janitor stand parked right outside the elevator doors. She steps out, throws the manuscript in the garbage can, and exits.

CUT TO:

ACT TWO
SCENE H

INT. JERRY'S APARTMENT—AFTERNOON

Jerry, George, Elaine and Kramer. George is on the phone.

GEORGE

Ma, will you stop? . . . It's just a statue! . . . How is it my fault?! . . . It was stolen. I didn't even touch it this time . . . Okay, fine . . . I don't see why this should affect the potatoes! Okay. Goodbye.

He hangs up.

GEORGE (CONT'D)

She doesn't react to disappointment very well . . . unlike me.

KRAMER

I'm not happy about this.

ELAINE

Why don't we just throw a Molotov cocktail through their window?

GEORGE

There's just no justice. This experience has changed me. It's made me more cynical, more bitter, more jaded.

JERRY

Really?

GEORGE

(CASUALLY) Sure, why not?

ELAINE

Well, how do you think I feel? Instead of editing the first novel of a major young writing talent, I am proofreading a food allergy cookbook.

JERRY

Can't you talk to your boss?

ELAINE

I did. He loves Rava . . . Worse . . . he loves Ray and he doesn't think you're funny at all.

KRAMER

I'm not happy about this.

JERRY

Well, perhaps we can take comfort in the knowledge that in the next world, Ray will be the recipient of a much larger and more harsh brand of justice . . .

GEORGE

Yeah . . . He'll have my parents!

DISSOLVE TO:

ACT TWO
SCENE J

INT. RAVA AND RAY'S APARTMENT—LATE AFTERNOON

*Ray is home alone. He putters about, admiring his "art collection."
Suddenly there's a brusque knocking on the door.*

KRAMER (O.S.)

Police! Open up!

RAY

Police?

He crosses to the door and cracks it open. Kramer barges in like a cop

THE STATUE

on a bust. He is wearing Jerry's grandfather's 'TV flatfoot suit' and he throws Ray against the wall, face first.

> **KRAMER**
>
> Freeze mother!

> **RAY**
>
> Hey . . .

Kramer shoves him roughly against the wall.

> **KRAMER**
>
> Shut up. Spread 'em. I said spread 'em! (LOOKS AROUND)
> You're in big trouble son. Burglary, grand larceny,
> possession of stolen goods and uh, uh . . . murder.

> **RAY**
>
> Murder?!

Kramer shoves him against the wall again.

> **KRAMER**
>
> Shut up! Keep 'em spread! Just make love to that wall,
> pervert!

> **RAY**
>
> I think you have me confused with somebody else.

> **KRAMER**
>
> Is your name's Ray?

> **RAY**
>
> Yeah.

> **KRAMER**
>
> Yeah, you're the punk I'm looking for.

Kramer looks at the array of statues. He grabs the statue. Puts it in a duffel bag.

> **RAY**
>
> Hey, hey, are you a cop?

> **KRAMER**
>
> Yeah, I'm a cop. I'm a good cop. I'm a damn good cop!
> Today's your lucky day, junior, 'cause I'm gonna let you

off with just a warning. Any more of this criminal
activity and you'll be sorry. You got me?

RAY

Got you? I don't even know what the hell you're talking
about.

KRAMER

Good. Good. Let's keep it that way.

Kramer exits *with the statue.*

DISSOLVE TO:

ACT TWO
SCENE K

INT. JERRY'S APARTMENT—EARLY EVENING

Jerry, Elaine and George are entering apartment with Kramer *who
is ushering them in.*

JERRY

Alright, alright, what's the big hubbub, bub?

Kramer dashes to his apartment and comes out *with the statue
concealed in the duffel bag. Kramer places the duffel bag on the table and
lowers it, revealing the statue.*

GEORGE

Kramer, I can't believe it. Oh, you're my hero.

KRAMER

Yeah.

JERRY

Kramer, what did you do?

KRAMER

Well, let's put it this way. I didn't take him to *People's
Court.*

THE STATUE

GEORGE

I feel like a huge weight's been lifted off my shoulders.
(HE BEAMS GIDDILY) I . . . I . . . I feel happy! Kramer, I
don't know how to thank you.

KRAMER

Well, I'll think of something . . .

*He slaps George on the back, sending the statue crashing to the ground.
On their stunned expressions, we:*

FADE OUT:

END OF ACT TWO

SHOW CLOSE

STAND-UP #3

INT. COMEDY CLUB—NIGHT

JERRY

People are going to steal from you. You can't stop them.
But everybody has their own little personal security
things, things that they think will foil the crooks, you
know? In your own mind, right? . . . You go to the
beach, go in the water, put your wallet in the sneaker,
who's gonna know? What criminal mind could
penetrate this fortress of security? I tied a bow, they
can't get through that. I put the wallet down by the toe
of the sneaker. They never look there. They check the
heel, they move on.

END OF SHOW

THE *Seinfeld* SCRIPTS

THE
REVENGE

WRITTEN BY

LARRY DAVID

DIRECTED BY

TOM CHERONES

AS BROADCAST APRIL 18, 1991

SHOW OPEN

STAND-UP #1

INT. COMEDY CLUB—NIGHT

JERRY

Whenever I see the news and they're hauling in some criminal/terrorist/ psycho/maniac/mass murderer guy, you notice he's always covering up his face with the newspaper, with the jacket, with the hat? What is he worried about? I mean, what is this man's reputation that he has to worry about this kind of exposure damaging his good name? I mean, what is he, up for a big job promotion down at the office or something? Afraid the boss is going to catch this on TV and go, "Isn't that Johnson from sales? He's up in that clock tower picking people off one by one. I don't know if that's the kind of man we want heading up that new branch office. He should be in bill collection. I think he's got aptitude."

ACT ONE

SCENE A

INT. GEORGE'S (RICK LEVITANS) BOSS'S OFFICE—DAY

George's boss, Rick Levitan, in his early forties, is on the phone.

LEVITAN
(INTO PHONE) She was great . . . You don't want to
know . . . Hey Brecky, remind me to tell you what we
did in Lake George . . . Get this, I got it all on video.

Suddenly George bursts into the room.

GEORGE
That's it! This is it! I'm done. Through. It's over. I'm
gone. Finished. Over. I will never work for you again.
Look at you. You think you're an important man? Is that
what you think? You're a laughingstock. You are a joke!
These people are laughing at you. You're nothing. You
have no brains, no ability. Nothing! I quit!

And with that he turns and storms out.

CUT TO:

ACT ONE
SCENE B

INT. JERRY'S APARTMENT—DAY

Jerry getting laundry ready. One bag is filled. He's working on a second.
Kramer enters.

KRAMER

Hey.

JERRY

Hey.

KRAMER

Boy, I have really had it with Newman. He wakes me up again last night at three o'clock in the morning to tell me he's going onto the roof to kill himself.

JERRY

What did you say?

KRAMER

I said "Jump." He's been threatening to do this for years. I said, "Look if you're going to kill yourself do it already, and stop bothering me." At least I'd respect the guy for accomplishing something.

JERRY

What's his problem?

KRAMER

No job, no women.

JERRY

He called the right guy.

KRAMER

What am I supposed to tell him, how much there is for him to live for? Why should I lie to him?

JERRY

Alright, I'm leaving. I'm going to the laundry.

KRAMER

Why don't you use the machines down in the basement?

JERRY

Fluff and fold, the only way to live. I drop it off. I pick it up. It's a delight.

THE REVENGE

KRAMER

(MOUSY) How about if I put a few things in your bag?

JERRY

Wait, wait a second. I don't want to do that.

KRAMER

Why? You're going over there.

JERRY

I don't want to mix in everything. My guys don't know your guys. You can't just lock 'em all in the same machine together. They'll start a riot.

KRAMER

You ever met my guys?

JERRY

No, I can't say as I have.

KRAMER

Well . . .

JERRY

Alright, put 'em on top.

Kramer removes his shirt.

JERRY (CONT'D)

Oh beautiful . . .

DISSOLVE TO:

**ACT ONE
SCENE C**

INT. LAUNDROMAT—DAY

Jerry enters *the laundromat and places his bag on the scale. Vic, the proprietor, appears. He's a man who is not familiar with pleasure.*

JERRY

This stuff on top is my friend's? Can I get it done in a separate machine?

VIC

I'll have to charge you for another machine.

JERRY

Whatever it costs. In fact, I would prefer it if the machines are not even touching each other. Because something could . . . you know, jump across.

George enters.

GEORGE

Guess what?

JERRY

How did you know I was here?

GEORGE

Kramer. Guess what?

JERRY

I don't know.

GEORGE

I quit my job.

JERRY

Get out of here.

GEORGE

I couldn't take it anymore.

VIC

You can have this on Monday.

JERRY

What happened? Levitan?

GEORGE

I go in to use his private bathroom . . . everybody uses it, and then I get a memo, a memo telling me to use the men's room in the hall. We share it with Pace Electronics. It's disgusting.

JERRY

You and your toilets.

THE REVENGE

GEORGE

I snapped. It was the last straw.

JERRY

So what are you going to do now? Are you going to look for something else in real estate?

GEORGE

Nobody's hiring now. The market's terrible.

JERRY

So, what are you gonna do?

Close-up on George's face as he searches for an answer.

CUT TO:

**ACT ONE
SCENE D**

INT. COFFEE SHOP—DAY

Jerry and George.

GEORGE

. . . I like sports. I could do something in sports.

JERRY

Uh-huh, uh-huh . . . In what capacity?

GEORGE

You know, like the general manager of a baseball team.

JERRY

Yeah, well . . . well that could be tough to get.

GEORGE

It doesn't even have to be the general manager. Maybe I could be like an announcer, like a color man. You know how I always make interesting comments during the game.

JERRY

Yeah, yeah. You make good comments.

GEORGE

So, what about that?

JERRY

Well you know they tend to give those jobs to ex-ballplayers and people that are, you know, in broadcasting.

GEORGE

Well, that's really not fair.

JERRY

I know . . . Well, okay, okay, what else do you like?

GEORGE

Movies. I like to watch movies.

JERRY

(NODS) Yeah. Yeah.

GEORGE

Do they pay people to watch movies?

JERRY

Projectionists.

GEORGE

That's true.

JERRY

But you gotta know how to work the projector.

GEORGE

Right.

JERRY

And it's probably a union thing.

GEORGE

Those unions. (THINKING OUT LOUD) Okay sports, movies . . . What about a talk show host?

JERRY

Talk show host, that's good.

GEORGE

I think I'd be good at that. I talk to people all the time.
Somebody even told me once they thought I'd be a
good talk show host.

JERRY

Really?

GEORGE

Yeah, a couple of people . . . How do you get that
though? Where do you start?

JERRY

Well that's where it gets tricky.

GEORGE

I can't just walk into a building and say I want to be a
talk show host.

JERRY

I wouldn't think so.

GEORGE

It's all politics.

A beat. George is at a loss for words.

JERRY

Alright, okay. Sports, movies, talk show host, what else?

George thinks for a beat, then:

GEORGE

This could have been a huge mistake.

JERRY

Yeah, well it doesn't sound like you completely thought
this through.

GEORGE

I guess not. What should I do?

JERRY

Maybe you can just go back.

GEORGE

Go back?

JERRY

Yeah, pretend like it never happened.

GEORGE

You mean just walk into the staff meeting on Monday morning like it never happened.

JERRY

Sure, you're an emotional person. People don't take you seriously.

GEORGE

Just go back, pretend the whole thing never happened.

JERRY

Never happened.

GEORGE

I was blowing off a little steam, so what?

JERRY

So what, you're entitled.

GEORGE

I'm emotional.

JERRY

That's right, you're emotional.

GEORGE

Never happened.

JERRY

Never happened.

DISSOLVE TO:

THE REVENGE

STAND-UP #2

INT. COMEDY CLUB—NIGHT

JERRY

To me, the most annoying thing about the couple of
times that I did work in an office is when you go in in
the morning you say hi to everyone and then for some
reason throughout the day you have to continue to
greet these people all day every time you see them. You
walk in in the morning, "Morning Bill, morning Bob,
how ya doin'? Fine." Ten minutes later you see them in
the hall, "How ya doin'?" Every time you pass you got
to come up with another little greeting. You know, you
start wracking your brains. You know, you do the little
eyebrow . . . you know. Start coming up with
nicknames for them, "Jimbo . . ."

DISSOLVE TO:

ACT ONE
SCENE E

INT. CONFERENCE ROOM—MONDAY MORNING

*Nine people, mostly in their thirties—some sitting, some standing, some
talking. George enters overly casual. Everyone takes note. George
addresses Glenda, a heavyset woman.*

GEORGE

How ya doin'?

GLENDA

What are you doing here?

GEORGE

What? I work here.

GLENDA

I thought you quit.

GEORGE

What quit? Who quit?

He takes a seat.

DAN

(TO BRECKY) Bill, how was your weekend?

BILL

Oh, excellent weekend. What about your weekend?

DAN

Fine weekend.

GEORGE

Yep. Good weekend.

DAN

Went up to the cape. Took the kids sailing. Lisa was a little scared at first, but that kid's gonna be a good sailor someday.

GEORGE

Ah, she's gonna be a fine sailor.

Levitan enters.

LEVITAN

Ava, what happened to you Friday afternoon?

AVA

Oh, I got tied up.

LEVITAN

I'll bet you did.

Polite chuckles.

LEVITAN (CONT'D)

I want to remind everyone that the tenth anniversary party for Rick-Bar Properties is gonna be Wednesday afternoon at four o'clock at Lasky's bar on Madison and Forty-eighth. I want all of you to be there. It really means a lot to me.

He turns to a person sitting next to him:

THE REVENGE

LEVITAN (CONT'D)

Is that Costanza over there? (TO GEORGE) What are you doing here?

GEORGE

(INNOCENT) What?

LEVITAN

Am I crazy, or didn't you quit?

GEORGE

When?

LEVITAN

Friday.

GEORGE

What, that? Are you kidding? I didn't quit. You took that seriously?

LEVITAN

You mean "laughingstock," all that stuff? . . .

GEORGE

Come on, will you stop it?

LEVITAN

No brains, no ability?

GEORGE

Teasing.

LEVITAN

. . . Okay, I want you outta here.

GEORGE

I don't know where you're getting this from . . . You're serious aren't you?

Levitan stares incredulously.

GEORGE (CONT'D)

. . . You see, you just . . . you don't know my sense of humor. I mean, Dan don't I joke around all the time?

DAN

I wouldn't say all the time.

LEVITAN

You can't win. You can't beat me. That's why I'm here and you're there. Because I'm a winner. I'll always be a winner and you'll always be a loser.

CUT TO:

ACT ONE
SCENE F

INT. LAUNDROMAT—DAY

Jerry and George. Jerry's picking his laundry up.

GEORGE

"I'll always be a winner and you'll always be a loser." This is what he said to me.

JERRY

Well, so that's that.

GEORGE

No, that's not that.

JERRY

That's not that?

GEORGE

No.

JERRY

Well, if that's not that, what is that?

GEORGE

I've got some plans . . . I've got plans.

JERRY

What kind of plans?

GEORGE

What's the difference?

JERRY

You don't wanta tell me.

George looks around conspiratorially, then:

GEORGE

. . . I'm gonna slip him a mickey.

JERRY

What? In his drink? Are you out of your mind? Who are you, Peter Lorre?

GEORGE

You don't understand. He's got this big party coming up. He's been looking forward to this for months. This is gonna destroy the whole thing.

JERRY

What if you destroy him?

GEORGE

No, no, no, no. Don't worry. It's perfectly safe. I've researched it, he'll get a little woozy.

He shoots him a look.

GEORGE (CONT'D)

He might keel over.

JERRY

What does that do? Big deal.

GEORGE

This is what they would do in the movies! It's a beautiful thing! It's like a movie. I'm gonna slip him a mickey!

JERRY

You've really gone mental. Where are you gonna get this mickey? I can't believe I'm saying "mickey."

GEORGE

I've got a source.

JERRY

You got a mickey source.

GEORGE

And Elaine is gonna keep him busy.

JERRY

Elaine? How'd you rope her into this?

GEORGE

I told her what a sexist he is and how he cheats on his wife.

JERRY

She knew that.

GEORGE

But she didn't know he doesn't recycle.

JERRY

What is the point of all this?

GEORGE

Revenge.

JERRY

Oh the best revenge is living well.

GEORGE

There's no chance of that.

FADE OUT:

END OF ACT ONE

ACT TWO

SCENE G

INT. HALLWAY—DAY

Jerry enters *and plops the laundry bag on a sofa.* Kramer enters.

> **JERRY**
> Did you get your laundry?

> **KRAMER**
> (UNSETTLED) Yeah.

> **JERRY**
> What's with you?

> **KRAMER**
> He jumped.

> **JERRY**
> What?

> **KRAMER**
> Newman jumped.

> **JERRY**
> Did he call you last night?

> **KRAMER**
> Oh, yeah, yeah, yeah, yeah, yeah.

> **JERRY**
> What did you say?

KRAMER

I said, "Wave to me when you pass my window . . ."

JERRY

Did he wave?

KRAMER

No, he jumped from the second floor. Mr. Papanickolas saw him from across the street. He's lying out there faking. See, he's trying to get back at me.

Jerry goes to laundry bag. As he opens it, he stops, frozen.

JERRY

Oh my god.

KRAMER

What's the matter?

Jerry dumps out the laundry bag going through the clothes frantically.

JERRY

On Thursday when I came home from Detroit I had fifteen hundred dollars on me. For some reason I decided to hide it in the laundry bag. And then I completely forgot about it. And then I took the laundry in on Friday. Oh, come on, let's go.

KRAMER

Where? Where?

JERRY

To the laundromat.

DISSOLVE TO:

ACT TWO
SCENE H

INT. LAUNDROMAT—DAY

VIC

I never saw it.

THE REVENGE

KRAMER

(TO VIC) Okay, c'mon give the guy his money. What . . .
what are you doing?

VIC

Hey, you see that sign up there?

Sign reads: "Not responsible for valuables."

JERRY

Oh, I see, so you put up a sign so you can do whatever
you want. You're not a part of society.

VIC

Yeah, that's right, because this place is my country. And
I'm the president, and that's my constitution: "I'm not
responsible."

JERRY

So anyone leaves anything here you can just take it, you
have a license to steal. You are like the James Bond of
laundry.

VIC

You ever hear of a bank?

JERRY

(TO KRAMER) Come on, let's go.

KRAMER

You can't let him get away with this.

CUT TO:

ACT TWO
SCENE J

INT. BAR—DAY

*The office party's in progress. Elaine and George are by the door trying
to look inconspicuous. Elaine is dressed, quite literally, to kill.*

ELAINE

Which one is he?

GEORGE

That's him over there, the one that looks like a blowfish.

ELAINE

Oh yeah, I see him.

GEORGE

Yeah . . . Hey, thanks for doing this.

ELAINE

Why pass up the opportunity to go to prison?

GEORGE

This is by far the most exciting thing I've ever done.

ELAINE

Yeah, it is kind of cool.

GEORGE

It's the first time in my life I've ever gotten back at someone.

ELAINE

I can't believe we're doing this. This is the kind of thing they do in the movies.

GEORGE

That's exactly what I told Jerry!

ELAINE

Really?

GEORGE

Yes. God, I've never felt so alive.

CUT TO:

ACT TWO
SCENE K

INT. LAUNDROMAT—DAY

Jerry and Kramer standing at the front. Jerry's carrying a laundry bag that appears much too heavy.

THE REVENGE

JERRY

Maybe we should call this off.

KRAMER

Oh, c'mon. What's the big deal? We're just gonna put a
little concrete in the washing machine.

JERRY

And what's going to happen?

KRAMER

Well, it'll mix up with the water and then by the end of
the cycle it'll be a solid block.

JERRY

If only you could put your mind to something
worthwhile. You're like Lex Luthor.

Jerry gives Kramer the bag.

KRAMER

You keep him busy.

*Kramer takes the bag and heads for the machine. Acting casually, he
inadvertently attracts Vic's attention, stumbles backwards with the bag
and crashes into the machine.*

CUT TO:

**ACT TWO
SCENE L**

INT. BAR—DAY

GEORGE

You go over there, you start flirting with him. Then I'll
come by, and while you're keeping him busy, I'll slip it
in his drink.

ELAINE

Wouldn't it be easier just to punch him in the mouth?

Elaine walks over to bar. Takes a seat on Levitan's left. Levitan is talking to a co-worker.

LEVITAN

Oh, c'mon, they're terrible. They got no infield.

Elaine bumps him with her elbow.

ELAINE

Ooop. Excuse me.

CO-WORKER

I'm gonna get some food. You want some?

LEVITAN

Nah.

ELAINE

Hi.

LEVITAN

Hi.

Levitan returns to his drink. Elaine plans her next move.

ELAINE

(TRYING TO GET HIS ATTENTION, MUSTERS A FAKE SNEEZE) Achoo!

He turns to her.

LEVITAN

God bless you.

ELAINE

Oh, thank you, thank you very much. (SHE BLOWS HER NOSE) Really I mean that. I am not one of those people who give insincere thank-yous. No sir, no sir, when I thank somebody, I really thank them . . . so thank you.

LEVITAN

You're welcome.

He turns away. He's not interested. A beat, then:

THE REVENGE

ELAINE

People don't say "God bless you" as much as they used to, have you noticed that?

LEVITAN

No.

A beat. She's really at a loss, then:

ELAINE

So, I'm going to a nudist colony next week.

LEVITAN

(ALL EARS) A nudist colony, really?

Elaine signals George.

ELAINE

Oh yeah, yeah. I love nudist colonies. They help me unwind.

LEVITAN

I've never been to a nudist colony.

ELAINE

Oh really? Oh you should go. They're great. They're great. Of course when it's over, it's hard to get used to all this clothing you know, so a lot of times I'll just lock the door to my office and I'll just sit there naked.

LEVITAN

Seriously?

ELAINE

I usually work naked a couple hours a day.

George arrives, but the seat on Levitan's right is occupied by Glenda, the heavyset woman from the office.

GEORGE

(WHISPERING) Glenda, could I ask you a favor? Could I have this seat?

GLENDA

(GROWLING) What do you have to sit here for? There are plenty of other seats.

GEORGE

(TRYING TO KEEP THEIR CONVERSATION LOW) I can't explain. It's very important that I sit here.

GLENDA

(LOUDER) What are you doing here anyway? I thought you were fired?

GEORGE

Okay, okay, fine.

Back to: Elaine and Levitan.

ELAINE

I cook naked, I clean . . . I clean naked, I drive naked. Naked, naked, naked.

LEVITAN

(IN AWE) Who are you?

ELAINE

Oh, you don't want to know, mister. I'm trouble, big trouble.

CUT TO:

ACT TWO
SCENE M

INT. LAUNDROMAT—DAY

Kramer, in the back of the laundromat, struggles with the bag, managing to get as much on himself as in the machine. Jerry's keeping Vic busy in the front.

JERRY

What about the gentle cycle? You ever use that?

He doesn't know what to make of Jerry.

JERRY (CONT'D)

Do you think it's effeminate for a man to put clothes in

the gentle cycle? . . . What about fine fabrics? How do you deal with that kind of temperament? What about stone washing? Ever witnessed one of those? That must be something. What do they just pummel the jeans with rocks?

Finally Kramer approaches, his work is done. He looks like a third base line.

KRAMER
(TO JERRY RE: HIS APPEARANCE) I didn't realize it was a full box.

DISSOLVE TO:

ACT TWO
SCENE N

INT. BAR—DAY

Angle on: Glenda.

George approaches Glenda.

GEORGE
I'm gonna count to three. If you don't give up the chair the wig is coming off.

GLENDA
I don't wear a wig.

GEORGE
One.

She leaves. Angle on: Elaine and Levitan.

ELAINE
No, no, no, no, no, I'm sorry, I don't really have a phone. In fact I don't really have an apartment. I kind of sleep around.

George gets ready to put the powder in Levitan's drink.

ELAINE (CONT'D)

I just like to have a few drinks and then just let the guy
do whatever he wants . . . Would you close your eyes a
second? I want to tell you a secret about my bra.

*Levitan closes his eyes. Elaine signals George to put the mickey in. As he
does, she whispers in Levitan's ear. They break out laughing.*

GEORGE

Hello, Rick.

LEVITAN

(LAUGHING) Hey, look who's here.

GEORGE

That's right, Ricky boy, it's me.

LEVITAN

(EBULLIENT) You know something Costanza, I'm a very
lucky man. I've always been lucky. Things just seem to
somehow just fall right in my lap. (HE GLANCES TO
ELAINE) You wouldn't believe it if I told you. In fact, I'm
glad you're here you know. Maybe I've been a little
rough on you. Why should we let petty personal
differences get in the way of business? I want you to
come back. You can use my bathroom anytime you
want.

GEORGE

You want me to come back?

LEVITAN

(CALLING OUT) Hey, how about a toast? Everybody, a
toast.

*Rick gets up with his drink. With one foot on the bar footrest and one
on his chair footrest, he rises above the crowd. He hits the side of his
glass with a spoon to get their attention. During the following, George
makes a series of gestures and noises searching for some way to stop him.*

LEVITAN (CONT'D)

Everyone, I want to propose a toast—to ten great years
at Rick-Bar Properties—

THE REVENGE

GEORGE

Uh, Rick.

LEVITAN

And all the people in this room that made that possible.

GEORGE

Uh, Rick.

LEVITAN

(HE PUTS HIS HAND ON GEORGE'S SHOULDER) And I'd also like to welcome back into the fold . . . our little shrimpy friend, George Costanza, who although he really didn't have a very good year, how you blew that McConnell deal I'll never know, but, what the hell, we've always enjoyed his antics around the office . . . (TO GEORGE) Anything you want to add to this?

GEORGE

Drink up.

And with that he downs his drink in one shot.

CUT TO:

ACT TWO
SCENE P

INT. JERRY'S APARTMENT—DAY

Jerry, Elaine and George, who is slumped on the sofa.

GEORGE

. . . I like history. The Civil War. Maybe I could be a professor or something.

ELAINE

Well, to teach something you really have to know a lot about it. I think you need a degree.

JERRY

Yeah, that's true.

Kramer enters *with an envelope.*

JERRY (CONT'D)

What?

Kramer slowly walks up to Jerry and holds it out.

JERRY (CONT'D)

Oh my god. The money. The fifteen hundred. Where'd you find it?

KRAMER

It was in my laundry.

JERRY

In your laundry?! The whole time?! Oh, I told you not to mix in our guys. What did we figure the damage on that machine would be?

KRAMER

It was about twelve hundred bucks.

NEWMAN (O.S.)

Kramer!

KRAMER

That's Newman!

NEWMAN (O.S.)

I'm on the roof!

Kramer heads for the window. He opens it and yells up:

KRAMER

Well, what are you waiting for?

JERRY

(TO ELAINE) Elaine come on, take a walk with me down to the laundromat. I gotta pay this guy the money.

GEORGE

(TO HIMSELF) I like horses . . . maybe I could be a stable boy.

KRAMER
(TO NEWMAN) You wanna shoot some pool tonight?

NEWMAN (o.s.)
I can't. I'm going to a movie.

Jerry and Elaine leave.

GEORGE
Nah, it's probably a union thing.

FADE OUT:

END OF ACT TWO

SHOW CLOSE

STAND-UP #3

INT. COMEDY CLUB—NIGHT

JERRY

People like the idea of revenge. Did you ever hear the expression "The best revenge is living well"? I've said this. In other words, it means, supposedly, the best way to get back at someone is just by being happy and successful in your own life. Sounds nice. Doesn't really work on that Charles Bronson kind of level, you know what I mean? Those movies where his whole family just gets wiped out by some street scum. You know. The guy could go up to him and go, "Charlie, forget the .357 magnum, you need a custom made suit and a convertible. New carpeting, a divan, French doors, that'll show those punks."

END OF SHOW

THE Seinfeld SCRIPTS

THE
HEART
ATTACK

WRITTEN BY

LARRY CHARLES

DIRECTED BY

TOM CHERONES

AS BROADCAST APRIL 25, 1991

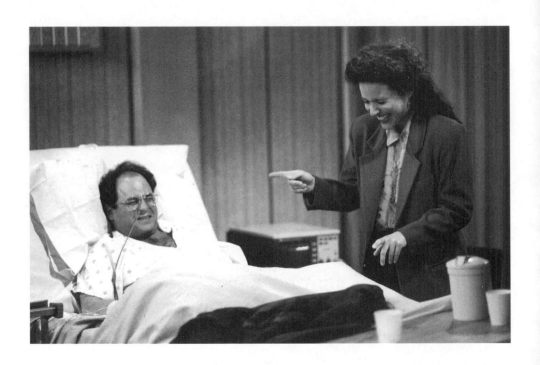

SHOW OPEN

STAND-UP #1

INT. COMEDY CLUB—NIGHT

JERRY

You know, I tell you, I gotta say that I'm enjoying
adulthood. For a lot of reasons. And I'll tell you reason
number one: as an adult, if I want a cookie, I have a
cookie, okay? I have three cookies or four cookies or
eleven cookies if I want. Many times I will intentionally
ruin my entire appetite. Just ruin it. And then I call my
mother up right after to tell her that I did it. "Hello,
Mom, yeah, I just ruined my entire appetite . . .
cookies." So what if you ruin . . . See because as an
adult we understand even if you ruin an appetite, there's
another appetite coming right behind it. There's no
danger in running out of appetites. I've got millions of
them, I'll ruin them whenever I want!

ACT ONE

SCENE A

INT. JERRY'S APARTMENT—NIGHT

It is dark. Jerry lies on couch watching TV, battling the urge to sleep. He is watching a cheesy foreign sci-fi flick, with bad accents and tinny music.

> **TV VOICE**
> (GERMANIC) Look Sigmund. Look in the sky. The planets are on fire. It is just as you prophesied. The planets of our solar system, incinerating. Like flaming globes Sigmund, like flaming globes. Ah, ha, ha, ha . . .

Jerry is asleep.

DISSOLVE TO:

ACT ONE
SCENE B

INT. JERRY'S BEDROOM—NIGHT

It is completely dark (Note: Read on, this does not require a set). Jerry picks up a pen and scribbles something down on a pad on the night table. He laughs, shakes his head, pretty proud of himself, and goes back to sleep still chortling.

DISSOLVE TO:

ACT ONE
SCENE C

INT. COFFEE SHOP—MORNING

Jerry looks like he didn't get much sleep. He stares intently at crumbled-up piece of note paper. The waitress places two salads down for George and Elaine. George removes a bag from his pocket and takes out a cucumber.

ELAINE

What do you got, a cucumber?

GEORGE

Yeah, so what?

ELAINE

You're bringing in an outside cucumber?

GEORGE

They refuse to put cucumber in the salad. I need cucumber.

JERRY

(READING THE NOTE) What have I done? I can't read this! Ful-hel-mo-nen-ter-val? I got up last night, I wrote this down, I thought I had this great bit. (HE FOCUSES ON PAPER) Wait a second, wait a second . . . "Fax me some halibut." Is that funny? Is that a joke?

ELAINE

No, let me see that.

She takes the paper.

ELAINE (CONT'D)

"Don't-mess-with-Johnny."

THE HEART ATTACK

JERRY

Johnny? Johnny who? Johnny Carson? Did I insult
Johnny on *The Tonight Show?*

ELAINE

Did you mess with Johnny, Jerry?

GEORGE

(RE: NOTE) Let me see that.

George studies the note.

ELAINE

Hey, where's Kramer?

JERRY

I don't know. That's like asking "Where's Waldo?"

GEORGE

(STILL HOLDING THE NOTE) I think I'm having a heart
attack.

JERRY

I don't think that's it.

GEORGE

I'm not kidding.

JERRY

What does that mean?

ELAINE

(CALMLY) I think what he's trying to say is that *he's*
having a heart attack.

JERRY

Oh, he's having a heart attack.

GEORGE

Tightness.

JERRY

C'mon.

GEORGE

Shortness of breath.

JERRY

Oh, this is ridiculous.

GEORGE

Radiating waves of pain.

JERRY

I know what this is. You saw that show on PBS last night, *Coronary Country*. (TO ELAINE) I saw it in the *TV Guide.* I called him and told him to make sure and not watch it.

GEORGE

There was nothing else on. Oh, the left arm, left arm.

JERRY

(TO ELAINE) He saw that show on anorexia last year and ate like an animal for two weeks.

GEORGE

Why can't I have a heart attack? I'm allowed.

JERRY

So what do you want? You want me take you to the hospital?

GEORGE

Manhattan Memorial, less of a line.

JERRY

I'll call an ambulance.

Jerry exits. The waitress approaches. *George is dying but the waitress doesn't notice.*

WAITRESS

Is everything alright?

GEORGE

We'll just take a check.

She *drops the check on the table and* exits. *George raises his head. He can't help but to check the check. Sure enough, he finds an error.*

THE HEART ATTACK

GEORGE

(WEAKLY CALLING AFTER HER) You made a mistake on
the . . .

ELAINE

George!

CUT TO:

ACT ONE
SCENE D

EXT. STREET—NIGHT

Stock footage of speeding ambulance.

CUT TO:

ACT ONE
SCENE E

INT. HOSPITAL ROOM—DAY

*George lies in the bed wallowing in self-pity. He has EKG cups attached
to his chest, a tube up his nose, and an IV tube in his arm. He is
attached to machines that beep and chart and monitor his progress. It's
a semi-private room. Next to him is another bed, but it's hidden by a
partition, a cubicle curtain. There is someone in there but we will not
see them. But, we hear his moans and groans.*

MAN IN OTHER BED (O.S.)

Ooooooh. . . . Arghhhh. . . .

GEORGE

Are . . . are you okay?

MAN IN OTHER BED (O.S.)

Oooooooooooh . . .

GEORGE

I'm George . . . George Costanza . . . I've never been in the hospital a day in my life, except when I had my tonsils out. You know, they never gave me any ice cream. I always felt that . . .

MAN IN OTHER BED (O.S.)

Shut up!

Angle on Jerry at doorway. He is bugging a nurse with the crumpled note paper.

JERRY

Well. What do you think?

NURSE #1

(LOOKING AT PAPER) "Salami, salami, bologna." Definitely.

JERRY

"Salami salami bologna"?

DOCTOR

(IN A HURRY) Oh, your friend's fine. He didn't have a heart attack. I'll be in, in a few minutes.

JERRY

What a surprise.

He enters George's room.

JERRY (CONT'D)

Hey, how ya doin' buddy? You need anything? Do you want me to go out and get you a Superman comic?

GEORGE

No, no thanks.

JERRY

You know, I was wondering . . . You know that Black Hawks jacket you have?

GEORGE

Oh, sure, my Black Hawks jacket. I love my Black Hawks jacket.

THE HEART ATTACK

JERRY

Well, you know, I was thinking if things don't exactly work out . . .

GEORGE

Well, it wouldn't fit you. The sleeves are too short.

JERRY

No, I tried it on. It fits good.

GEORGE

Well I didn't really think about what I was gonna do with all . . .

JERRY

Well, you know . . .

GEORGE

(RELUCTANTLY) Well, okay.

JERRY

Oh, and . . . Do you think it would be alright if I called Susan Davis?

GEORGE

Susan Davis . . . hey, wait a second.

JERRY

Well, it's not like we'd be bumping into you.

GEORGE

I don't know . . . you and Susan Davis?

JERRY

You know, if your future was a little more certain . . .

GEORGE

Okay, go ahead. Call her, get married, have babies, have a great life . . . What do I care? I'm finished. It's all over for me. In fact let's end it right now. Jerry, kill me, kill me now. I'm begging you. Let's just get it over with. Be a pal. Just take the pillow and put it over my face.

JERRY

Well, ah, (TAKING PILLOW) what, kind of like this?

GEORGE

Whadya doing? Whadya, crazy?

Elaine enters. *Jerry turns.*

ELAINE

Jerry!

JERRY

Elaine, what are you doing here?

GEORGE

Jerk off.

Jerry crosses to her.

JERRY

(WHISPERING) There's nothing wrong with him, I saw
the doctor, he's fine.

They walk to the bed.

ELAINE

Hi, George, how ya feeling? Is anybody getting your
apartment?

*Elaine sits with Jerry and they have their own conversation, ignoring
George.*

GEORGE

I'll tell ya, if I ever get out of here I'm gonna change my
life. I'm gonna do a whole Zen thing. Take up yoga,
meditate, I'll eat right, calm down, lose my anger . . .
(THEN SNAPPING) Hey, is anybody listening?!

The doctor enters. *The doctor and Elaine exchange a romantic,
awkward glance.*

DOCTOR

(TO ELAINE) Uh, hello. (TO GEORGE) Uh, Mr. Costanza?

GEORGE

(PANICKY) Uh yeah, you know Doctor, I gotta tell you,
I feel a lot better.

THE HEART ATTACK

DOCTOR

Well, we looked at your EKG's, ran some tests, did a complete work-up.

GEORGE

(ULTRA-PANICKY) Oh God, Mommy!

DOCTOR

And you simply haven't had a heart attack.

GEORGE

I haven't? I'm okay? I'm okay? Oh thank you, thank you, Doctor. I don't know how to thank you.

JERRY

Hey, that was really fun, George. Can we go home now?

DOCTOR

No, actually, we'd like to keep him here overnight for observation, just to be safe.

GEORGE

Oh sure, sure, anything. Can you believe it? There's nothing wrong with me.

DOCTOR

Well, I wouldn't go that far.

GEORGE

(PANICKING) What? Oh my God. What? Is it meningitis? Scoliosis? Lupus? Is it lupus?

DOCTOR

Have you ever had your tonsils taken out?

GEORGE

My tonsils? Yeah, when I was a kid.

DOCTOR

Well, they've grown back. Your adenoids are swollen too.

GEORGE

(WITH MOUTH OPEN) Really?

ELAINE

Whose tonsils grow back?

DOCTOR

It happens.

JERRY

Yeah, if you've been exposed to gamma rays.

ELAINE

I still have my tonsils. Everyone in my family has their tonsils. In fact, we were forbidden to socialize with anyone who didn't have their tonsils.

DOCTOR

That's interesting, because no one in my family has their tonsils and we were forbidden to socialize with tonsil people.

JERRY

Well it's like the Capulets and the Montagues.

GEORGE

Excuse me?

DOCTOR

Anyway, I strongly recommend they come out.

GEORGE

What, you mean with a knife?

DOCTOR

Yes. With a knife. You know, snip snip. Anyway, you'd be completely under, you wouldn't feel a thing. And when you wake up, you can have some ice cream.

GEORGE

Yeah, that's what they told me the last time.

DOCTOR

Think about it.

He turns and bumps into Elaine.

DOCTOR (CONT'D)

Excuse me.

THE HEART ATTACK

ELAINE

(FLUSTERED) Oh, I'm sorry.

He exits.

ELAINE

I just . . . have to ask that doctor one more question.

She leaves.

JERRY

Women go after doctors like men go after models. They want someone with knowledge of the body . . . we just want the body.

Kramer enters. *He is carrying a tray of hospital food.*

KRAMER

Hey.

JERRY

Hey.

KRAMER

Boy, they got a great cafeteria downstairs. Hot food, sandwiches, a salad bar. It's like Sizzler's opened up a hospital.

Kramer sits and begins to eat.

KRAMER (CONT'D)

So, how did you have a heart attack? You're a young man. What were you doing? Are they gonna do a zipper job? Oh, they love to do zipper jobs.

JERRY

Kramer.

KRAMER

The really bad thing about the heart is the sex thing. See, you gotta be careful about sex now. You get that heart pumping and suddenly, boom! Next thing you know you got a hose coming out of your chest attached to a piece of luggage.

JERRY

Kramer, George didn't have a heart attack.

KRAMER

No? . . . That's good.

GEORGE

I have to have my tonsils taken out.

KRAMER

Oh man . . . No . . . George we gotta get you outta here. Get out! Right now! They'll kill ya in here.

JERRY

It's routine surgery.

KRAMER

Oh yeah? My friend, Bob Saccomanno, he came in here for a hernia operation . . . Oh yeah, routine surgery . . . now he's sittin' around in a chair by a window going, (IN A FALSETTO VOICE) "My name is Bob" . . . George, whatever you do, don't let 'em cut you, don't let 'em cut you . . .

GEORGE

Well, what should I do, Kramer?

JERRY

Well, for one thing, don't listen to him.

KRAMER

I'll tell you what to do, I'll tell you what to do. You go to Tor Eckman. Tor, Tor, he'll fix you right up. He's an herbalist, a healer, George. He's not just gonna fix the tonsils and the adenoids, he is gonna change the whole way you function—body and mind.

JERRY

Eckman? I thought he was doing time.

KRAMER

No, no, he's out. He got out. See, the medical establishment, see they tried to frame him. It's all politics. But he's a rebel.

THE HEART ATTACK

JERRY

A rebel? No. Johnny Yuma was a rebel. Eckman is a nut. George, you want to take care of your tonsils, you do it in a hospital, with a doctor.

KRAMER

He's holistic. George. He's holistic.

GEORGE

Holistic . . . that sounds right.

JERRY

George, you need a medical doctor.

GEORGE

(TO JERRY) Let me ask you something . . . How much do you think it would cost to have tonsils and adenoids removed in the hospital?

JERRY

Well, an overnight stay in a hospital? Minor surgery? I dunno, four grand.

GEORGE

Uh-huh, and how much does the healer charge?

KRAMER

First visit, thirty-eight bucks.

GEORGE

Oh, yeah, holistic . . . that's what I need. That's the answer.

FADE OUT:

END OF ACT ONE

ACT TWO

SCENE E

On his wall are pictures of famous clients. 8 × 10 glossies, posters of Broadway musicals. Jerry and George are sitting on pillows, while Kramer fiddles with an acupuncture model.

GEORGE

So how do you like the way I talked you into comin' down here?

JERRY

Don't flatter yourself my friend. I'm here strictly for material, and I have a feeling this is a potential gold mine . . . I still think you're nuts though.

GEORGE

All I know is I've been going to doctors all my life. What has it gotten me? I'm thirty-three years old. I haven't outgrown the problems of puberty, I'm already facing the problems of old age. I completely skipped healthy adulthood. I went from having orgasms immediately to taking forever. You could do your taxes in the time it takes me to have an orgasm. I've never had a normal, medium orgasm.

JERRY

I've never had a really good pickle.

GEORGE

Besides, what's it gonna cost me? Thirty-eight bucks.

Tor enters. *He hugs Kramer for too long. Tor walks to the pillows. He studies Jerry and George for a moment, then:*

TOR

(TO JERRY) Would you not put your foot on that, please?

JERRY

Sorry.

Tor sits. He turns to George.

TOR

(TO GEORGE) What month were you born?

GEORGE

April.

TOR

You should've been born in August. Your parents would have been well-advised to wait.

GEORGE

Really.

TOR

Do you use hot water in the shower?

GEORGE

Yes.

TOR

Stop using it.

GEORGE

. . . Okay.

KRAMER

I'm off hot water.

TOR

Kramer tells me that you are interested in an alternative to surgery.

GEORGE

Yes, yes I am.

TOR

(HE BLOWS INTO GEORGE'S FACE) I think *we* can help you. See, unfortunately, the medical establishment is a business like any other business. And business needs customers. And they want to sell you their most expensive item which is unnecessary surgery.

GEORGE

Can I use hot water on my face?

TOR

No . . . You know I am not a business man. I'm a holistic healer. It's a calling, it's a gift. You see, it's in the best interest of the medical profession that you remain sick. You see, that insures good business. You're not a patient, you're a customer.

JERRY (V.O.)

And you're not a doctor, but you play one in real life.

GEORGE

What about shaving?

TOR

(TO JERRY) You're eating too much dairy. (TO GEORGE) May I?

Tor reaches over to touch George's face.

GEORGE

I guess so.

Tor feels George's face.

TOR

You see, you are in disharmony. The throat is the gateway to the lung. Tonsillitis, adenoiditis, is, in Chinese medical terms, an invasion of heat and wind.

JERRY (V.O.)

There's some hot air blowing in here.

THE HEART ATTACK

TOR

You know, I lived with the Eskimos many years ago and
they used to plunge their faces into the snow.

GEORGE

Could it be lukewarm?

JERRY (V.O.)

Too much dairy? You really think I'm eating too much
dairy?

CUT TO:

**ACT TWO
SCENE F**

EXT. NEW YORK STREET—NIGHT

Angle on: parked car.

CUT TO:

**ACT TWO
SCENE G**

INT. DOCTOR'S CAR—NIGHT

*Close-up of Dr. Fein. He speaks sincerely, almost seductively. As he does,
camera pans slowly to Elaine, in passenger seat.*

DOCTOR

. . . The tongue . . . yes, the tongue . . . or, in medical
terms, the glossa . . . It's a muscular organ . . . Consists
of two parts . . . the body and the root . . .

*Reveal Dr. Fein is holding Elaine's tongue with a piece of paper between
his fingers. Elaine's expression is perplexed.*

> **DOCTOR (CONT'D)**
> ... You see, it's covered by this mucous membrane ...
> These little raised projections are the papillae, which
> give it that furry appearance. Very tactile ...

Fein, still holding her tongue.

> **ELAINE**
> Uh-huh.

DISSOLVE TO:

ACT TWO
SCENE H

INT. HEALER'S APARTMENT—NIGHT

Tor is pouring tea.

> **TOR**
> Your tea is ready now. This will solve your so-called
> tonsil problem. It's a special concoction. It contains
> crampbark.

> **JERRY**
> I love crampbark.

> **TOR**
> Cleavers.

> **JERRY**
> Cleaver, I once had cleaver as a kid. I was able to lift a
> car.

> **TOR**
> And some couchgrass.

> **JERRY**
> Couchgrass and crampbark? You know, I think that's
> what killed Curly.

THE HEART ATTACK

Tor hands the tea to George who looks at Jerry and Kramer who give him opposite reactions. Jerry's is skeptical. Kramer's very enthusiastic.

> **KRAMER**
> Go ahead, drink it George.

> **JERRY**
> Excuse me, Tor. May I ask you a question? You have intuitive abilities. You're in touch with a lot of this cosmic kind of things . . . I have this note I can't read, I was wondering if . . .

Tor takes the note.

> **TOR**
> (LAUGHING) Oh, yes . . . yes . . . "Cleveland 117, San Antonio 109 . . ."

He hands note back to Jerry.

> **KRAMER**
> Go ahead, drink it George.

George begins to drink the tea.

> **GEORGE**
> Hey, it's not too bad.

CUT TO:

ACT TWO
SCENE J

INT. AMBULANCE—NIGHT

George strapped down on a gurney. His face is a shade of purple. He is screaming. He looks like human eggplant. Jerry and Kramer try to calm him, but it is very difficult because the ambulance is swerving back and forth as if it's about to tip over. As if it's driving a hundred miles an hour around curves. Meanwhile, the ambulance attendant in the back and the driver are in the midst of a gigantic argument.

GEORGE

(PANIC, HYSTERIA) I'm an eggplant! I'm an eggplant! I'm a minstrel man!

DRIVER

I didn't take your Chuckle, man!

ATTENDANT

I had five Chuckles. I ate a green one and the yellow one and the red one is missing.

DRIVER

I don't even like Chuckles!

JERRY

(TO ATTENDANT) Maybe he doesn't like them. That's possible.

GEORGE

My face! My face! Get me to the hospital!

ATTENDANT

I want that Chuckle back—you hear me?

JERRY

(TO ATTENDANT) I'll get you a Chuckle. You want me to get you a Chuckle?

ATTENDANT

(TO DRIVER) Pull over!

DRIVER

Pull over? Did you say pull over? You wanna piece of me?

ATTENDANT

Yeah.

JERRY

You're gonna fight?

GEORGE

Now? I'm a mutant!

KRAMER

(TO DRIVER) Hey, let me drive.

THE HEART ATTACK

ATTENDANT

Come on man, pull over!

DRIVER

Alright! I'm gonna mess you up, man.

The ambulance comes to a screeching halt. The driver gets out and the attendant heads for the back door.

JERRY

Really gentlemen, please.

GEORGE

My heart! My heart!

GEORGE (CONT'D)

Where you going? Are you crazy?

ATTENDANT

I'm gonna kick his ass.

KRAMER

Hey, you have keys.

GEORGE

You can't leave. This is an ambulance! This is an emergency!

He leaves. *Hold on the three of them for a beat, then:*

JERRY

All this for a Chuckle.

KRAMER

What's a Chuckle?

JERRY

It's a jelly candy. It comes in five flavors.

CUT TO:

ACT TWO
SCENE K

INT. DOCTOR'S CAR

He's still holding her tongue.

DOCTOR

You see taste buds run on grooves along surfaces.

ELAINE

Can you let go of my tongue now?

DOCTOR

What?

ELAINE

Let go of my tongue!

DOCTOR

Oh, sorry.

ELAINE

Well, I should get going . . .

Doctor leans in for a kiss.

ELAINE (CONT'D)

(RECOILING) What are you doing?

DOCTOR

I was going to kiss you good night.

ELAINE

A kiss? With the tongue? The glossa with the bumps and the papillae? . . . Yech, I don't think so.

And she leaves.

CUT TO:

ACT TWO
SCENE L

INT. AMBULANCE

It's moving again. The driver's behind the wheel, but there's no attendant.

THE HEART ATTACK

JERRY

You just can't leave him out there.

DRIVER

(OVER HIS SHOULDER) I told him I was gonna mess him up.

KRAMER

Well can you call him an ambulance?

DRIVER

(OVER HIS SHOULDER) I told him I didn't take his Chuckle. I don't eat that gooey crap!

KRAMER

Hey, watch the road! Watch the road man!

DRIVER

(TURNING BACK) Hey man, you want some of what he got?

JERRY/KRAMER

Watch out!!

SFX: crash

CUT TO:

ACT TWO
SCENE M

INT. HOSPITAL ROOM—EVENING

George lies in the hospital bed. He's watching TV He wears a neck brace. There is cream all over his face. Jerry enters. He is limping and wearing a neck brace. He talks to George, but George cannot respond except facially.

JERRY

How ya doing?

George nods.

JERRY (CONT'D)

Can't talk?

George shakes his head.

JERRY (CONT'D)

Hey, how'd you get the plastic one?

George lifts his eyebrows, knowingly.

JERRY (CONT'D)

I like that.

George sticks out his tongue.

JERRY (CONT'D)

So how's life without tonsils?

George gestures quickly with his arm to indicate he wants ice cream.

JERRY (CONT'D)

What? What's that? . . . So how much is this thing gonna cost you now? Like, five, six thousand? . . .

George signals that it will cost even more than that.

JERRY (CONT'D)

Well, live and learn . . . at least we lived. Kramer went to Eckman . . . He feels all better already . . .

George motions again for the ice cream.

JERRY (CONT'D)

What are you doing?

Elaine enters.

ELAINE

Oh, poor George. Oh I'm sorry but I can't stay long. I don't want to run into Doctor Tongue . . . Here, I brought you something.

She removes a pint of ice cream. George can't contain himself.

ELAINE (CONT'D)

Oh please, come on, it was nothing.

Nurse enters.

THE HEART ATTACK

JERRY

Hey, check out the TV.

TV VOICE

(GERMANIC) It's just as you prophesied. The planets of
our solar system, incinerating. Like flaming globes
Sigmund, like flaming globes. Ah, ha, ha, ha . . .

Jerry pulls the note from his pocket.

JERRY

That's it. That's it! Flaming globes of Sigmund! Flaming
Globes of Sigmund! That's my note! That's what I
thought was so funny?! . . . That's not funny . . . There's
nothing funny about that.

MAN IN OTHER BED (O.S.)

Shut up!

George pitches the ice cream carton over the curtain.

MAN IN OTHER BED (O.S.)

Ahhhgg.

FADE OUT:

END OF ACT TWO

SHOW CLOSE

STAND-UP #2

INT. COMEDY CLUB—NIGHT

> **JERRY**
>
> I have a friend who's a hypochondriac, always thinks he's sick, never is. And then you have another type of person, always thinks they're well, no matter how bad they really are. You know this type of person? Very annoying. "Feel great . . . like being on a respirator . . . intravenous heart/lung machine, I never felt better in my life." Medical science is making advances every day to control health problems. In fact, it's probably only a matter of time before a heart attack, you know, becomes like a headache. We'll just see people on TV going, "I had a heart attack this big (GESTURES BIG WITH HIS HANDS) . . . but I gave myself one of these, clear (PUTTING ELECTRODE PANELS TO CHEST) Brrhht . . . and it's gone!"

END OF EPISODE

THE Seinfeld SCRIPTS

THE
DEAL

WRITTEN BY

LARRY DAVID

DIRECTED BY

TOM CHERONES

AS BROADCAST MAY 2, 1991

SHOW OPEN

STAND-UP #1

INT. COMEDY CLUB—NIGHT

JERRY

I was watching women in the department store the other day trying on clothes and I noticed that they do it differently from men. Women don't try on the clothes, they get behind the clothes. They take a dress off the rack and they hold it up against themself. They can tell something from this. They stick one leg way out. 'Cause they need to know, "If someday I'm one-legged at a forty-five-degree angle, what am I gonna wear?" You never see a man do that. You don't see a guy take a suit off the rack, put his head in the neck and go, "What do you think about this suit, I think I'll get it . . . Yeah, it looks fine, put some shoes by the bottom of the pants, I wanta make sure. Yeah, perfect, now what if I'm walking, move the shoes, move the shoes, move the shoes, move the shoes."

ACT ONE

SCENE A

Elaine and Jerry are watching TV. Elaine controls the remote, changing stations at a furious pace.

JERRY

What are you doing? Alright, alright . . . What's a matter with that? What about that one?

ELAINE

Robert Vaughn? *The Helsinki Formula?*

JERRY

He was good in *Man from U.N.C.L.E.*

ELAINE

. . . So guess whose birthday's coming up soon?

JERRY

I know, I know. I'm having my root canal the same week.

ELAINE

Oh, right . . . I hope you got a good oral surgeon because that can be very serious. (RE: THE TV) Hey look, naked people.

JERRY

No, I don't want to look at the naked people.

ELAINE

Been awhile?

JERRY

I have a vague recollection of doing something with
someone, but it was a long, long time ago.

ELAINE

I think my last time was in Rochester, my hair was a lot
shorter.

JERRY

I remember that it's a good thing. And someday I hope
to do it again.

*Elaine looks back to the TV. Then Jerry casts a quick nonplatonic glance
at Elaine.*

ELAINE

What?

JERRY

What?

ELAINE

What was that look?

JERRY

What look?

ELAINE

The look you just gave me.

JERRY

I gave a look?

ELAINE

Yes.

JERRY

What kind of a look?

ELAINE

I know that look.

Jerry looks for an answer.

THE DEAL

ELAINE (CONT'D)

Why should I tell you?

JERRY

Well, you're the big look expert. I want to see how smart you are.

ELAINE

Trust me, I know the look.

A beat. They turn back to the TV. Then:

ELAINE (CONT'D)

So?

JERRY

What?

ELAINE

What about the look?

JERRY

I don't know.

ELAINE

. . . You got something on your mind?

JERRY

No. Things pop into your head . . . You?

ELAINE

Things occur to me from time to time.

JERRY

Yeah, me too.

They turn back to the TV. . . .

JERRY (CONT'D)

Well you can't expect to just forget the past . . . completely.

ELAINE

Well no, of course not.

JERRY

I mean it's something we did, probably about, what?
Twenty-five times?

ELAINE

Thirty-seven.

JERRY

(TURNING TO BEDROOM) Yeah, we pretty much know
what we're doing in there.

ELAINE

We know the terrain.

JERRY

No big surprises.

ELAINE

Nope.

They turn back to the TV. . . . Then:

JERRY

. . . What do you think?

ELAINE

I don't know. What do you think?

JERRY

Well . . . it's something to consider.

ELAINE

Yeah.

JERRY

I mean, let's say . . . What if we did?

ELAINE

What if?

JERRY

Is that like the end of the world or something?

ELAINE

Certainly not.

THE DEAL

JERRY

Why shouldn't we be able to do that once in a while if we want to?

ELAINE

I know.

JERRY

I mean really what is the big deal? We go in there, we're in there for a while, then we come back out here. That's not complicated.

ELAINE

It's almost stupid if we didn't.

JERRY

It's moronic.

ELAINE

Absurd.

JERRY

. . . Of course, I guess, maybe some little problems could arise.

ELAINE

Well, there's always a few.

JERRY

I mean if anything happened and we couldn't be friends the way we are now, that would really be bad.

ELAINE

Devastating.

JERRY

Because "this" is very good.

ELAINE

And "that" would be good.

JERRY

"That" would be good too. The idea is to combine the "this" and the "that." But "this" cannot be disturbed.

ELAINE

We just want to take "this" and add "that."

A beat.

JERRY

But of course, we'd have to figure out a way to avoid the things that cause the little problems. Maybe some rules or something.

ELAINE

Huh.

JERRY

For example, you see I call you whenever I'm inclined and vice versa.

ELAINE

Right.

JERRY

But if we did "that" we might feel a certain obligation to call.

ELAINE

Well why should that be? Oh! I have an idea. I have an idea. No calls the day after "that."

JERRY

Beautiful. Let's make it a rule.

ELAINE

Alright, Sir.

JERRY

And here's another rule. When we see each other now, we retire to our separate quarters. But sometimes, when people get involved with "that," they feel pressure to sleep over. When "that" is not really sleep. Sleep is separate from "that" and I don't see why sleep got all tied up and connected with "that."

ELAINE

Okay, okay, rule number two, spending the night is optional.

THE DEAL

JERRY

Well, now we're getting somewhere.

ELAINE

What about the kiss good night?

JERRY

Tough one. Your call.

ELAINE

It's bourgeois.

JERRY

Fine. Well . . .

ELAINE

Well.

JERRY

(STANDS) You ready?

ELAINE

(STANDS) Ready.

They start making their way toward the bedroom.

JERRY

So you think you can handle this?

ELAINE

Definitely.

DISSOLVE TO:

**ACT ONE
SCENE B**

INT. JERRY'S APARTMENT—NEXT MORNING

*Jerry pours some juice. We hear a knock and then a key turn. It's
Kramer.*

KRAMER

Hey.

JERRY

Hey.

KRAMER

Got the paper?

JERRY

Not yet.

KRAMER

No paper?

JERRY

I haven't been out yet.

KRAMER

Well, what's taking you so long?

Elaine enters *from the bedroom wearing nothing but a big button down shirt. Kramer looks at Elaine, looks at Jerry, computes, then starts exiting.*

KRAMER (CONT'D)

Oh . . . Yeah . . .

DISSOLVE TO:

ACT ONE
SCENE C

INT. COFFEE SHOP—DAY

Jerry and George.

GEORGE

What's the deal with Aquaman? Could he go on land or was he just restricted to water?

JERRY

I think I saw him on land a couple times.

A waitress *puts the food down and* leaves.

THE DEAL

Jerry (cont'd)

So, how's the job situation coming along?

George

Still looking. It's pretty bad out there. What about you?

Jerry

Nothing much. I slept with Elaine last night.

George, suddenly out of breath.

George

Oxygen. I need some oxygen. This is major.

Jerry

I thought you'd like that.

George

Oh, this is huge.

Jerry

I know.

George

Alright, okay, let's go. Details.

Jerry

Nah, I can't give details.

George

You what?

Jerry

I can't give details.

George

No details?

Jerry

I'm not in the mood.

George

You ask me here to have lunch, tell me you slept with Elaine and then say you're not in the mood for details? Now you listen to me, I want details, and I want them

right now. I don't have a job. I have no place to go.
You're not in the mood? Well, you get in the mood.

JERRY

Alright, okay. Well we were in my apartment, watching
TV. . .

GEORGE

Where were you sitting?

JERRY

We were on the couch.

GEORGE

Next to each other?

JERRY

No, separated.

GEORGE

Time?

JERRY

Around eleven.

GEORGE

Okay, go ahead.

JERRY

So she's flipping around the TV and she gets to the
naked station.

GEORGE

Oh, see, that's why I don't have cable in my house. The
naked station. If I had that in my house I would never
turn it off. I wouldn't sleep, I wouldn't eat. Eventually
firemen would have to break through the door, they'd
find me sitting there in my pajamas with drool coming
down my face. Alright so you're watching the naked
station . . .

JERRY

And then somehow, we started talking about what if we
had sex.

THE DEAL

GEORGE

Boy, these are really bad details.

JERRY

It pains me to say this, but I might be getting too mature for details.

GEORGE

Oh, I hate to hear this. Any kind of growth really irritates me.

JERRY

Well I'll tell you though, it was really passionate.

GEORGE

Better than before?

JERRY

She must have taken some kind of seminar or something.

GEORGE

This is all too much. So, what are you feeling? What's going on? Are you like a couple again now?

JERRY

Not exactly.

GEORGE

Not exactly? What does that mean?

JERRY

Well, we've tried to arrange a situation where we'll be able to do this once in a while, and still be friends.

George starts laughing.

JERRY (CONT'D)

What?

GEORGE

Where are you living? Are you here? Are you on this planet? It's impossible. It can't be done. Thousands of years, people have been trying to have their cake and eat it too. So, all of a sudden, the two of you are gonna come along and do it. Where do you get the ego? No one can do it. It can't be done.

JERRY

I think we've worked out a system.

GEORGE

Oh, you know what you're like? You're like a pathetic gambler. One of those losers in Las Vegas who keeps thinking he's gonna come up with a way to win at Blackjack.

JERRY

No, this is very advanced. We've designed a set of rules. That we can maintain the friendship by avoiding all the relationship pitfalls.

GEORGE

Alright, alright, tell me the rules.

JERRY

Okay . . . no calls the next day.

GEORGE

(TO HIMSELF) So you have sex, the next day you don't have to call . . . that's pretty good. Go ahead.

JERRY

You ready for the second one?

GEORGE

I have to tell you I'm very impressed with the first one.

JERRY

. . . Spending the night, optional.

GEORGE

Nah. Ya see, ya got greedy.

JERRY

No. That's the rule, it's optional.

GEORGE

I know less about women than anyone in the world, but the one thing I do know is that they are not happy if

you don't spend the night. It could be a hot, sweaty room with no air-conditioning and all they have is a little army cot this wide, you're not going anywhere.

JERRY

I think you're wrong.

GEORGE

I hope I am.

CUT TO:

ACT ONE
SCENE D

INT. ELAINE'S APARTMENT—NIGHT

Living room—kitchen. Jerry has his pants on, but is disheveled. Shirt out, etc. He is snacking at Elaine's refrigerator. Elaine emerges from bedroom just wearing a big T-shirt.

JERRY

(RE: PIECE OF CAKE) Is this yours or the roommate's?

ELAINE

The roommate's.

JERRY

Would she mind?

ELAINE

She keeps track of everything.

JERRY

Well, too bad 'cause I'm taking it.

ELAINE

Thanks.

Jerry tucks in his shirt.

JERRY

Well . . . I guess I'll get going.

ELAINE

Oh . . .

JERRY

I've got that root canal tomorrow morning, it'll be easier if I go home.

ELAINE

Fine. Go ahead.

JERRY

I don't understand. Is there a problem? . . . I'm getting the impression there's a problem.

ELAINE

Just go.

JERRY

I'm having surgery tomorrow!

ELAINE

Oh surgery, you're going to the dentist.

JERRY

But you said it could be very serious.

ELAINE

Okay, so fine, go.

JERRY

What happened to the rules? Remember sleeping over was optional?

ELAINE

Yeah, it's my house, it's my option.

JERRY

It has nothing to do with whose house it is!

ELAINE

Of course it does!

Door opens. Elaine's roommate, Tina, enters. She always arrives when you least want to see her, which is not often.

THE DEAL

TINA
Hi.

ELAINE
Hi.

TINA
Oh, hi Jerry.

JERRY
Hi.

TINA
I had such a great improv class tonight.

ELAINE
Oh really.

TINA
I did this improv where I pretended I was working in one of those booths, you know at an amusement park where you have to shoot the water in the clown's mouth and you blow up the balloon . . .

ELAINE
Uh, Tina, could you excuse us for just a second?

TINA
(HURT) Oh, yeah, I'll excuse you.

Tina exits. *Jerry starts to take his shoes off.*

ELAINE
What are you doing?

JERRY
I can't go if you're mad.

ELAINE
I'm not mad.

JERRY
You still seem a little mad.

ELAINE
No, no, Jerry, I'm fine, really. It's okay.

JERRY

. . . So you're okay with everything?

ELAINE

Definitely. Are you?

JERRY

Definitely.

Jerry goes to the door.

JERRY (CONT'D)

Well, good night.

ELAINE

Good night.

He moves to kiss her.

ELAINE

What are you doing?

JERRY

What?

ELAINE

. . . The rules.

They stand there awkwardly.

TINA (O.S.)

Hey, who took my cake?

FADE OUT:

END OF ACT ONE

ACT TWO

SCENE E

INT. GIFT SHOP—DAY

Jerry and George shopping.

GEORGE

What about jewelry? That's a nice birthday gift.

JERRY

No, no. I have to be very careful here. I don't want to send the wrong message, especially after the other night.

GEORGE

Maybe I'll get her some jewelry.

JERRY

No, no, you can't get her anything better than me. Whatever I spend, you have to spend half.

GEORGE

What am I supposed to get her, Bazooka?

JERRY

You don't understand I'm in a very delicate position. Whatever I give her, she's going to be bringing in experts from all over the country to interpret the meaning behind it.

GEORGE

What does she need? Maybe there's something that she needs.

JERRY

I think I heard her say something about a bench.

GEORGE

A bench? What kind of a bench?

JERRY

I don't know. She mentioned a bench.

GEORGE

What, like at a bus stop?

JERRY

I don't know.

GEORGE

Like a park bench?

JERRY

I have no idea.

GEORGE

Who puts a bench in their house?

JERRY

Forget the bench.

GEORGE

I got it. You want to get her something nice? What about a music box?

JERRY

No, too "relationshippy." She opens it up, she hears that Lara's theme, I'm dead.

GEORGE

Okay, then what about a nice frame with a picture of another guy in it? The frame says, "I care for you, but if you want to get serious perhaps you'd be interested in someone like this."

JERRY

Nice looking fellow.

GEORGE

What about candle holders?

JERRY

Too romantic.

GEORGE

Lingerie.

JERRY

Too sexual.

GEORGE

Waffle maker.

JERRY

Too domestic.

GEORGE

Bust of Nelson Rockefeller.

JERRY

Too gubernatorial.

GEORGE

Let's work on the card.

CUT TO:

STAND-UP #2

INT. COMEDY CLUB—NIGHT

JERRY

I had to buy a gift for someone, the hardest part to me
is that card, that card is the killer, I never know what
it's supposed to say. And, it's getting so tough 'cause the
relationships are becoming so complicated, greeting
card companies now put out cards that are blank on the
inside. Nothing. No message. I mean it's like the card
company says, "We give up, you think of something."
You know, "For seventy-five cents, I don't want to get
involved."

CUT TO:

ACT TWO
SCENE F

INT. JERRY'S APARTMENT—NIGHT

Jerry and Elaine. Elaine is opening her gift. It's in a cake-sized box.

JERRY

Maybe you won't like it.

ELAINE

Oh, how could I not like it? Of course I'll like it.

JERRY

You could not like it.

ELAINE

Just the fact that you remembered means everything.

JERRY

Of course I remembered. You reminded me every day
for two months.

Elaine laughs and hits Jerry playfully just as she takes the top off the box.

JERRY (CONT'D)
(REMEMBERING) Oh, the card.

Jerry crosses to desk. Elaine sees her gift and is speechless.

ELAINE

. . . Cash?

JERRY

What do you think?

ELAINE

You got me cash?

JERRY

Well, this way I figured you could go out and get
yourself whatever you want. No good?

ELAINE

Who are you, my uncle?

THE DEAL

JERRY

Hey, come on. It's a hundred and eighty-two dollars there. I don't think that's anything to sneeze at.

ELAINE

Let me see the card.

Jerry hands her the card. She reads it aloud.

ELAINE (CONT'D)

"To a wonderful girl, a great pal, and more."

Kramer enters.

KRAMER

Hey. (TO ELAINE) Oh, Elaine, I'm glad you're here. Stay, stay right here. I'm gonna be right back.

Kramer exits *leaving the door open.*

ELAINE

(SEETHING, BUT CONSCIOUS OF THE OPEN DOOR) "A pal," you think I'm your pal?

JERRY

I said, "and more."

ELAINE

I am not your pal.

JERRY

What's wrong with pal? Why's everybody so down on pal?

Kramer comes back *carrying a large gift.*

ELAINE

What's this?

KRAMER

Yeah!

ELAINE

You got me something?

KRAMER

Yeah. Yeah, open it.

ELAINE

Oh, Kramer . . .

She rips it open quickly. It's a hand-crafted Santa Fe style bench seat.

ELAINE (CONT'D)

A bench? You got me the bench? This is just what I
wanted.

Elaine hugs Kramer.

KRAMER

(TO JERRY) Pretty good, huh?

JERRY

Great.

KRAMER

Remember when we were standing here and she
mentioned it? I made a mental note of it.

JERRY

Well, goodie for you.

KRAMER

Oh yeah, I'm very sensitive about that. I mean
someone's birthday comes up, I keep my ears open. So,
what did you get her?

JERRY

A hundred eighty-two bucks.

KRAMER

(LAUGHING) Cash? You've gotta be kidding.
What kind of gift is that? That's like something her
uncle would give her.

Elaine reads Kramer's card aloud.

ELAINE

"Think where man's glory most begins and ends, and
say my glory was I had such a friend."

Elaine looks up at him.

THE DEAL

KRAMER

Yeats.

ELAINE

Oh Kramer.

She kisses him.

JERRY

(TO KRAMER) Could you excuse us, please?

KRAMER

What?

JERRY

We're talking.

KRAMER

Oh, the relationship.

Kramer leaves.

JERRY

. . . You know, we never had one fight before this deal.

ELAINE

I know.

JERRY

Never.

ELAINE

Ever.

JERRY

We got along beautifully.

ELAINE

Like clams.

JERRY

It was wonderful.

ELAINE

A pleasure.

JERRY

. . . So I think we should just forget the whole deal and
go back to being friends.

ELAINE

I can't do it.

JERRY

You what?

ELAINE

I can't do that.

JERRY

You mean, it's . . .

Jerry gestures, "it's over." She nods.

JERRY (CONT'D)

No "this?"

She shakes her head.

JERRY (CONT'D)

No "that?"

She shakes "no" again.

JERRY (CONT'D)

No "this" or "that"? Oh boy . . . mmhmm (A BEAT)
What do you want?

ELAINE

This, that, and the other.

JERRY

Oh sure, of course. You're entitled. Who doesn't want
this, that and the other?

ELAINE

You.

JERRY

. . . Well.

CUT TO:

THE DEAL

ACT TWO
SCENE G

INT. COFFEE SHOP—DAY

Jerry and George.

GEORGE
Oh, those birthdays, I told you they're relationship killers. If a relationship is having any problems whatsoever, a birthday will always bring it out.

JERRY
I never should have made up those rules.

GEORGE
What is it about sex that just disrupts everything? Is it the touching, is it the nudity?

JERRY
Well, it can't be the nudity. I never got into these terrible kind of fights and misunderstandings when I was changing before gym class.

GEORGE
You know, this means I can't see her anymore either.

JERRY
Why?

GEORGE
It's break-up by association . . . Besides, she's mad at me anyway because of my birthday present.

JERRY
Why, what did you wind up giving her?

GEORGE
Ninety-one dollars.

JERRY
Sorry about that.

GEORGE
So, what are you gonna do?

JERRY
Well, if I do call her there's no joking around anymore. This is pretty much it.

GEORGE

So, maybe this should be it.

JERRY

It could be it.

GEORGE

She seems like an "it."

JERRY

She's as "it" as you get. Imagine bumping into her on the street in five years with her husband and she tells me he's a sculptor, they live in Vermont.

GEORGE

We'd have to kill him.

JERRY

We'd get caught and I'd get the chair.

GEORGE

I'd go to prison as your accomplice. I'd have to wear that really heavy denim. Get on that cafeteria line and have the guy who slops those mashed potatoes on my plate . . . Go to the bathroom in front of hundreds of people.

JERRY

You know what else . . .

GEORGE

You better call her.

CUT TO:

ACT TWO
SCENE H

INT. JERRY'S APARTMENT—MORNING

Jerry is at the kitchen counter drinking a glass of juice. Kramer enters.

KRAMER

Hey.

THE DEAL

JERRY

Hey.

KRAMER

You got the papers yet?

JERRY

Yeah.

KRAMER

Well, where, where is it?

Elaine enters *from the bedroom carrying the paper.*

KRAMER (CONT'D)

Hey, you done with that?

ELAINE

No.

KRAMER

Well you're not reading it now?

ELAINE

Alright, you can take it but I want it back.

Kramer heads for door.

KRAMER

Yeah, yeah . . . So uh, what are you guys gonna do
today?

ELAINE

Oh this and that . . .

JERRY

. . . And the other.

Kramer shakes his head.

KRAMER

Well I really liked the two of you much better when
you weren't a couple.

He exits.

FADE OUT:

END OF ACT TWO

SHOW CLOSE

STAND-UP #3

INT. COMEDY CLUB—NIGHT

JERRY

Why is commitment such a big problem for a man? I
think that, for some reason, when a man is driving
down that freeway of love, the woman he's involved
with is like an exit. But he doesn't want to get out, he
want's to keep driving. And the woman is like, "Look,
gas, food, lodging, that's our exit, that's everything we
need to be happy, get out, here, now!" But the man is
focusing on the sign underneath it says, "Next exit
twenty-seven miles." And he thinks, "I can make it."

FADE OUT:

END OF EPISODE

THE SEINFELD SCRIPTS

THE
BABY
SHOWER

WRITTEN BY

LARRY CHARLES

DIRECTED BY

TOM CHERONES

AS BROADCAST MAY 16, 1991

SHOW OPEN

STAND-UP #1

INT. COMEDY CLUB—NIGHT

JERRY

Men flip around the television more than women, I think. Men get that remote control in their hands, they don't even know what the hell they're not watching. You know we just keep going, "Rerun, don't wanna watch it." "What are you watching?" "I don't care, I gotta keep going." "Who was that?" "I don't know what it was, doesn't matter, it's not your fault, it doesn't matter, I gotta keep going." Women don't do this. See now, women will stop and go, "Well let me see what the show is, before I change the channel." You see. Men just fly. Because women, you see, women nest and men hunt. That's why we watch TV differently. Before there was flipping around. Before there was television, kings and emperors and pharaohs and such had story-tellers that would tell them stories 'cause that was their entertainment. I always wonder, in that era, if they would get like thirty story-tellers together so they could still flip around. Just go, "Alright start telling me a story, what's happening? I don't want to hear anymore, shut up. Go to the next guy. What are you talking about? Is

there a girl in that story? . . . No? Shut up, go to the next guy. What do you got? I don't want to hear that either, shut up. No, go ahead, what are you talking about? . . . I don't want to hear that. No, the all of you, get out of here. I'm going to bed."

ACT ONE

SCENE A

INT. COFFEE SHOP—DAY

Jerry, George and Elaine sitting at booth.

GEORGE

(INDIGNANT, AGHAST) She's pregnant? *Leslie* is pregnant?
Oh see, there is no justice.

JERRY

She's the performance artist, right?

GEORGE

(DRIPPING WITH SARCASM) Yeah, performance artist.
She's a real performer, a real trooper.

JERRY

What's her husband's name, again? Chip? Kip? Skip?

ELAINE

Todd.

JERRY

Todd. Oh yeah. (TO GEORGE) He's a Kennedy.

ELAINE

No, he's not.

JERRY

C'mon, he's a third cousin or something.

ELAINE

By marriage.

JERRY

Oh, by marriage, yeah. (TO GEORGE) We went to their wedding. You should have heard him talking about Chappaquiddick, trying to blame the whole thing on bad directions.

GEORGE

That woman was unequivocally the worst date of my life.

ELAINE

Oh, pardon me for trying to set you up with a beautiful, intelligent woman.

GEORGE

What, you don't think I can attract beautiful, intelligent women?

JERRY

Thin ice, George. Very thin ice . . .

GEORGE

Maybe for her new performance piece she'll give birth on stage.

ELAINE

She stopped performing.

GEORGE

Oh, what a huge blow to the culture.

JERRY

You believe this guy. He holds a grudge like Khomeini.

GEORGE

She dragged me down to that warehouse on the waterfront in Brooklyn to see one of her "performances?"

JERRY

Oh, and she cooks dinner onstage for some celebrity?

GEORGE

God! She's cooking dinner for God! She's yelling and screaming, and the next thing I know, she throws a big can of chocolate syrup all over my new red shirt.

ELAINE

(EXASPERATED) It was an accident.

GEORGE

Oh, yeah, sure, accident, right. She was aiming right at me like she was putting out a fire. Then, for the rest of the show, I'm sitting there with chocolate all over my shirt. Flies are landing on me. I'm boiling. I'm fantasizing all the things I'm gonna say when I see her. And later, finally, backstage when I talk to her, I'm a little groveling worm. "What kind of chocolate was that? Do you throw any other foods?"

JERRY

(TO ELAINE) He thought he still had a shot.

GEORGE

And then, then, then she leaves with somebody else! Never even, never even said goodbye. Never called me back. Never apologized. Nothing. Like I was dirt.

JERRY

What ever happened with the shirt?

GEORGE

I still have it. The collar's okay. I wear it under sweaters.

ELAINE

I don't know what I'm gonna do. She asked me to give her a baby shower.

JERRY

Asked you? You're not going to do that are you?

ELAINE

Anyone else, never. But, Leslie, I have a problem saying no to. For some reason I seem to want her approval.

GEORGE

Let Maria Shriver give her a baby shower.

JERRY

Ask not what I can do for you. Ask what you can do for me.

GEORGE

(IN GERMAN) *Ich bin ein* sucker.

ELAINE

Oh, would you two stop with the Kennedys? Why does everybody make such a big deal about the Kennedys? What is this fascination? Who cares? It's all so boring.

GEORGE

She doesn't deserve a baby shower. She deserves a baby monsoon. She deserves Rosemary's baby!

ELAINE

(TO JERRY) I do have one teeny little problem, though.

GEORGE

Never said goodbye. Never apologized. Nothing.

ELAINE

See, I was gonna give the shower in my apartment.

JERRY

But?

ELAINE

My roommate has Lyme disease.

JERRY

Lyme disease? I thought she had Epstein-Barr Syndrome?

ELAINE

She has this in addition to Epstein-Barr. It's like Epstein-Barr with a twist of Lyme disease.

JERRY

How did she get Lyme disease?

ELAINE

I don't know. She did some outdoor version of *Hair* in Danbury, Connecticut.

JERRY

They still do that play?

ELAINE

It's a classic.

JERRY

With the nudity?

ELAINE

I guess. She must've rolled over on a tick during the love-in.

GEORGE

Never said goodbye. Goodbye!

JERRY

Explain to me how this baby shower thing works.

ELAINE

What do you wanna know?

JERRY

Well, I mean does it ever erupt into a drunken orgy of violence?

ELAINE

Rarely.

JERRY

There's no hazing of the fetus or anything, is there?

ELAINE

No.

JERRY

When is this supposed to be?

ELAINE

Saturday.

JERRY

Saturday . . . Well, I have a show in Buffalo on Saturday
. . . They're not gonna bust up my apartment or
anything, are they?

ELAINE

I'll take full responsibility. You won't regret it.

JERRY

'Cause I've seen these pregnant women. And they
sometimes misjudge their fetal girth. Just like one
wrong turn and *boom*—an entire buffet is swept off the
table.

GEORGE

Someday, before I die, mark my words, I'm gonna tell
that woman exactly what I think of her. I'll never be
able to forgive myself until I do.

JERRY

And if you do?

GEORGE

I still won't be able to forgive myself, but at least it
won't be about this.

DISSOLVE TO:

ACT ONE
SCENE B

INT. JERRY'S APARTMENT—DAY

*Close-up on TV screen. It broadcasts a completely snowy picture, with
horizontal lines, virtually unwatchable. Pull back to reveal Jerry, sitting
on his knees in front of TV adjusting dials. Kramer hovers over him.*

KRAMER

What are you doing this for? Look at you.

JERRY

Quiet. I'm trying to get a picture.

KRAMER

But you don't have to do this! The guy is waiting in my house.

JERRY

Leave me alone.

KRAMER

It's a one-time fee. A hundred and fifty bucks, why live like this?!

JERRY

I'm not getting illegal cable!

KRAMER

Oh, so what are you gonna do? You gonna wait for the cable companies to resolve their dispute? They're gonna be in court for years.

JERRY

No, I read in the paper . . .

KRAMER

Oh, oh, the paper . . .

JERRY

Well they might hook us up again.

KRAMER

Oh God, you're so naive. All the cable companies care about is the "Big Mammoo."

Jerry smacks the TV.

KRAMER (CONT'D)

(RE: THE SMACKING) Oh, look at you. You're banging on things. Pathetic. Just wasting your life. I'm offering you fifty-six channels—movies, sports, nudity. And it's free! For life!

JERRY

Stop shouting! You're ruining the reception.

THE BABY SHOWER

KRAMER

Can you hear yourself? Can, can, do you know what you're saying?

JERRY

What you're suggesting is illegal.

KRAMER

It's not illegal.

JERRY

It's against the law.

KRAMER

Well, yeah.

JERRY

(RE: RABBIT EARS) Just, just, hold this. Can you hold that?

KRAMER

(HOLDING RABBIT EARS) Look, will you at least let me bring the guy over. He's an amazing man. He's a Russian immigrant. He escaped from the Gulag. He's like the Sakharov of cable guys . . . He'll slow down your gas meter. He sells slugs, Jerry. Slugs for the subway.

JERRY

A real human rights nut, huh?

KRAMER

Yeah. He's intense, man.

JERRY

I don't know. What if I get caught?

KRAMER

Oh, you're not gonna get caught. Look, let me get him. Man, it's the nineties, it's Hammer time. Come on. Just let me get him.

Kramer drops rabbit ears. Jerry throws up his hands in exasperation. Kramer exits and returns with a Russian cable guy, Anatoly Tabachnick, and his assistant. Tabachnick mumbles, shakes, laughs. Wanders around the apartment. Jerry is confused.

JERRY

You know, why don't we wait. Because I'm going out of town tomorrow.

TABACHNICK

Tomorrow okay.

KRAMER

No problem. Yeah, you'll have the whole thing installed by the time you get back.

JERRY

(MUTTERING TO HIMSELF) Every time I turn on the TV, sirens are gonna go off. They're gonna track me down like a dog, I know it.

KRAMER

No, no, now look now, Jerry, Jerry, it's no risk. I swear. The Mets have seventy-five games on cable this year.

Jerry pauses. He is stunned. Then, with sudden resolve:

JERRY

Put it in.

KRAMER

You won't regret it.

While Jerry mutters, Kramer rubs his hands together with glee. He begins to do a shimmy with a reluctant Jerry while he chants.

KRAMER

(CHANTING) Jerry's gonna be a cable boy, a cable boy, a cable boy . . .

DISSOLVE TO:

ACT ONE
SCENE C

INT. JERRY'S APARTMENT

Jerry enters. *He is carrying his luggage.* A group of men, officious, in suits, wait for him. *Two are examining the cable, others simply look around.*

THE BABY SHOWER

> MAN

Mr. Steinfeld?

> JERRY

Seinfeld.

> MAN

We're with the FBI. You wanna tell us about your cable hook-up?

> JERRY

My cable hook-up? What about it?

> JERRY

It's been illegally installed, Mr. Steinfeld.

> JERRY

It has? I've been out of town. How did you know?

Another agent leads Kramer out of the bedroom.

> KRAMER

Jerry, I had to tell them. I had to. I had no choice. They were onto the scam from the very beginning.

> MAN

You're in very serious trouble, Mr. Steinfeld.

> JERRY

Wait a minute. Wait a minute, hold on. We're just patsies. We're just a couple of users. We never sold the stuff. What about the Russian guy? The Russian guy is the guy you want.

Tabachnick steps out of the bedroom. *He is dressed like the other FBI men. He speaks with no trace of an accent.*

> TABACHNICK

Mr. Seinfeld, Agent Stone. FBI. Undercover.

Jerry glances around, makes a mad dash for the door.

> KRAMER

No, Jerry!

Jerry is gunned down in a hailstorm of bullets. Kramer leans next to a fallen Jerry, cupping his head in his hands.

KRAMER
Cable boy, cable boy. What have you done to my little cable boy . . .

CUT TO:

ACT ONE
SCENE D

INT. AIRPLANE

Jerry shudders. A stewardess approaches.

JERRY
Excuse me. Can I get something to drink?

STEWARDESS
I'm afraid not.

JERRY
What's with this airline? What are you, cutting out the drinks now?

STEWARDESS
No, sir. We're flying into a blizzard. Please fasten your seat belt. We're making an emergency landing.

JERRY
Are they gonna go over the instructions again?

We pull back to see the passenger sitting next to Jerry. Passenger offers his hand.

PASSENGER
My name is Bill. I might be the last person you ever see.

FADE OUT:

THE BABY SHOWER

STAND-UP #2

Int. COMEDY CLUB—NIGHT

JERRY

I'm not afraid of flying, although many people do have
fear of flying and, I have no argument with that. I think
fear of flying is quite rational because, human beings
cannot fly. Humans have fear of flying same way fish
have fear of driving. Put a fish behind the wheel and
they go, "This isn't right. I shouldn't be doing this. I
don't belong here."

END OF ACT ONE

ACT TWO

SCENE E

INT. GEORGE'S CAR—NIGHT

George drives. He wears an unzipped coat, and a sweater revealing a bright red collar. Jerry is in the passenger seat.

GEORGE

Sounds like a rough trip.

JERRY

Oh, fire engines, ambulances all along the runway. And then when we landed safely, they all seemed so disappointed.

GEORGE

So the college cancelled the gig?

JERRY

Well, there was so much snow, the roads were closed. I really appreciate it you picking me up. Thanks again.

GEORGE

(MODESTLY) Forget it.

JERRY

No, really . . . an airport run.

GEORGE

It's nothing.

JERRY

Hey, it's one thing if I asked you, "Could you do me a favor?" . . . but to suggest it . . .

GEORGE

When you told me what you went through on the plane, it makes you stop and think. You appreciate having a real friend.

JERRY

(KIDDINGLY) You know, if Richie Brandes did this, I'd be suspicious. You know how he's always got some ulterior motive?

GEORGE

(LAUGHING NERVOUSLY) . . . Ulterior motive.

JERRY

Oh, wait a minute. Wait a minute. Don't take the bridge. Get off here. We can't go back to my place. Elaine's having the shower.

GEORGE

What, tonight? Now?

JERRY

Yeah, yeah. I forgot all about it. Alright. It's no big deal. We'll just go back to your place.

GEORGE

My place? No, no, no. I hate my place. I don't wanna go back to my place.

JERRY

You want to get a bite?

GEORGE

Yeah, I would, it's just, you know I just ate a whole pot roast.

JERRY

Well, so what should we do?

GEORGE

Shouldn't we at least drop off your bag?

Suddenly Jerry zeroes in on George's shirt collar, then reaches over and yanks the sweater down.

JERRY

Red shirt! Red shirt! That's the red shirt.

GEORGE

What are talking about?

JERRY

You're wearing the chocolate shirt.

GEORGE

I am? What a strange coincidence.

JERRY

A-ha! Nice try my friend. But you gotta get up pretty early in the morning.

GEORGE

You gotta let me go over there.

JERRY

What are you gonna do, badger a pregnant woman at her own baby shower?! What are you gonna take it off and make her rinse it in club soda?

GEORGE

No, I'm gonna hold it under her nose so she can smell the scent of stale Bosco that I had to live with for three years and I'm gonna say, "Remember this shirt, baby? Well, now, it's payback time!"

CUT TO:

**ACT TWO
SCENE F**

INT. JERRY'S APARTMENT

Leslie is talking to a group of girls, including Elaine.

LESLIE

We just bought an apartment on Riverside Drive. Bernard Goetz's mother used to live there.

ELAINE

So, where's Todd?

LESLIE

Up in Hyannisport.

ELAINE

Oh my God, Hyannisport? With the Kennedys? Who
else is up there? Is Rose up there?

WOMAN

So, when's your due date?

LESLIE

March twentieth, nine a.m.

WOMAN

You know the time!

LESLIE

I'm having a planned C-section. My therapist told me if
I go through labor, I might get psychotic.

The girls mull this over.

ELAINE

Leslie, Leslie, whatever happened to Sargent Shriver? Is
he still with them? You don't hear much about him
these days. Is he out of the loop?

Leslie takes a bite of food.

LESLIE

Elaine, who catered this, Sears?

*Suddenly, the door opens. Kramer, Tabachnick and his assistant
enter. Tabachnick looks over this bevy of women and nods approvingly.
The women stop dead in their tracks, then nervously, disperse.*

ELAINE

(TO KRAMER) What is this? What are you doing here?

KRAMER

We're putting in the cable.

ELAINE

The cable? No, no, no. I'm having a party here. You can't do this now.

KRAMER

Oh, we have to do this now.

Tabachnick and assistant are leering at the "American chicks."

ELAINE

Who's this guy?

KRAMER

Which one?

ELAINE

Both of them.

KRAMER

Oh, they're Soviet cable guys.

ELAINE

Okay . . . Does Jerry know about this?

KRAMER

Oh yeah . . . it's all authorized, yeah.

ELAINE

You can't. You can't do this, now.

KRAMER

Elaine, do you know how booked up this guy is? Now, if I send him away now it's gonna take Jerry months to get him back . . . He won't like that.

ELAINE

Alright. Just do it fast and then get out.

Kramer snaps his finger, crisply giving the order.

KRAMER

Anatoly! (TO ELAINE) Look, it's only gonna take a few minutes. Then, you and the gals can take a load off and watch something on Lifetime.

CUT TO:

THE BABY SHOWER

ACT TWO
SCENE G

INT. GEORGE'S CAR—NIGHT

> **JERRY**
>
> And what if we go up there? What are you going to say to her?

> **GEORGE**
>
> (HEATING UP) What am I going to say?

> **JERRY**
>
> Yeah.

> **GEORGE**
>
> What did you go out with me for? Just to dump chocolate on my shirt and then just dump me altogether?! I don't deserve that kind of treatment! What, you don't have the common courtesy to return my calls! To apologize! You think I'm some sort of a loser, that likes to be abused and ignored! Whose shirt can be ruined without financial restitution?! Some sort of a masochist who enjoys being humiliated. You think you can just avoid me like I have some sort of a disease! You have the disease! You have the disease! You may be beautiful and rich and physically . . . just . . . unbeliev-able . . . but you sicken me, you disgust me, you and everyone like you.

> **JERRY**
>
> You'll never say that to her face.

> **GEORGE**
>
> Watch me.

CUT TO:

ACT TWO
SCENE H

INT. JERRY'S APARTMENT—NIGHT

Kramer is flirting with a female guest.

> **KRAMER**
> Yeah, I eat the whole apple. The core, stem, seeds,
> everything.

> **ELAINE**
> (TO KRAMER RE: TABACHNICK) Kramer, Kramer, look at
> him. Look. He's eating all the food.

> **KRAMER**
> Yeah, yeah. Well, you know, there are many differences
> between American and Soviet cultures that you're not
> aware of. See, in Russia, the cable guy, they got the
> whole run of the house. Yeah, that's tradition.

Kramer turns back to the woman. The TV sound is turned off.

> **KRAMER (CONT'D)**
> Did you ever eat the bark of a pineapple?

*Tabachnick and assistant start arguing in front of TV. It escalates into
stiff-arm choke holds.*

> **ELAINE**
> Kramer!

Kramer sees the fight in progress.

> **KRAMER**
> Uh . . . excuse me.

*As women watch, horrified, Kramer breaks it up. Tabachnick then walks
to bathroom while assistant returns to work. Kramer returns to woman
with whom he was flirting. Tabachnick at bathroom door. Banging on it
and shouting in Russian. Woman finally opens it. She can barely get out
as he pushes his way in and slams door shut. Jerry enters with George
behind him. Elaine immediately confronts him.*

THE BABY SHOWER

ELAINE

What are you doing here? I thought you were out of
town for the weekend.

JERRY

The show was cancelled. There was a blizzard.

ELAINE

I can't believe you told Kramer it's okay to put the cable
in during the shower, Jerry. Look, look, they've eaten
everything.

Leslie approaches.

LESLIE

Jerry, what a surprise. I thought you were out of town.

JERRY

Well Leslie, sometimes the road less travelled is less
travelled for a reason.

Elaine heads for George:

ELAINE

(TO GEORGE) George, don't even think about it. Don't
even dream about it.

GEORGE

(UNCONVINCINGLY) About what?

Tabachnick sticks head out of bathroom.

TABACHNICK

Kramer, Kramer, Kramer.

*Kramer rushes over. Kramer quickly closes the door and he and
Tabachnick slink away. Tabachnick is joined by assistant at the food
table. They begin eating again. George is ready. He takes his sweater off
and heads for Leslie by the dessert table. Leslie is eating a large chunk of
chocolate cake. George approaches her.*

GEORGE

Leslie.

LESLIE

Yeah.

GEORGE

George . . . George Costanza.

LESLIE

Hi.

GEORGE

(LAUGHS) You I guess you don't remember me . . . but
we actually, kind of um . . . went out . . . a couple of
years ago . . . once . . . Remember?

LESLIE

Vaguely.

GEORGE

You took me to one of your shows . . .

LESLIE

And?

GEORGE

And, um it was quite good. In fact, you even
incorporated me into the show. I'm not actually a
performer. Although, my parents felt I had talent . . .

Suddenly we hear off camera:

MARY

Jerry?!

*Angle—a woman, with vengeance in her eyes, approaches Jerry. Jerry
looks at her puzzled. Slowly, all attention is focused on this exchange.*

MARY

Remember me?

JERRY

I'm sorry. I . . .

MARY

(LIVID) Mary Contardi. No? Doesn't ring a bell, Jerry?
We had a date, three years ago. You took me to one of
your shows.

JERRY

(STAMMERING) Oh, I, I, think I remember.

THE BABY SHOWER

MARY

Told me you had a great time! Said you'd call me the next day.

JERRY

Well, I'm sure I meant to call. I probably just lost your . . .

MARY

Liar! Liar! You were never going to call me! You thought you could waltz through the rest of your life and never bump into me again! But you were wrong, Jerry! You were wrong! What do you think, I'm some sort of poor, pathetic wretch?

JERRY

No I don't think that . . .

MARY

Some person who could be dismissed and ignored?! Some insignificant piece of dust?! Some person who doesn't deserve your respect and your attention?! You're the one that doesn't deserve my respect and my attention! You're the insignificant piece of dust!

She feigns spitting on the floor and storms away. Angle—George and Leslie. She's bored to tears.

GEORGE

Actually, I never had any formal training. I guess I'd be better suited for improvs, or something . . .

Mary, in a mad rush for the door, shoves Leslie into George, depositing her chocolate cake on his shirt. It's a bullseye.

LESLIE

Thanks a lot.

Angle—front door—a few women begin filing out saying goodbyes to a dejected Elaine at the door.

ELAINE

I'm sorry you have to go.

WOMAN #1

Yeah. I really have to be going.

Angle—Jerry, spotting Tabachnick, assistant and Kramer by the TV, crosses to them.

JERRY

Alright listen, I've changed my mind about this whole thing. I don't want the cable.

KRAMER

Jerry, don't be a fool.

TABACHNICK

You don't want?

JERRY

No, I don't want. So just tell me what I owe you for your trouble . . .

Tabachnick confers with assistant in Russian, then:

TABACHNICK

Four hundred dollars.

JERRY

(TO KRAMER) Four hundred dollars? You told me one-fifty.

Angle—front door—Elaine is still by the door. Leslie has her coat on, about to leave.

LESLIE

I'm going . . . obviously.

ELAINE

Oh, Leslie, I am so sorry about everything that went on here tonight. You know, I had no idea . . .

LESLIE

Elaine, you know, I was watching you tonight and I realized something. You're just like you were in college.

ELAINE

Oh, thank you.

Leslie leaves.

THE BABY SHOWER

ELAINE (CONT'D)

(TO HERSELF, TOTALLY CONFUSED) "Like you were in college"?

Leslie reenters, *calls out to bedroom:*

LESLIE

Come on! Let's go!

George emerges from bedroom, *carrying gifts, obviously embarrassed.*

GEORGE

(SHEEPISHLY, TO ELAINE) I'll be right back.

George exits. *Back to: Jerry, Tabachnick and Kramer.*

JERRY

(DEFIANTLY) I'm not paying four hundred dollars. I don't even want the thing. What are you going to do?

CUT TO:

**ACT TWO
SCENE J**

INT. JERRY'S APARTMENT—LATER

Close-up of TV screen. The screen is cracked, creating a spider-webbed fissure. The set is on, but merely makes some unrecognizable electronic noise. Pull back to reveal: Jerry, George and Elaine slumped on chairs—staring at the TV.

GEORGE

Every woman on the face of the earth has complete control of my life. And yet I want them all . . . Is that irony?

ELAINE

Why can't I meet a Kennedy? . . . I saw John Junior once

downtown. I was on a bus. I hit the ding but . . . it didn't stop.

JERRY

Alright, I said I had a good time and I'd call, but who takes that literally?

Kramer enters and sticks his head in the door.

KRAMER

Hey, come on over, *Dr. Zhivago*'s on cable in five minutes . . . I'm making popcorn.

Kramer leaves. *On their reaction:*

FADE OUT:

END OF ACT TWO

SHOW CLOSE

STAND-UP #3

INT. COMEDY CLUB—NIGHT

JERRY

What do you do at the end of a date when you know you don't want to see this person ever again, for the rest of your life? What do you say? What do you say? No matter what you say, it's a lie. "I'll see you around. See you around. If you're around, and I'm around, I'll see you around that area. You'll be around other people. You won't be around me. But you will be around." "Take care now." Did you ever say that to somebody? "Take care now. Take care, now. Because I'm not going to be taking care of you. So you should take care, now." "Take care, take care." What does that mean? "Take off!" Isn't that what you really want to say, "Take off now."

FADE OUT:

END OF EPISODE

THE Seinfeld SCRIPTS

THE
CHINESE
RESTAURANT

WRITTEN BY
LARRY DAVID & JERRY SEINFELD

DIRECTED BY
TOM CHERONES

AS BROADCAST MAY 23, 1991

SHOW OPEN

STAND UP #1

INT. COMEDY CLUB—NIGHT

JERRY

I'm on the street the other day, make a pay phone call,
go overtime on the call, hang up the phone, walk away.
You've had this happen? Phone rings. It's the phone
company, they want more money. Don't you love this?
And you've got them right where you want them for
the first time in your life. You're on the street, there's
nothing they can do. I like to let it ring a few times, you
know, let her sweat a little over there. And then just
pick it up, "Yeah, hello operator . . . oh, I've got the
money . . . I've got the money right here, you hear that
(TAPS "PHONE"), that's a quarter . . . yeah, you want that
don't ya?"

ACT ONE

SCENE A

INT. CHINESE RESTAURANT—NIGHT

Dinnertime, a crowded Sunday night. Jerry, George and Elaine enter. *They are in the middle of a conversation. They wait to be seated.*

ELAINE
No, they just have to get more cops on the force. It's as simple as that.

GEORGE
Cops. I don't even care about cops. I wanna see garbagemen. It's much more important. All I wanna see are garbage trucks, garbage cans and garbagemen. You're never gonna stop crime. We should at least be clean.

JERRY
I tell ya what they should do, they should combine the two jobs. Make it one job, cop slash garbageman. I always see cops walking around with nothing to do. Grab a broom. Start sweeping. You sweep sweep sweep sweep, catch a criminal, get right back to sweeping.

ELAINE
You should run for mayor.

JERRY

Ah, nobody listens.

ELAINE

Where is someone? I'm starving.

GEORGE

This is him, right here.

The host, Bruce, appears at the podium. He's Chinese, speaks with an accent, mid forties.

ELAINE

Is there a table ready?

BRUCE

How many?

ELAINE

(TO THEM) How many?

JERRY

(TO GEORGE) Is Tatiana coming?

GEORGE

I don't know. I have to call her, tell her where we are. I'm very lucky that she's even considering seeing me at all.

JERRY

Really? I thought things were going okay.

GEORGE

They were . . . It's kind of complicated.

JERRY

What is it?

George indicates he can't talk now.

ELAINE

How many?

JERRY

Alright . . . Four, Seinfeld.

Bruce looks at a list.

THE CHINESE RESTAURANT

BRUCE

Four. Oh, be five, ten minutes.

GEORGE

What do you want to do?

ELAINE

Let's go someplace else. I'm too hungry.

JERRY

We might as well just stay here. We haven't got that much time, if we're gonna make the movie.

GEORGE

I'm gonna call Tatiana. Where's the phone?

George moves away.

JERRY

Tatiana.

The phone is directly across from them. A well-heeled man is talking on it. He's pure GQ in the most obnoxious way.

GEORGE

Excuse me, are you going to be very long?

The man looks back at him without giving him any information . . .

BRUCE

(CALLING OUT) Lashbrook, four.

The Lashbrook's get up.

JERRY

So, did I do a terrible thing?

ELAINE

You mean lying to your uncle?

JERRY

I couldn't have dinner with him. *Plan Nine from Outer Space,* one night only, the big screen—my hands are tied.

George returns, still looking at the man on the phone.

GEORGE

(TO JERRY AND ELAINE) You know, it's a public phone. You're not supposed to just chit chat.

ELAINE

Jerry, get menus so when we sit down we'll be able to order right away.

JERRY

Can't look at a menu now. I gotta be at the table.

GEORGE

He knows I'm waiting. He sees me. He doesn't want to look.

ELAINE

(TO JERRY) Everything's gotta be just so all the time with you, doesn't it?

JERRY

I offered you those cookies in my house.

ELAINE

Health cookies. I hate those little dustboard fructose things.

GEORGE

I just can't believe the way people are. What is it with humanity? What kind of world do we live in?

Jerry's eyes suddenly lock on a woman at a table.

ELAINE

What?

JERRY

There's a woman over there who looks really familiar. Dark hair, striped shirt.

ELAINE

(TURNS BACK) I've never seen her before.

JERRY

I know this woman. This is gonna drive me crazy.

A party of four comes up behind and accidentally bumps into Elaine.

THE CHINESE RESTAURANT

MAN
Excuse me.

ELAINE
Oh, I'm sorry.

They walk past Jerry, Elaine and George right to the host. They're immediately escorted to a table.

ELAINE (CONT'D)
Did you see that?! Those people, look, they're getting a table.

JERRY
Well maybe they were here from before.

ELAINE
No, no, no, they weren't here before.

GEORGE
(TO PHONE MAN, WHOSE BACK IS TO GEORGE) Excuse me, are you gonna be much longer? I have to make a very important call.

The phone man looks at George uncomprehendingly and returns to his conversation.

ELAINE
(TO JERRY) Find out what's going on.

Elaine and Jerry approach Bruce.

JERRY
Excuse me, didn't those people just come in? I believe we were ahead of them.

BRUCE
What's your name?

JERRY
Seinfeld.

He looks at his list and then turns to his wife and starts talking to her in Chinese. After a fairly long exchange varying in tone with Elaine hanging on every incomprehensible word, the host finally turns to them:

BRUCE

No, no, they were here before. (CALLING OUT) Kekich, two?

Kekiches come from behind.

ELAINE

You ever notice how happy people are when they finally get a table? They feel so special that because they've been chosen. It's enough to make you sick.

JERRY

Boy, you are really hungry . . .

George is still locked on the phone guy . . .

GEORGE

(WHISTLES) Hey!

The man turns, looks at George and continues talking.

GEORGE (CONT'D)

(TO JERRY) Hey, if anything happens here can I count on you?

JERRY

What?

GEORGE

If we decide to go at it.

JERRY

Yeah, I want to get into a rumble.

GEORGE

I have to get in touch with Tatiana.

GEORGE

(RE: THE MAN) Look at his little outfit. It's all so coordinated. (UTTER CONTEMPT) The little socks match the little shirt . . . I really hate this guy.

ELAINE

I'm gonna faint.

JERRY

George, who is that woman in the stripes?

GEORGE

I don't know her.

JERRY

She looks so familiar.

ELAINE

It's not fair that people are seated first come, first served. It should be based on who's hungriest. I feel like just walking over there and taking some food off somebody's plate.

JERRY

I'll tell you what—there's fifty bucks in it for you if you do it.

ELAINE

What do you mean?

JERRY

You walk over to that table, you pick up an egg roll, you don't say anything, you eat it, say "Thank you very much," wipe your mouth, walk away. I'll give you fifty bucks.

GEORGE

What are they gonna do?

JERRY

They won't do anything, in fact you'll be giving them a story to tell for the rest of their lives.

Elaine's toying with the idea.

ELAINE

Fifty bucks? You'll give me fifty bucks?

JERRY

Fifty bucks . . . that table over there, the three couples.

ELAINE

Okay, I don't want to go over there and do it and then

come back here and find out there was some little
loophole like I didn't put mustard on it, or something.

JERRY

No, no tricks.

ELAINE

Should I do it, George?

GEORGE

For fifty bucks? I'll put my face in their soup and blow.

ELAINE

Alright . . . alright. Here, hold this. I'm doing it.

*She steels herself as she prepares to defy a social law, millions of years
old—private ownership of food. She approaches the table. There are three
elderly couples. She talks like a ventriloquist trying not to move her lips.*

ELAINE (CONT'D)

(SMILING, WITHOUT MOVING LIPS) I know this sounds
crazy, but the two men who are standing behind me are
going to give me fifty bucks if I stand here and eat one
of your egg rolls. I'll give you twenty-five if you let me
do it.

ELDERLY COUPLES

(RANDOMLY AND OVERLAPPING) What? What are you
talking about? Egg roll? What is it? Who is she? What
did she say?

*Elaine totally caves in, does an about face and slinks back. Jerry and
George are laughing and applauding.*

JERRY

Well, what happened?

ELAINE

(ALSO HYSTERICAL) Did you see that?

GEORGE

What were you telling them?

THE CHINESE RESTAURANT

ELAINE

I offered them twenty-five (BREAKS UP LAUGHING) They
had no idea . . . (BREAKS UP AGAIN)

Now the man gets off the phone.

JERRY

George, the phone's free.

GEORGE

Hallelujah.

*Jerry notices George rubbing leg as he walks to the phone. But a woman
beats him to the phone by the thinnest of margins.*

GEORGE (CONT'D)

Excuse me, I was waiting here.

WOMAN

Where? I didn't see you.

GEORGE

I've been standing here for ten minutes.

WOMAN

Well, I won't be long.

GEORGE

Uh, that's not the point. The point is I was here first.

WOMAN

Well, if you were here first, you'd be holding the phone.

She puts her quarter in and ignores him completely. She starts to dial.

GEORGE (CONT'D)

You know, we're living in a society! We're supposed to
act in a civilized way . . .

George returns to Jerry and Elaine.

GEORGE (CONT'D)

Does she care? . . . No. Does anyone ever display the
slightest sensitivity over the problems of a fellow
individual? No, no, a resounding no!

Right on cue, he's stopped by the first phone guy who's on his way out.

PHONE GUY

Hey, sorry I took so long.

GEORGE

(COMPLETE ABOUT FACE) Oh, that's okay, really don't worry about it.

Phone guy leaves.

ELAINE

How do people fast? Did Gandhi get this crazy? I'm gonna go walk around and see what dishes look good.

She leaves.

JERRY

I told my uncle I had a stomachache tonight. You think he bought that?

GEORGE

Yeah, he probably bought it.

JERRY

So what happened with Tatiana?

GEORGE

I shouldn't even tell you.

JERRY

Come on.

GEORGE

Well, after dinner last week she invites me back to her apartment . . .

JERRY

I'm with ya.

GEORGE

Well, it's this little place with this little bathroom . . . it's like right there. It's not even down a little hall, or off in an alcove, you understand? There's no . . . buffer zone. So we start to fool around and it's the first time and it's early in the going and I begin to perceive this impending intestinal requirement, whose needs are going to

surpass by great lengths anything in the sexual realm.
So I know I'm gonna have to stop. And as this is
happening I'm thinking even if I can somehow manage
to momentarily extricate myself from the proceedings
and relieve this unstoppable force, I know that
bathroom is not going to provide me with the privacy
that I know I'm going to need . . .

JERRY

This could only happen to you.

GEORGE

So I finally stop—and say—"Tatiana, I hope you don't
take this the wrong way, but I think it would be best if
I left."

JERRY

You said this to her . . . after?

GEORGE

(SHAKES HIS HEAD) No . . . during.

JERRY

Oh boy.

GEORGE

Yah.

JERRY

Wow, so?

GEORGE

(GEORGE TAKES A DEEP BREATH) So I'm dressing, and
she's staring up at me struggling to compute this
unprecedented turn of events. I don't know what to say
to reassure this woman and worst of all, I don't even
have the time to say it. The only excuse she might
possibly have accepted is if I told her that I am in reality
Batman, and I'm very sorry, I just saw the Batsignal. It
took me three days of phone calls to get her to agree to
see me again. And now she's waiting for me to call. (RE:
WOMAN ON PHONE) And she's still on the phone.

Elaine returns.

ELAINE

I hate this place. I don't know why we came here. I'm
never coming back here again.

JERRY

Who is that woman?

ELAINE

(WISTFULLY) Remember when you first went out to eat
with your parents? Remember . . . It was such a special
treat, you go and they serve you this different food that
you never saw before and they put it in front of you and
it was such a delicious and exciting adventure. And now,
I just feel like a big sweaty hog waiting for them to fill
up the trough.

GEORGE

(RE: WOMAN ON PHONE) Oh she's off.

George moves to the phone.

ELAINE

Jerry, talk to that guy again.

JERRY

What am I going to say?

ELAINE

Tell him we want to catch a movie, that we're late.

*Mr. Cohen—a fortyish, garrulous, expansive country club type
approaches the podium.*

MR. COHEN

Hey, what stinks in here?

BRUCE

(BRIGHTENING) Ah, Mr. Cohen! Haven't seen you
couple weeks.

MR. COHEN

I've been looking for a better place.

Host howls at this remark.

THE CHINESE RESTAURANT

BRUCE

You want table?

MR. COHEN

No, just bring me a plate and I'll eat here.

BRUCE

(LAUGHING) Bring him a plate, he'll eat here. Come on, I'll get you a table.

Bruce seats Mr. Cohen. Jerry and Elaine approach Bruce again.

JERRY

(TO OWNER) Excuse me, we've been waiting here, now I know we were ahead of that guy, he just came in.

BRUCE

Oh no, Mr. Cohen always here.

ELAINE

He's always here? (TO JERRY) What does that mean? (TO HOST) What does that mean?

BRUCE

Oh Mr. Cohen, very nice man. He live on Park Avenue.

Bruce walks away.

ELAINE

Where am I? Is this a dream? What in God's name is going on here?

George returns stricken.

GEORGE

She's not there. She left. She must have waited and left, because those people wouldn't get off the phone.

JERRY

Did you leave a message?

GEORGE

Yeah, I told her to call me here and to tell anyone who answers to ask for a balding, stocky man with glasses. I'd better tell them I'm expecting a call.

George leaves.

ELAINE

Jerry, here comes that woman.

JERRY

Where do I know her?

The woman (Lorraine) approaches *and looks at Jerry with a glimmer of recognition. She's attractive, 40ish woman.*

LORRAINE

Hi, Jerry.

JERRY

(HAS NO IDEA WHO SHE IS) Hey! How you doing?

LORRAINE

How is everything?

JERRY

Good. Good. Good. What's going on? . . .

LORRAINE

Working hard. And you?

JERRY

(FLOUNDERING) Oh, you know, working around, same stuff, doing, whatever . . .

LORRAINE

You haven't been around in a while.

JERRY

I know. I know. Well, you know.

LORRAINE

You should come by.

JERRY

Definitely, I plan to. I'm not just saying that.

Elaine sticks her hand out.

ELAINE

Hi, I'm Elaine.

LORRAINE

Lorraine Catalano.

THE CHINESE RESTAURANT

JERRY

Oh, I'm sorry. Lorraine this is Elaine.

They ad-lib hellos, then:

LORRAINE

Well, it was nice seeing you Jerry. (TO ELAINE) Nice
meeting you.

ELAINE

Oh, nice to meet you too, Lorraine.

She exits. Suddenly, Jerry remembers:

JERRY

Oh my God, Lorraine! That's Lorraine from my uncle's
office . . . I am in big, big trouble.

ELAINE

The one you broke the plans with tonight?

JERRY

Yeah. She works in his office. Now she's going to see
him tomorrow and tell him she saw me here tonight.
He's going to tell his wife. His wife's going to call my
mother. Oh this is bad. You don't know the chain
reaction of calls this is going to set off. New York, Long
Island, Florida . . . it's like the Bermuda Triangle,
unfortunately nobody ever disappears. My uncle to my
aunt, my aunt to my mother, my mother to my
uncle . . .

FADE OUT:

END OF ACT ONE

ACT TWO

SCENE B

INT. CHINESE RESTAURANT—NIGHT

JERRY

. . . My uncle to my cousin, my cousin to my sister, then my sister to me.

ELAINE

You just should've had dinner with your uncle tonight and gotten it over with. It's just a movie.

JERRY

Just a movie? You don't understand, this isn't plans one through eight from outer space. This is plan nine. This is the one that worked. The worst movie ever made.

ELAINE

I'm looking forward to it.

JERRY

(LOOKING AT HIS WATCH) Hey, I got news for you. If we're making this movie, we gotta get a table immediately.

ELAINE

Alright lookit, let's stop fooling around. Let's just slip him some money.

JERRY

In a Chinese restaurant? Do they take money?

ELAINE

(MOCKING) Do they take money? Everyone takes money. I used to go out with a guy who did it all the time. You just slip him twenty bucks.

GEORGE

Twenty bucks? Isn't that excessive?

ELAINE

What do you want to give him, change?

GEORGE

It's more than the meal.

JERRY

Oh, come on, we'll divide it up three ways.

GEORGE

(POINTING TO THEM) Alright, seven, seven, (TO HIMSELF) six. (OFF THEIR LOOK) I'm not going to eat that much.

JERRY

I'm counting your shrimps . . . Okay who's gonna do it?

GEORGE

Oh no, I can't do it. I'm not good at these things. I get all flustered. Once I tried to bribe an usher at the roller derby. I almost got arrested.

ELAINE

I guess it's you, Jer.

JERRY

Me? What about you?

ELAINE

Oh, I can't do that . . . It's a guy thing.

JERRY

The women's movement just can't seem to make any progress in the world of bribery, can they?

ELAINE

. . .Give me the money.

Jerry hands Elaine the money. Elaine coughs, wets her lips—approaches the host. She clenches the money in her fist, and stands in front of him for a moment nodding uncomfortably.

ELAINE (CONT'D)

How's it going?

BRUCE

Very busy.

A beat, then:

ELAINE

Boy we are really anxious to sit down.

BRUCE

Very good specials tonight.

Now she reveals the money.

ELAINE

If there's anything you can do to get us a table, we'd really appreciate it . . .

BRUCE

(OBLIVIOUS) What is your name?

ELAINE

(MORE URGENTLY) No, no. I want to eat now!

BRUCE

Whole Sea Bass dinner tonight, very fresh.

ELAINE

(ALMOST SCREAMING) Here, take this. I'm starving! Take it. Take it.

Bruce seems puzzled for a moment, then takes the money.

BRUCE

(CALLING OUT) Dennison, four. Your table is ready.

ELAINE

No, no, I want that table! I want that table.

THE CHINESE RESTAURANT

He leaves followed by the Dennisons. Elaine looks at the Dennisons, then looks at her hand in disbelief. Defeated, she heads back . . .

ELAINE

Oh come on, did you see that? What was that? He took the money! He didn't give us the table!

JERRY

You lost the twenty?

ELAINE

Well . . . how could he do that?

GEORGE

You didn't make it clear.

ELAINE

Make it clear?!

JERRY

What a sorry exhibition that was. Alright, let me get the money back.

Jerry goes to host's station.

JERRY (CONT'D)

Excuse me, I realize this is extremely embarrassing, my friend here apparently made a mistake.

BRUCE

Your name?

JERRY

Seinfeld.

BRUCE

(CHECKING HIS LIST) Yeah, Seinfeld, four.

JERRY

No, no, no, do you see the girl over there with the long hair?

BRUCE

(ACKNOWLEDGING ELAINE) Oh, yes, yes, very beautiful girl, very beautiful. Your girlfriend?

JERRY

Well, actually we did date for a while but that's really not relevant here.

BRUCE

Oh, relationships are very difficult. It is very hard to stay together.

JERRY

Alright listen, how much longer is it gonna be?

BRUCE

(LOOKING AT LIST) Oh, about five, ten minutes.

Jerry heads back to George and Elaine.

GEORGE

So?

JERRY

There seems to be a bit of a discrepancy.

ELAINE

So when are we going to eat?

JERRY

Five, ten minutes.

GEORGE

(TO JERRY ACCUSINGLY) We should've left earlier. I told you!

JERRY

I don't see any way we can eat and make this movie.

ELAINE

I have to eat!

JERRY

Well let's just order it to go and we'll eat it in the cab.

ELAINE

Eat in the cab? Chinese food in a cab?

JERRY

We'll eat it in the movie.

THE CHINESE RESTAURANT

ELAINE

Where do you think you're going? Do you think they have big picnic tables there?

JERRY

Well what do you suggest?

ELAINE

I say we leave now, we go to Skyburger and we scarf 'em down . . .

JERRY

I'm not going to Skyburger. Besides, it's in the opposite direction. Let's just eat popcorn or something.

BRUCE

(CALLING OUT) Cartwright.

ELAINE

(A BEAT, THEN PICKING RIGHT UP) I can't have popcorn for dinner.

BRUCE

Cartwright.

ELAINE

I have to eat!

JERRY

They have hot dogs there.

ELAINE

Oh movie hot dogs. I'd rather lick the food off the floor.

GEORGE

I can't go anyway. I have to wait for Tatiana's call. Let me just check.

George approaches the podium.

GEORGE (CONT'D)

Excuse me, I'm expecting a call . . . Costanza.

BRUCE

Yes. I just got a call. I yell Cartwright, Cartwright. Just like that. Nobody came up, I hang up.

GEORGE

Was it for Costanza or . . .

BRUCE

Yes, yes, that's it! Nobody answer.

GEORGE

Was it a woman?

BRUCE

Yes, yes, I tell her you not here, she said curse word, I
hang up.

The slowest of burns. He walks back to Jerry and Elaine.

GEORGE

(ALMOST INAUDIBLE) She called . . . he yelled
"Cartwright" . . . I missed it.

JERRY

Who's Cartwright?

GEORGE

I'm Cartwright . . .

JERRY

You're not Cartwright.

GEORGE

(EXPLODING) Of course I'm not Cartwright . . . Look
why don't you two just go to the movies by yourself.
I'm not in the mood.

ELAINE

Me either, I'm going to Skyburger.

JERRY

So you're not going?

ELAINE

You don't need us.

JERRY

I can't go to a bad movie by myself. What am I, gonna
make sarcastic remarks to strangers? I guess I'll just go
to my uncle's.

THE CHINESE RESTAURANT

GEORGE

Should we tell him we're leaving?

ELAINE

What for? Let's just get out of here.

They leave, *then:*

BRUCE

Seinfeld, four.

FADE OUT:

END OF ACT TWO

SHOW CLOSE

STAND-UP #2

INT. COMEDY CLUB—NIGHT

JERRY

Hunger will make people do amazing things. I mean the proof of that is cannibalism. Cannibalism? What do they say? I mean, they're eating, "This is good, who is this? I like this person." You know, I mean, I really think the hardest thing about being a cannibal is trying to get some really deep sleep. You know what I mean? I would think you'd be goin', "Who's is that? Who's there? Who's there? Is somebody there? What do you want? What do you want? You look hungry, are you hungry? Get outta here!"

END OF EPISODE

THE Seinfeld SCRIPTS

THE
BUSBOY

WRITTEN BY

LARRY DAVID & JERRY SEINFELD

DIRECTED BY

TOM CHERONES

AS BROADCAST JUNE 26, 1991

SHOW OPEN

STAND-UP #1

INT. COMEDY CLUB—NIGHT

JERRY

I'm not a foodie. I don't, "Oh, this is too rare. Oh, it's too salty." Just eat it and shut up. I'll eat anywhere, whatever they're having. I have eaten rolls off of room service trays in hotel hallways. I have. It's not a joke. This is my life. I don't know, somebody left it. Why would someone poison a roll and leave it in a hallway for some comic coming down at two o'clock in the morning? Why would they do that? Sometimes you go to a nice restaurant, they put the check in a little book. What is this? The story of the bill? "Once upon a time, there were some very hungry people . . ." What is this? A little gold tassle hanging down? Am I graduating from the restaurant? What is this about?

ACT ONE

SCENE A

INT. RESTAURANT—EARLY EVENING

Nouvelle Italian, candles on the table. Jerry, George and Elaine are finishing dinner. George sits across from them, hasn't eaten a thing.

ELAINE
Do you want some of mine?

JERRY
Take some of mine.

GEORGE
Why do I get pesto? Why do I think I'll like it? I keep trying to like it, like I have to like it.

JERRY
Who said you have to like it?

GEORGE
Everybody likes pesto. You walk into a restaurant, that's all you hear—pesto, pesto, pesto.

JERRY
I don't like pesto.

GEORGE
Where was pesto ten years ago?

JERRY

(NODDING AT A MAN) Look at that guy.

Elaine starts to look but Jerry stops her.

JERRY (CONT'D)

I'll bet you he's gettin' hair transplants. Any time you see a guy that age wearing a baseball cap, ten to one, plugs.

ELAINE

(SHE TURNS NONCHALANTLY) The thing about that painting . . . is with the colors and um . . . oh yeah, plugola.

During this, George has started eating Elaine's food, which he will continue eating throughout.

JERRY

(TO ELAINE) Oh, one more thing about the car. Let it warm up for a minute.

GEORGE

That's a tough minute. It's like waiting in the shower for the conditioner to work.

JERRY

I don't understand why he couldn't take a cab.

GEORGE

Who?

JERRY

Elaine is having a "houseguest." She's picking him up at the airport tonight.

GEORGE

A guy?

ELAINE

(SLIGHTLY EMBARRASSED) Yes, a guy.

JERRY

He's from a . . . Yakima, right.

ELAINE

Seattle.

JERRY

Everybody's moving to Seattle.

GEORGE

It's the pesto of cities. . . (LEADING) So . . .

ELAINE

(TO JERRY) You tell him.

JERRY

Well, from what I can piece together our friend here met a gentleman.

ELAINE

Ed.

JERRY

Who was in town on a business venture and um . . .

Looks to Elaine for help.

ELAINE

. . . We shared an interpersonal experience.

George tings glass with fork.

ELAINE (CONT'D)

(TO JERRY) Go on.

JERRY

So they went out a few times, but apparently when the fellow returned home he discovered that the Benes tattoo does not wash off so easily.

ELAINE

On some people.

GEORGE

Oooh.

JERRY

So, he's coming in to stay with her for a week.

ELAINE

It was just gonna be a weekend but then somehow it became a week.

Now the menu on the next table catches on fire from the candle . . . Elaine picks up a wine glass. She's about to douse it. Now George springs into action. He tosses the menu on the floor and stomps it out. They ad-lib congratulations. The manager approaches *the table.*

MANAGER

What happened?

GEORGE

Oh, the busboy left the menu a little close to the candle.

MANAGER

I'm sorry for the disturbance.

ELAINE

(KIDDING) I'm never eating here again.

The manager leaves.

JERRY

(PATS GEORGE ON THE SHOULDER) Nice going. Thank you, that ought to get us a free dessert.

From their P.O.V. we see the manager giving the busboy a severe dressing down.

JERRY (CONT'D)

I think the busboy's in trouble.

GEORGE

Did I get him in trouble—because of what I said?! I just told him what happened . . . he didn't do it on purpose.

The manager is still arguing. We see him point at George. Then the busboy points at George.

GEORGE (CONT'D)

He pointed at me. Why did they point at me?

ELAINE

I said I would never eat here again. But I . . . I . . . He had to know I was kidding.

JERRY

(BUTTERING A ROLL) I didn't say anything.

Now the busboy takes his apron off, throws it and storms out.

GEORGE

I can't believe it. He's going! He's fired!

ELAINE

Oh, I said it in a kidding way.

GEORGE

I didn't know he'd get fired.

JERRY

He'll probably kill his family over this.

GEORGE

What if he's waiting for me outside? He pointed at me! Did you see him point?

JERRY

A lot of ex-cons become busboys. They seem to gravitate towards 'em.

GEORGE

Was it my fault?

ELAINE

Was it my fault?

JERRY

. . . Maybe I'll try that pesto.

CUT TO:

ACT ONE
SCENE B

INT. JERRY'S APARTMENT—LATER

JERRY

Look I feel bad for him too, but he'll get another job. I

mean, let's face it, it's not a profession where you embellish your resume and undergo a series of grueling interviews.

George, still hungry, is eating a sandwich.

GEORGE

Oh, like you really know busboys.

JERRY

Oh, like you do.

GEORGE

Hey, at least I was a camp waiter.

JERRY

Camp.

GEORGE

It was a fat camp. Those kids depended on me.

SFX: buzzer sounds

JERRY

Elaine?

ELAINE (O.S.)

Yeah.

Jerry buzzes back.

JERRY

Busboys are always changing jobs. That's the business. I know. I work with these guys. I talk to them in the kitchen at the comedy clubs.

GEORGE

Then why don't *you* try and get him another job.

JERRY

I'd love to, but I don't know anything about him. He could be one of those people that walks around the street pricking people with pins.

Elaine enters.

THE BUSBOY

ELAINE

I don't know if you people are aware of this, but I am one clever chickadee.

GEORGE

What, did you get the busboy's number?

ELAINE

His phone's been disconnected, but I was able to obtain an address, 1324 Amsterdam Avenue, apartment 4D. (HANDING HIM A CARD) Now, I did my job. (TO JERRY) May I have the car keys, please?

Jerry hands her the keys.

GEORGE

How did you get all this?

ELAINE

Does the word "charm" mean anything to you?

JERRY

No.

George grabs his jacket.

JERRY (CONT'D)

(TO GEORGE) So now you're going to his apartment? I really think this is nuts.

GEORGE

(PUTTING HIS JACKET ON) I'd like to apologize. I want to tell him I . . . I . . . I didn't mean to get him in trouble.

JERRY

You, you're going now?

GEORGE

Yeah, I want to see if there's anything I can do . . . maybe get him another job . . . maybe I'll hear of something.

JERRY

Maybe the fat camp. (TO ELAINE) You're not going?

ELAINE

I would, but I have to pick up Ed at the airport.

JERRY

I just don't think you should go alone. Can't you wait
till after my set?

GEORGE

(TORN) It'll take too long.

Kramer enters.

JERRY

Take the K-man. A little support.

GEORGE

(NOT SURE) I don't a . . .

KRAMER

Take me where? Where?

CUT TO:

ACT ONE
SCENE C

INT. HALLWAY—NIGHT

Kramer and George have arrived at the busboy's door. George appears
nervous.

GEORGE

Look, I really appreciate your coming, but if you
wouldn't mind, try not to say too much.

KRAMER

What am I gonna say?

GEORGE

I don't know.

KRAMER

Well, I'm not an idiot.

GEORGE

Certainly not.

KRAMER

Then we're cool.

GEORGE

Yeah . . . yeah, we're—we're cool.

George knocks lightly, then Kramer knocks loudly. After a few beats the busboy opens up as if they're narcotics officers. He is short, menacing.

GEORGE (CONT'D)

Uh, I'm sorry to bother you, I was in the restaurant earlier and I was wondering if I could talk to you for a few minutes about what happened.

He signals them to come in.

GEORGE (CONT'D)

(HALTINGLY) I hope I'm not interrupting anything, it's just that I think I may have without realizing it been responsible for getting you fired (NERVOUS LAUGH) and . . . and . . . and I just want you to know that I didn't intend for that to happen.

KRAMER

(PATTING GEORGE ON SHOULDER) He's a helluva guy.

GEORGE

This is a guy I know . . . Kramer.

He's watching them suspiciously.

KRAMER

Habla espanol?

GEORGE

(TO HIMSELF) Oh my God.

ANTONIO

Si.

KRAMER

Como se dice . . . waterbed?

GEORGE

(INTERRUPTING) Anyway, I just wanted to let you know I'm really sorry that happened and if I can help out in any way, I'll certainly be glad to do that . . . Well, I guess that's about it.

KRAMER

(INTERRUPTING) You got anything to drink? *Agua?*

GEORGE

Oyuyuy. (ANTONIO POINTS TO THE SINK) We really should get going.

KRAMER

Let me get a glass of water.

Kramer heads for the sink.

GEORGE

(INTO HIS OWN SHOULDER) Hurry up.

Antonio suddenly notices his cat is missing.

ANTONIO

Pequita? Pequita? (HE'S STARTING TO PANIC)

Antonio starts talking quickly in Spanish.

KRAMER

His cat's gone.

Now Antonio walks to the door and notices it's open.

ANTONIO

La puerta esta abierta. (SCREAMING) *La puerto esta abierta!* (TO THEM) Who left the door open? Who left the door open?!

George and Kramer look at each other.

ANTONIO (CONT'D)

Come on, come on, help me look!

As they head out:

FADE OUT:

END OF ACT ONE

THE BUSBOY

ACT TWO

SCENE D

INT. ANTONIO'S APARTMENT—LATER

They sit in silence, then:

KRAMER

(TO ANTONIO) . . . You know cats run away all the time.
You know, my aunt, she had a cat, ran away, showed
up three years later, you never know. They got things
in their brains where they remember where they're
from. Unless of course somebody else starts feeding
him. See, that's what you gotta worry about.

George looks at Kramer to stop him.

GEORGE

Once again, Antonio, I can't even begin to say how
deeply, deeply sorry I am about everything—the job,
the cat . . .

SFX: *crash.*

GEORGE (CONT'D)

. . . the lamp.

KRAMER

The wire was sticking out. (HE TRIES TO FIT A BROKEN
PIECE TOGETHER) Yeah.

GEORGE

(GEORGE HANDS HIM A BUSINESS CARD) Here's my card. I'm in real estate, so if you're ever looking for something bigger, something nicer . . . maybe not right away. Anyway . . .

George reaches out to shake hands. Antonio doesn't budge.

KRAMER

You oughta get that wire fixed.

As they exit:

KRAMER (CONT'D)

(HOLDING HIS HAND UP) I got the door.

He shuts the door and the broken piece of lamp falls to the floor.

CUT TO:

ACT TWO
SCENE E

INT. JERRY'S APARTMENT—NIGHT

Jerry's on the phone.

JERRY

George stop worrying about this guy. It wasn't your fault . . . Come on, he's not stalking you.

Kramer enters.

KRAMER

Hey.

JERRY

(TO KRAMER) Hey. (INTO PHONE) He doesn't even know where you live . . . Who told you to give him your business card? . . .

SFX: *buzzer*

THE BUSBOY

JERRY (CONT'D)

(TO KRAMER) That's Elaine.

Kramer buzzes her in.

JERRY (CONT'D)

(INTO PHONE) Kramer . . . (THEN TO KRAMER) George
wants to know when you want to look for the cat again.

KRAMER

It's been a week. It's up to the cat now.

JERRY

(INTO PHONE) Kramer says it's up to the cat now. (TO
KRAMER) It'll be on your conscience.

KRAMER

Oh, how do you figure?

JERRY

(INTO PHONE) How do you figure? (TO KRAMER) 'Cause
you're the one who left the door open.

KRAMER

Why was I in charge of closing the door?

JERRY

(INTO PHONE) Why was he in charge of closing the
door? (IRRITATED, TO KRAMER) 'Cause you came in after
him!

KRAMER

So!

JERRY

(INTO PHONE) So! (TO KRAMER—MORE IRRITATED) So,
the last person in should close the door!

KRAMER

Let me talk to him.

JERRY

(TO KRAMER) Talk—call him from your house.

Elaine enters. Kramer leaves.

JERRY (CONT'D)

(INTO PHONE) He's calling you now . . . okay.

He hangs up.

ELAINE

Ed's downstairs. Can I have the car keys?

He pitches her the keys. Elaine gets aspirin from bathroom.

JERRY

No hello?

ELAINE

Got any aspirin? Hello. Now, lookit, you guarantee this car will get me to the airport tomorrow? No problems?

JERRY

Guarantee? . . . Hey, it's a car.

ELAINE

Because if there's even the slightest chance of any problem at all, I don't want to take it. Because if I don't get this guy on a plane to Seattle and out of my life, I'm gonna kill him and anyone who tries to stop me.

JERRY

So did you have a nice week together?

ELAINE

I heard a little ping in the car the last time. What was that ping?

JERRY

There's no ping. Why are you so wacky?

ELAINE

Jerry, you cannot imagine how much I hate this guy . . . And he hasn't even done anything! It's the situation. He's a wonderful guy, but I hate his guts!

JERRY

(SUGGESTIVELY) So, have you two been, uh . . .

ELAINE

No! . . . I told him I've been having my period for the

THE BUSBOY

last five days. I'm sleeping all squished over on the edge
of my bed. But I've only got fourteen hours to go.
Nothing can go wrong now. I think I've taken care of
everything. I've confirmed the plane reservation. I've
checked the weather.

JERRY

What's your airport route?

ELAINE

I've got it all mapped out—I'm taking the tunnel.

JERRY

(OMINOUSLY) . . . What about the Van Wyck?

ELAINE

I spoke to a cab driver. For five bucks he turned me on
to the Rockaway Boulevard shortcut.

JERRY

Ooh.

ELAINE

Now lookit, his plane leaves at 10:15, we're gettin' up at
about eight. That gives us enough time, right?

JERRY

You still using that old alarm clock?

ELAINE

Oh, no, no. I bought a new one today. It's got
everything. It's got everything. If you oversleep more
than ten minutes a hand comes out and slaps you in the
face.

DISSOLVE TO:

STAND-UP #2

INT. COMEDY CLUB—NIGHT

JERRY

Flying doesn't make me nervous—driving to the airport
can make you very nervous because when you're flying,

when you're getting on a plane, if you miss that plane, there's no alternative. On the ground you have options. You have buses, you have taxis, you have trains. But when you're taking a flight, if you miss it, that's it. No airline goes, "Well, you missed the flight, we do have a cannon leaving in about ten minutes. Would you be interested in that? It's not a direct cannon, you have to change cannons after you land." (HE PANTOMIMES AS THE CANNON OPERATOR) "I'm sorry, where you goin'? Chicago?" (HE CRANKS CANNON TO CHICAGO) "Oh, Dallas? Alright, wait a second." (HE CRANKS CANNON BACK TOWARD DALLAS) "Dallas, that's about Dallas. Texas, anyway, you should hit Texas. Are you ready? Make sure you get out of the net immediately because we shoot the luggage in right after you."

DISSOLVE TO:

ACT TWO
SCENE F

INT. ELAINE'S APARTMENT—MORNING

Elaine and Ed are in bed. Ed is sleeping peacefully. Elaine opens her eyes and groggily leans over to see the time. She looks once—then picks up the clock to get a better look. CU—alarm. It reads 9:15 . . . the sky has fallen. In a state of frenzy she throws all tact to the wind.

ELAINE
(ROUSTING HIM) Get up! The alarm didn't go off!! (NOW SHE SHAKES HIM) It's 9:15! You're gonna miss the plane! It's 9:15!

EDDIE
9:15?

ELAINE
Yes! 9:15!

THE BUSBOY

EDDIE

We'll never make it. I'll leave tomorrow.

ELAINE

Tomorrow? Are you crazy? No, now, now! Let's go!

She gets his suitcase from the closet, throws it on her bed and furiously begins packing.

ELAINE (CONT'D)

You get dressed! Get dressed!

EDDIE

Can I shower!

ELAINE

Shower?! Are you out of your mind?!

EDDIE

I gotta shower. I'll feel dirty all day.

ELAINE

Forget the shower! The shower's out. Move it! Put your clothes on! Put your clothes on!

She pulls drawers out of the dresser and turns them over into the suitcase. He starts walking toward the bedroom door.

ELAINE (CONT'D)

Where are you going?

EDDIE

The kitchen.

ELAINE

The kitchen?!

EDDIE

I've got a bag of cashews in there.

ELAINE

They're not making it! Let's get your pants on!

EDDIE

What's the big deal if we don't make it? I'll just go tomorrow or the next day.

ELAINE

No! You have your ticket! You have to go now!

EDDIE

I'll never make it.

ELAINE

Don't say that!

EDDIE

But it takes forty-five minutes to get there. That'll only leave me five minutes to get to the plane.

ELAINE

Shut up and pack!

EDDIE

And what if I don't make the plane? You'll have already left. Then what will I do?

ELAINE

You're talking too much!

EDDIE

Where's my sweater?

ELAINE

What?!

EDDIE

My brown sweater.

ELAINE

What? What sweater?

EDDIE

My brown sweater.

ELAINE

You didn't bring a brown sweater.

EDDIE

I brought a brown sweater.

ELAINE

Here! Here! You want a brown sweater? (REACHING INTO ANOTHER DRAWER) You got a brown sweater!

EDDIE
That's not mine. I can't take your sweater.

ELAINE
It's brown!

She takes clothing on hangers and dumps them in.

EDDIE
(RE: THE HANGERS) What are you doing!

ELAINE
No time for folding . . . I think that's it.

She zips the suitcase up.

EDDIE
My shoes. You packed my shoes.

ELAINE
Shoes? Shoes? Shoes?! Shoes weren't invented till the fourth century! People walked around for thousands of years without them!

She puts a coat on over her nightie. He picks up the suitcase. She grabs it from him and shoves him aside.

ELAINE (CONT'D)
I got this. Let's go!

CUT TO:

ACT TWO
SCENE G

INT. JERRY'S APARTMENT—DAY

JERRY
Anywhere in the city?

GEORGE
Anywhere in the city I'll tell you the best public toilet.

JERRY

Okay . . . Fifty-fourth and Sixth?

GEORGE

Sperry Rand Building, 14th floor. Morgan Apparel.
Mention my name—she'll give you the key.

JERRY

Alright . . . Sixty-fifth and Tenth.

GEORGE

(SCOFFING) Are you kidding? Lincoln Center, Alice Tully
Hall, the Met, magnificent facilities.

Elaine enters, *still wearing her nightclothes under her coat. She's been
through an ordeal.*

ELAINE

(AS IF RECOUNTING A DREAM) I never knew I could drive
like that. I was going faster than I've ever gone before
and yet it all seemed to be happening in slow motion. I
was seeing three and four moves ahead, weaving in and
out of lanes like an Olympic skier on a gold medal run.
I knew I was challenging the very laws of physics. At
Queens Boulevard I took the shoulder. At Jewel Avenue
I used the median. I had it. I was there . . . and then . . .
I hit the Van Wyck. They say no one's ever beaten the
Van Wyck, but gentlemen I tell you this—I came as
close as anyone ever has. And if it hadn't been for that
five-car pile-up on Rockaway Boulevard, that numbskull
would be on a plane for Seattle right now instead of
looking for a parking space downstairs.

Kramer enters, *excited.*

KRAMER

. . . The busboy's coming! The busboy's coming!

GEORGE

The busboy's coming?

JERRY

You don't mean here?

THE BUSBOY

KRAMER

Yeah, I just buzzed him in. He's on his way up . . .

GEORGE

He's coming up?! (GEORGE HEADS FOR THE DOOR) I'll check you out later.

JERRY

Where are you going?

GEORGE

I'm the one he wants! He's coming to settle the score.

JERRY

(ATTEMPTING TO USHER THEM OUT) No. You three all know each other. There's no point in me getting involved at this stage of the game.

KRAMER

No, he's not going to do anything. I guarantee it.

GEORGE

Oh, the hell with it. Let him kill me. I . . .

We hear a knock in the hallway.

KRAMER

(WAVING) Antonio, in here.

Antonio enters.

GEORGE

(VOICE CRACKING) Hey, Antonio, how's it going?

Antonio, with great purpose, crosses to George and throws his arms around him.

ANTONIO

Three nights ago a gas main beneath the restaurant exploded, killing five people in my section, including the busboy who replaced me. If I am not fired that night because of you and your thoughtless, stupid, insensitive remarks, it would have been me. You saved my life.

Antonio grabs George and hugs him.

GEORGE

(SLOUGHING IT OFF) Ah, come on.

SFX: buzzer

ELAINE

Yeah?

EDDIE (O.S.)

It's Eddie.

ELAINE

He's coming up.

Elaine buzzes him in.

ELAINE (CONT'D)

He's coming up.

ANTONIO

And that very same night of the accident while looking for Pequita, I found a job in a restaurant where they pay me almost twice what I was making before—and when I returned to the apartment, Pequita, perhaps frightened from the explosion, had miraculously returned. Well, but now I must go, for today I am starting my new and wonderful job. And I am very late. Thank you, thank you. Thank you all.

And with that he goes . . . They ad-lib congrats to George. After a few beats we hear a disturbance in the hallway.

EDDIE (O.C.)

Hey, watch where you're going. You almost knocked my head off.

ANTONIO (O.C.)

Hey, why don't you watch where you're going, okay? 'Cause you bumped into me!

EDDIE (O.C.)

Who do you think you're talking to pal?

ANTONIO (O.C.)

Hey, get your hands off me!

THE BUSBOY

THE
SCRIPTS

EDDIE (O.C.)

You, go to hell!

ANTONIO (O.C.)

(LAUNCHING INTO SPANISH CURSING)

We hear a scuffle accompanied by fighting sounds as they all watch hallway.

DISSOLVE TO:

ACT TWO
SCENE H

INT. COFFEE SHOP—DAY

We join Jerry, George and Elaine at a table.

JERRY

He'll get another job. He's a busboy!

GEORGE

It won't be for a while. At least not until after the cast comes off.

JERRY

(EATING) It was that fall down the stairs. That's what did it.

GEORGE

That's not how it happened. It's when he fell on him with his knee.

ELAINE

Oh, that was awful. Poor Antonio.

The waiter comes with two bags of food to go.

ELAINE (CONT'D)

Thanks . . .

GEORGE

So, much longer?

ELAINE

Till when—till he goes back to Seattle or till he can feed himself?

GEORGE

(THINKING BETTER OF IT) I guess it's not important.

ELAINE

Take care of yourselves.

She leaves.

GEORGE

I should probably get going too. If I don't feed Pequita by seven, she goes all over everything . . . Take it easy.

JERRY

Yeah . . .

As Jerry takes another bit of his sandwich, the waiter starts to clear the table.

JERRY (CONT'D)

How ya doing?

FADE OUT:

END OF ACT TWO

SHOW CLOSE

STAND-UP #3

INT. COMEDY CLUB—NIGHT

JERRY

First of all, I can't believe that people actually do fight. People have fist fights in life. I can't really believe that we have boxing either. It's really kind of an amazing thing. To me, the problem with boxing is you have two guys having a fight that have no prior argument. Why don't they have the boxers come into the ring in little cars, drive around a little bit, have a little accident, they get out, "Didn't you see my signal?" "Look at that fender!" . . . Then you'd see a real fight.

END OF EPISODE